Pants
A History Afoot

To B. K.

Translated by
Laurel Hirsch

Design and layout: Laurent Romano
Editor: Léonore Lara
Iconography: Maryse Hubert and Delphine Pietri
Copyeditor: GEDEV, Paris

© Les Éditions de l'Amateur,
25, rue Ginoux, 75015 Paris
Authorized English Language Edition
© Vilo Publishing 2001,
30, rue de Charonne, 75011 Paris
ISBN : 2-84576-035-3
Printed in Italy

Laurence Benaïm

Pants
A History Afoot

ViLO

PUBLISHING

Contents

Acknowledgments

I, in particular, would like to thank Alexia, Bruno, Charlotte, Françoise and Hugo Krief, as well as Nicole, Paul, Alexandre and Franck Benaïm. Denis Krief, Pierre Zins and Bernard Zins who inspired this work. Patrick Arfi who supported this project, and those who contributed to its realization: Michel Jullien, Léonore Lara, Laurent Romano (Éditions de L'Amateur). My deepest gratitude to Céline Bokobsa, Barbara Jeauffroy, Léonore Lara, Delphine Pietri, Delphine Priollaud and Anne Laure Quilleriet, as well as Maria Ter Markarian and Alexandre Vassiliev for their invaluable assistance.

Thanks also to Per Kaufman, Cécile François, Fatiha Habchi, Catherine Royer and Isabelle Salomon of Le Printemps who gave such great faith and energy to this book. And further thanks to Géraldine de Friberg, Emmanuelle Mayer and Amélie Rouyer for their support during the realization of this work and during the Affaire de Libertés exhibition held at Le Printemps de la Mode on October 8 to 30, 1999.

I extend my sincerest gratitude to all the couturiers and fashion designers who created original drawings and photo-montages expressly for this book, to the couture houses, museums of fashion, public relations departments, those working in the archives and institutions and the photographers who accepted with all enthusiasm and kindness to participate in this project.

Azzedine Alaia, assisted by Thomas Vasseur; Agnès B and Florence Callot; the house of Allard; Jean Touitou (APC); Marc Acoli; Marc Aubidet; Françoise Auguet; Marithé Arlabusse; Jean Michel Pereira, Isabella Capece, the house of Giorgio Armani; Maïmé Arnodin; Madame Greta Stroh of the Fondation Arp; Pierre Bergé and Yves Saint Laurent, as well as Laurence Comte, Caroline Deroche, Dominique Deroche, Eléonore de Musset, Clara Saint and Danièle Leclerc, Maryvonne Numata at Yves Saint Laurent; Elena Bertacchini, Monica Sacchetti (Averix); Éric Bergère; Jean Charles Blais; Christine Blanc; Sylvie Grumbach, Nicolas Delarue and Marie-Anne Capdeville; Denise Dubois, Didier Grumbach, Chambre Syndicale de la Haute Couture, Paris; Patrick Bensard, Anne-Marie Cholet, Bernard Emi, Nicolas Villodre (Cinématèque de La Danse); Rosanda Meier, Le Cachemirien; Pacal Collet, the house of Jean Charles de Castelbajac; Lean Claude Chiroutte; Marion Brenot (Pierre Cardin); Cerutti; Mareka Genty, the Chanel Archives; Brigitte Chouet; Jean Colonna; Sophie Favre et Coqueline Courregès (Courregès); Rei Kawakubo and Yelka Music (Comme

des Garçon); Christie's; Gérald Cohen; Lisbeth Pernot, Différences Communication
(for Levi's); Diesel; Carla Buzzi; Paola Locati (Dolce e Gabbanna); Bibliothèque
Marguerite Durand; Duthilleul and Minart; Yves Dumora; the offices of Edelman
(for United Colours of Benetton); Timothy Everest; Evisu; Minouche Fenech; Chiara
Casalotti of the Salvatore Ferragamo Museum, Florence; Jean Paule Goude and Irène
McBride; Bettina Graziani; Philippe Guez; Monsieur Grauer at the Musée des Archives
de la Police; Béatrice Keller and Caroline Gobert; Lionel Vermeil, Colette Lacoste
(Jean Paul Gaultier); Jaques Gavard; Muriel de Lamarzelle; the house of Marithé
and François Girbaud; Alix de Chabot, Calvin Klein; Eric Lanuit, Mylene Lajoix,
the house of Givenchy; Christina Malgara, Tom Ford (Gucci); Valérie Courbot,
archives services at Hermès; Jean-Claude Jitrous and Yann Patry; Helena Jorosova;
Sidonie Schoeff and Camille, the house of Joseph; the house of Karting; Ruth Obadia,
the house of Kenzo; William Klein; Elisabeth Bonnel, Laure du Pavillon, the house of
Christian Lacroix; Hannah Lawrence (Helmut Lang); Pacale Landot, Hania Destell,
Philippe Salva, Odile Fraigneau, the house of Jeanne Lanvin; Madame Lee Young Hee;
Véronique Leroy; Ling Fei; Christian Louboutin; the house of Alexander McQueen;
Patrick Scallon, the house of Martin Margiela; Chief Officer Mestdagh, Musée des
Traditions des Troupes de Montagnes; Agence Metropolitan; Musée de la Marine, Paris;
archives of the Musée de la Mode et du Costume, Palais Galliera; British Golf Museum
St. Andrews, Edinburgh; Victoria and Albert Museum, London; Marie Claude Beaud,
general curator of the Musée des Arts Décoratifs; Ludia Kamitsis, Pamela Golbin,
curators at the Musée de la Mode; Marie Hélène Poix, Jérôme Recour (resource center
of UFAC) Musée de la Mode, Paris; Catherine and Alain Miran; Margalette Presse;
the house of Missoni; Marie Chalmel, Valérie Dufournier, Jean de Mouy, the house
of Jean Patou; Hector Pascual, curator of the Fondation Pour le Rayonnement
de L'Œuvre d'Yves Saint Laurent, assisted by Romain Verdure; Hélène Pichenot,
Premiere Vision; Isabelle Picard; Laudomia Pietri, Agence Pietri (for Gap); Phyléa;
Valérie Houdaille of Rendez-Vous Extérieurs (for Dockers); Joelle Reneaud, the house
of Renoma; Safia Bendali; Nathalie Rykiel, the house of Sonia Rykiel; Virginie
Berthelot, the house of Fred Sathal; the offices of Annie Schneider; Jeremy Scott;
Martine Sitbon; Sophie Boiley, the house of Paul Smith; Miloslav Sebek; Olivier
Saillard, curator at the Musée de la Mode de Marseille; the offices of Kuki de Salvertes;
Girault/Totem; Bruno Suet; Olivero Toscani for United Colours of Benetton; Mario
Testino/Art Partners; Laurent Bérangerm Bruno Danto, Luc Guichard, Aurélia Maes
and the entire team at Toute Petite Agence; Angleo Sensini (Trussardi); Max Vadukul;
Olivia Berghauer, the house of Valentino, the offices of VDRP; Patricia Cucco,
Staefania Sacchi Di Gilio, the house of Versace; Viktor and Rolf; Vivienne Westwood;
Ghyslain Yarhi; Nathalie Ours; Irène Silvagni, the house of Yohji Yamamoto; Gaspard
Yurkievich; Jean Claude Zana; Zmirov Communication (for Helly Hansen).

Foreword

"Customer: God made the world in six days and you,
you can't make me a pair of pants in six months.
Tailor: But Sir, look at the world and look at your pants."
(Samuel Beckett, Le Monde et le Pantalon, 1945)

Duds, trousers, ducks, slacks, cords, plus fours. Fantasy pants. Sports pants. Cassimere pants. Sunday pants. Baggy, skin-tight, narrow, hugging, Hussar pants, bellbottoms, cuffed, with foot straps, Oriental *sarouels*, Indian *dhotis*, Korean *pajis*, Japanese *hakamas*, pants have spanned centuries and civilizations with the self-assurance of a sage, robust enough to hide within its pockets and seams the secrets of a past replete sudden revivals, the evolution from "wrapping the leg" to "making pants" worn by populations subjected to the rigors of the Central Asian climate. It was with the nomads of the steppes — the Huns, the Scythes and the Alans — who made pants their attire for war, and clearing these first steps, they were adopted by the Persians and the Hittites, but with the exception of Alexander the Great, were rejected by the Greeks.

Pants drag with them a scandalous identity. Saint Pantaleon, a doctor from Bithynia in Asia Minor who was martyred in the fourth century, was the patron saint of the Doges, and more specifically, of sailors and fishermen. In Italy, his name was first and foremost a sobriquet applied to Venetians, the *Pantaloni*, according to Agrippa d'Aubigné *(Confessions du Très Catholique Sieur de Sancy, 1660)*. Pantaloon was a character in the Commedia dell'Arte who wore long culottes, "an amorous and salacious old man, base and miserly, ever the target of all servants of intrigue. ... a hypocritical buffoon of a character," according to the cardinal of Retz *(Mémoires, 1717)*. And according to the *Dictionnaire de L'Académie*, he was "a man who assumed all sorts of shapes and played all sorts of roles to achieve his ends."

It was this gouty, snorting, coughing, spitting, hooked-nosed old man who gave his name to the most universal article of clothing in the world. Miserly, pretentious, Pantaloon is the dupe *par excellence*, libidinous to excess. Pants, we slip into them, we wear them, we leave them. We've place their bottoms on school benches. There are those that "have nothing in them," and others that "wear for two." From George Sand who, according to Alfred de Vigny was "a man in dress, in language, in the sound of her voice and in the daring of her intentions," to Colette who sensed in her "the soul of an extraordinarily intelligent man and an loving woman." Outfits of the "horsewomen" and of eccentrics, for a long time, pants led a licentious life, even if the first to advocate their use were hygienic Suffragettes like Amelia Bloomer. Hugging too much, they were already suspected of all evils. "The young men of our age have had the foolishness to cover their thighs in a kind of very tight casing, that is so bothersome that they cannot, as others can, execute an sort of movement," Monsieur Macquart deplored as early as 1798 in his article "Culotte" in *L'Encyclopédie Méthodique de la Médecine.* Two centuries later, inspired by prisoners who had no belts to hold them up, teenagers were wore them too big and were deemed indecent by American conservatives.

Never has an article of clothing been so popular, yet so tainted with taboo. It is through them, in declaration of movement, of body, of all freedoms, that veritable revolutions in fashion have occurred. Their name remains linked to Levi's, Poiret, Chanel, Yves Saint Laurent, who made them a classic part of the woman's wardrobe. Today, a classic, subjected to hijackings, metamorphoses, blends that led fashion into the world of high technology. Why pants more than the blouse or the skirt? Because its unique, manifold, complex history is tied to struggles — struggles of power, struggles of love. For western women, they defend a way of living, of surviving, of promoting their differences within indifference, devoid of dependence based upon gender, social status or nationality.

With them, both protector and seducer, all is permitted. The small step, the race, the great leap to the next millennium. The two legs of this daredevil have walked without rest during all of the twentieth century. In their way, they are its memory and its fabric. And it is through pants that we have the desire to cross the bridge to the third millennium. They, whom the future continues to succeed in unbuttoning. "Of the universal culotte and the universal pants, what they will bring, such could not be known or said. But what can be confirmed, is that with the culotte, it is still a woman wearing the mark, the exterior label of her sex. Whereas with pants, it is the woman absolutely masculinized, completely incognito, with the possibility to see, to move with all ease through the streets, and travel the world without being the object of indiscreet eyes." So wrote the fashion historian John Grand-Carteret in his 1899 work *La Femme en Culotte.*

L. B.

Figure carrying a *barsom* (detail).
Gold plaque, Mede, treasure from the
Oxus, Bactrian (7th-6th century BC),
British Museum, London.

In the Beginning

From the Baggy Pants of the Persians to the Leggings of the Romans

I t was in Persepolis in southern Iran along the stone walls of the staircase leading to the "Apadana" reception hall that the long, flowing baggy pants, emblem of the all-powerful Persian Empire (557-330 BC) were first depicted. Medes, Aryans, Cappadocians, Scythes, Bactrians, Sogdians and Drangianins, as bearers of offerings, march past, sculpted and motionless, with their horses or camels and dressed in purple trousers that were often covered by gold-bejeweled tunics. These treasures of Achaemenian art are testimony to a civilization whose legend fired Herodotus' imagination. "They wore on their heads soft felt hats called tiaras, and over their bodies tunics with sleeves of different colours and cuirasses fashioned in iron layers, giving the appearance of fish scales."

Offering protection from the cold and for combating the enemy, pants emerged as the outfit *par excellence* of

warriors, and the bas-reliefs found in Persepolis depict them beneath a belted tunic for holding large daggers. The Huns, nomads of the Steppes and so-called "cruel men", and ancestors of the Turks, Mongols, Alans, and above all, the Scythes and the Sarmates, were the first to adopt the tunic with a pointed hood, along with leather

In the Beginning

From the Baggy Pants of the Persians to the Leggings of the Romans

3

pants, which distinguished them from the dress of the Mediterranean region. These "Barbarians of the North" wore pants under a long, belted garment that had long sleeves — a caftan, which has survived for more than three millennia.

4

Great horsemen, known for their taste for entertainment and luxury, for sleeping in grand silver beds and for drinking from goblets adorned with precious stones, the Persians, who were dignitaries of the Achaemenian Empire, a paradise filled with magnificent wildcats, appeared to have worn pants in response to their passion for hunting. "They hunted on horseback, shooting arrows, using bows and slings," as historians from Herodotus to Xenephon would write. Some accounts emphasize Persian women who, without ever having been depicted on a bas-relief, inspired portraits of horsewomen more than prisoners, in contrast to the Greeks, for example. And didn't the Persian women, according to the Latin historian Quintus Curtius, consider working wool "with their hands" as the greatest affront (v. III, 19)? The warrior and nomadic tradition was a part of the life of royal princesses. Ctesias, Cyrus' doctor, cited the example of Roxanne, the sister of Teritouchmes, in his work Persica. "She was very beautiful and most adept in the art of the javelin." In the court of Darius III, princesses were attended by "women on horseback" (Quintus Curtius, v. III, 1-22) and their travel rations were no dif-

1- Fighting barbarian warriors. Detail of a gold comb, Scythian (beginning of the 4th century BC), Hermitage Museum, Petersburg.

2- Persian and Mede guards. Detail of the east staircase of the Apadana, Persepolis (6th-5th century BC).

3- Parthian pants and tunic. Funerary relief, Palmyra, Syria (1st half of the 2nd century AD), Louvre Museum, Paris.

4- Donor dressed in Kushan garb. Buddhist monastery of Shotorak, Kappis, Afghanistan (4th-5th century AD), Guimet Museum, Paris.

ferent from the men's. They were trained in the traditional martial arts. Western antiquity had a long-held
aversion to pants and considered them indecent. The
wearing of tight-fitting pants, for example, were restrict-

ed to the slaves of the Greeks, probably to indicate their
barbarian origins. Pants, however, ended up becoming
essential in the eyes of Alexander (356-323 BC) when he
formed his calvary.

5

From the Baggy Pants of the Persians to the Leggings of the Romans

La Gallia braccata

The pants of the Scythes, introduced by the Germans and the Celts, served as a model for the Gauls. A sort of breeches called *femoralia*, they were the traditional dress. These long leggings with an ample seat opened in the front, came down to the calves and occasionally were laced to the shoes. In 325 BC, the Greek historian Polybius referred to them by the Greek word *peison*, or Persian pants. They can be seen on the coins of the Santons and the Pictons, as well as on the *arc de triomphe* in Orange. "After first having found them rather odd, the Romans adopted them for their troops, baptizing the Gaul from Narbonne, *Gallia braccata*, and calling tailors *bracaricus faber*," according to the clothing historian François Boucher.

During the second century BC, breeches reached the Romans from the Gauls, having first passed through Germania. Roman women took to wearing short underpants, almost panties, called *sugbligatus*, as can be seen in the mosaics of the Villa Casale in Sicily (fourth century AD). Initially used only by acrobats and gymnasts, a two-piece outfit composed of a brassiere and panties was adopted by both matronly and free-minded women, as was revealed during the nineteenth century with the excavation of Pompeii. "Thighs were covered in a fine cloth fashioned into a veritable pair of leggings," as was noted in an article on the frescoes of Pompeii in *La Revue des Deux Mondes* in July 1870. "On the thighs, very fine leggings can be perceived, in contrast with the coarse fabric of the rest of the clothing. Torn in places, it allows glimpses of firm and polished flesh with contours so realistic as to be almost embarrassing."

7

5- Alexander the Great. Persian miniature (16th century), Topkapi Museum, Istanbul.

6- Roman soldier. Detail of a sarcophagus depicting the submission of a Barbarian before a troop of Romans (2nd century AD), Thermes Museum, Rome.

7- Bronze statuette of Attis. Roman, Guimet Museum, Paris.

6

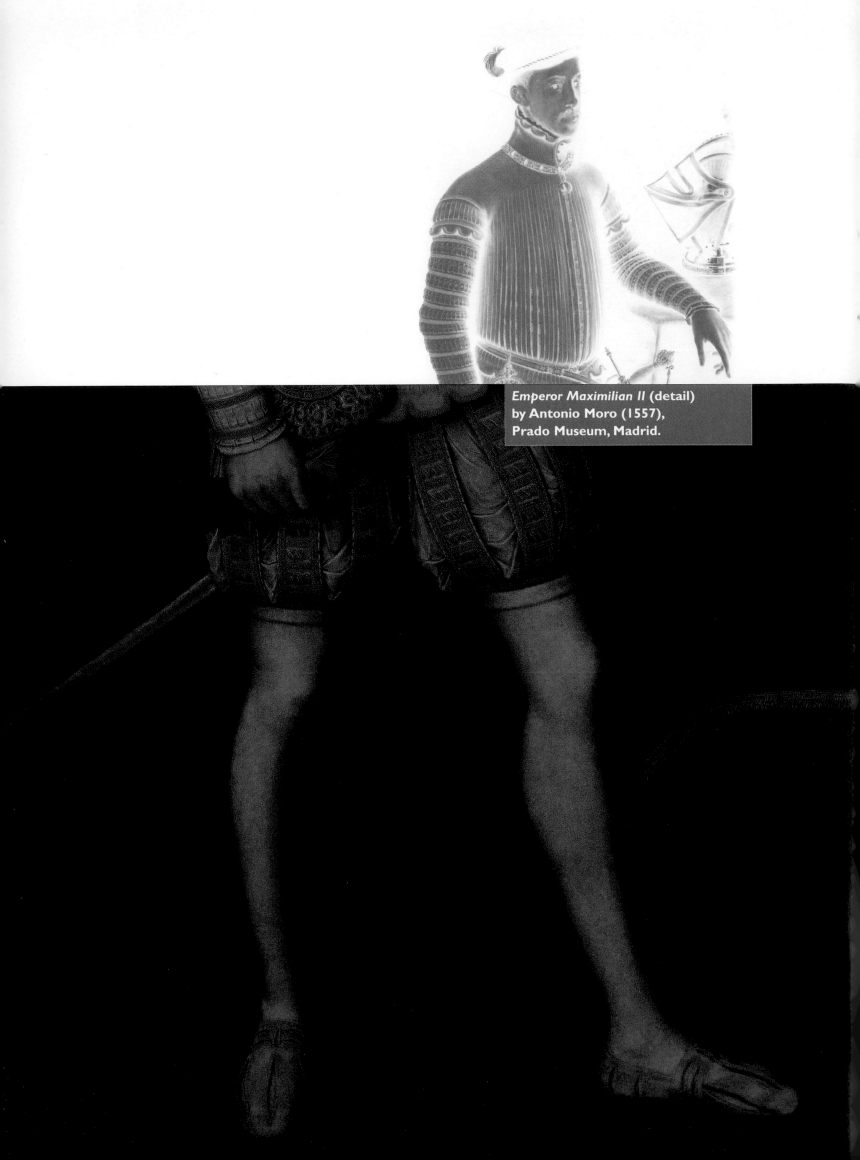

Emperor Maximilian II (detail)
by Antonio Moro (1557),
Prado Museum, Madrid.

**Breeches,
Knickers
and Leggings**

The
Trials
and Tribulations
of the
culotte

Won over by horse-women, adopted by princes who celebrated their virility with splendor and stylishness, pants made their entry into the history of style discreetly, yet at the same time, heroically. Breeches, their ancestors that were used by both sexes, were the object of controversy, confusion and discussion, as is evidenced by the abundance of illustrations dating as far back as the fifteenth century that were devoted to the "dispute of the culotte". The most famous engraving remains that by E. Van Mecken (1480). Here, with blows from lances, brooms and shuttles Pétronille Largottée snatches the fabric trophy from Jeannot Dindonnet. "With a blow from this step stool, I'll shine your brains. I'm the one wearing the pants! Fa la la! I'm in pants!" Or, the unfortunate husband who defends himself in vain. "And me, says Jean, I shall smash your eyes out with one punch if you bother me," he shoots at Margot in another engraving dating from the sixteenth century. Thus the quarrel of the pants, that "sheath for the legs" according to John Grand-Carteret, lays bare the war of the sexes. And to cite an old proverb, "He who has pants, has freedom".

According to historians, it was in 1340 that the difference in masculine and feminine attire became clear. Prior, ever since the beginning of the Christian Era, the only distinctions lay in the drape and the stitching, in the stylishness or the simplicity. It was also in the fourteenth century that the nature of attire (then, ample dresses for both sexes) became transformed with the appearance of separate legs. From that point on, the female body became defined by garments that allowed the shoulders and the throat to be seen above a low-cut neck. The breasts and the belly, symbols of femininity and maternity, were accentuated. Dresses were very long, close-fitting at the bust, clinching

at the waist and with plunging necklines. Hairstyles became far more complicated than they had been in the past. The controversy over pants took off, and the accusation against Joan of Arc, "a maid of twenty years, dressed like a man" serves as substantiation. "The spoken of Jeanne had her hair cut in the style of valets, and that she started wearing shirts, breeches, gipon, long knickers of a single piece that were attached to the aforementioned gipon by twenty aglets," Delivered to the English after her capture, in 1429, the Maid of Orleans was condemned by the court to burn at the stake as a witch. "This maid bears a respectable elegance, she has the presence of a man, she speaks little," as Perceval de Bowlainvilliers, a contemporary of hers, noted. Other woman sporting pants and who disguised their sex under armor can be found at the head of various insurrections.

1

Breeches, Knickers and Leggings.
The Trials and Tribulations of the Culotte

The "Bouffant" Style

Giving shelter to the power struggles, the ancestor to the pants took off by leaps and bounds. Already by the Middle Ages, breeches (the name deriving from the Latin braccae and referring to "the kind of pants worn by different peoples of Antiquity") worn under a blouse or a tunic that went down almost to the feet, slowly crept into use. Unknown in Rome during the Republican period, breeches still considered there as a primitive accessory. Were it not the Romans who called a part of transalpine Gaul by the condescending term *Gallia Braccata?*

In the fifteenth century men adopted the doublet or a long vest fastened by aglets to pants that reached the hips. The chest was artificially embellished by well-placed padding, and the flanks sculpted by the coat or gipon. As to the legs, they were tightly sheathed in long knickers. Coinciding with the advent of aglets, such as those used with the doublet, came the adaptation of military styles for civil dress. The French term for the doublet, "pourpoint," comes from the verb "pourpoindre," meaning stitched, indicating that they were stuffed with cotton or fibers and then quilted with stitches. Doublets were worn under a coat of mail to protect from being wounded by iron lances. This modification in clothing

1- Scene of net fishing. Detail from a miniature of the Fables of Bidpai (circa 1480), Condé Museum, Chantilly.

2- *Les Moissinneurs* (detail). Bruegel the Elder (circa 1565), Metropolitan Museum, New York.

3- Threshing with a flail. Detail of a page from an illuminated psalter; the month of August (circa 1330-1340), Corpus Christi College, Oxford.

4- Detail of a foxhunt scene. *Livre de la Chasse* by Gaston Phebus (circa 1405-1410), Bibliothèque Nationale de France, Paris.

5- Martyr of an Evangelist (detail). Hans Fries (1514), Kunst Museum, Basel.

corresponds to the appearance of the "gentleman soldier," who, sporting in blousy sleeves and short, bouffant
silk knickers, spread throughout the Habsburg Empire
beginning in the first half of the sixteenth century.

These military-style breeches soon disappeared as in
Italy, they were transformed into luxurious leggings fashioned, for the first time, out of knitting.

During the Renaissance, breeches with separated legs
became the distinctive symbol of aristocratic society, as

6- *Adoration of the Magi* (detail of a predella).
   Luca Signorelli (1482), Uffizzi Museum, Florence.

7- Venetian courtesan. *Modes de Gaigmières en Italie*
   (16ᵗʰ century), engraving.

8- Charles V. Titian (1532), Prado Museum, Madrid.

the paintings of Signorelli illustrate, notably his
Adoration of the Magi at the Uffizzi in Florence.

Venetian courtesans, who, according to Racinet "dressed
like men," and adopted "sailor-like, Provençal, squab-
bler's, codpiece" trousers that provoked jealousies and
reprisals. From the middle of the fifteenth century, Venice
took measure against gender cross-dressing. These mea-
sures extended to Rome and were the backing for all
denunciations. In *Les Courtisanes et la police des mœurs
à Venise*, the deposition of a servant shocked by the audacious outfit of her mistress states, "She had pants and a
turquoise blue overblouse adorned with gold or silver,
green silk stockings, a coat of textured silk and a feathered hat". Was not one of the first famous women to wear

Breeches, Knickers
and Leggings.
The Trials and Tribulations of the Culotte

8

pants Catherine Cornaro, a Venetian who was queen
of Cyprus?

As the codpiece ceaselessly swelled, taking on the
appearance of a metal shell or a padded crotch, sarcastic engravings multiplied, associating a woman in pants
with an undesirable crazy person. "If your hen behaves
like a cock, if your woman behaves like a master,
straightaway, put the hen in the pot and the woman in
Bissetre [the asylum]." The argument over pants became
more overt. "Women go to the country and leave their
husband cornered, obliged to abandon everything and to
struggle desperately with the woman's world. They
would cry and bemoan, hopeless about being so alone,"
as an 18th-century German stamp reads. Some people did
not hesitate to make pants an existential concern. "These

Breeches, Knickers
and Leggings.
The Trials and Tribulations of the Culotte

knickers, being an object of my strong affections, I just must have them, as they are the source of my joy," declares Dame Florence, a character in *Combat des Femmes à qui aura l'haut de chausse*, an anonymous engraving published by Banthazar-Montcornet in Paris around 1635.

Trousers, which were adopted by some women up until the sixteenth century in the spirit of a religious crusade, by the seventeenth century became something of a claim for independence and movement. In accounts by "army irregulars" such as Madame de Chevreuse, Mademoiselle de Montpensier, Madame de Montbazon and Madame de Saint-Balmont, the so-called "horsewomen of the seventeenth century," beautiful women with huge plumed hats who, according to John Grand-Carteret, "in petti-

12

coats… are ready to put on large canioned boots and slip into pants".

Rhinegraves, Canions and Lace

The flaunting of virility engendered an evermore overt stylishness. From the France of the Vallois, to the Spain of Charles I, the sophistication was extreme, codifying a particular appearance from the "split-stave barrel-like" knickers, to the "bears' paws" shoes. The distinction

13

9- **Man wearing a ruff and woman's hairstyle. Frontispiece from** *Les Hermaphrodites* **(c. 1605).**

10- **Louise Labbé in men's dress. Sketch by Gustave Girrane.**

11- **Emperor Rudolph II taking his cure. Lucas van Valckenborch (after 1593), Kuntsthistorisches Museum, Vienna.**

12- *Promenade de Magistrats,* **in Paris during the 17th century. Drawing by Bocourt after François Chauveau.**

13- **Coronation sword.** *Louis XIV, Roi de France* **(detail), Hyacinthe Rigaud (1701), Louvre Museum, Paris.**

between the sexes became more pronounced as the birth of the farthingale used by women coincided in 1575 with the appearance of men sporting swords at their sides and wearing pants that went down to the knee, replacing the bouffant knickers. Men's garb was ornamented in rash of silk and velvet, and Louis XIV, the Sun King, asserted himself as the organizer of France's royal attire.

Thus, in the seventeenth century, the French court began to create its own style. In 1655, breeches were replaced by petticoated breeches in the style of the rhinegraves xwith cascades of ribbons and lace that marked the triumph of Baroque fashion. Paris, where the Grand Condé set the tone, became the center of clothing manufacture for the civilized world. At the end of the century, men's attire took form that it maintains to the present: a white shirt and pants, most often those that fold over and are fitted at the waist. The three-piece suit came to being with the vest replacing the doublet. In 1678, trousers replaced the "rhinegrave".

Leaving men to give themselves over to such capricious frivolity as make-up and beauty marks, women of the Great Century, through the sport of hunting, discovered new finery for their seduction. In 1615, in *Le Livre des Bigarrures et Touches*, the chronicler Estienne Tabourot evoked the advent of the horsewoman. "It is said that when women of the court started wearing breeches, they made a general inquiry into how they would call these pants to differentiate from the men's. Finally, they unanimously agreed to call them *caleçons* (leggings)."

Thus, leggings, "a sign of virility," became feminized. A woman's outfit adapted from equestrian sports began to emerge starting at the beginning of the seventeenth century. This was the *hongreline*, a sort of slim doublet worn over a dress fashioned from the same fabric. In the court of Louis XVI, women sported hunting outfits that were inspired by military garb, with a lace jabot replacing the plunging neckline. Madame la Duchesse d'Orléans would make her appearance wearing a peruke and plumed three-cornered hat. Just where were women going? The English diarist Samuel Pepys noted in his journal, "Today, I am using a muff that my wife wore last year. I have now bought her a new one, and the other suits me fine".

Trousers: A Symbol of Independence

14

Along side the legendary Geneviève Prémoy, the so-called "Chevalier Bantazar" and musketeer heroine, the most famous horsewomen remain Louise Labbé, who appeared at the siege of Perpignan (1542) dressed in shining armor astride her spirited horse "Princesse Palatine," and Christine de Suède who in 1654 exchanged the royal purple, "symbol of enslavement" for the trousers, "symbol of independence".

"If I prefer men, it is not because they are men, it is because they are not women," declared she who engraved the helmeted profile of Minerva on one side of a medallion and a phoenix upon a pyre on the other, and inscribed the word *Makelos*, which is to say, "without equal and unmarried". "She is dressed like a man, has his tone of voice and almost all his actions," said the Duke de Guise.

14- Geneviève Prémoy in men's garb after a period document.

15- "Bad Omen: Unhappy Household and Debates over Pants." Print extract from *Moralités* by Nicolas Guérard (17th century).

Breeches, Knickers and Leggings.
The Trials and Tribulations of the Culotte

Among the pioneers was Catherine de Médicis who introduced the *vertugade* into French fashion. This was a roll that the Italians placed under a skirt to puff it up. She also initiated the ladies of France in the wearing of leggings *(caleçons)*, the name for which undoubtedly derives from the Italian *calzone*, and which was also called "bridles for the buttocks". Pierre de Bourdeille, abbot and lord of Brantôme, man of the sword and of pleasures recounted in the *Vie des Dames Illustres* (circa 1584), "By this curiosity in which she had kept so beautiful a leg, it must be believed that it was so as not to hide it under a skirt, nor a petticoat, nor a dress, but to show it off, sometimes with beautiful leggings of gold or silver cloth or some other fabric, very smartly and properly fashioned, which she would usually wear".

Brantôme observed that there were designs intended to be shown and others "made of satin" and "nicely padded" for thin ladies "of the kind not knowingly, one comes to touch them finding nothing but good and firmly believing that it is their natural stoutness, as underneath this satin, there were flouncy white leggings. […] And thus, a lover, taking his lady dressed […] would leave her, happy and satisfied believing that she in fact, was really a looker". If the countrywomen remain faithful to "serge knickers" similar to the breeches of the Middle Ages, ladies of standing did not hesitate wearing leggings while travelling or hunting, even if the eccentrics at the Rambouillet Hotel preferred to forget them when lunching in the meadows. Angélique Paulet, known as the "Beautiful Lioness," was even the inspiration for Voiture's *Stanzas on a Woman Whose Skirt Hikes Up While Pouring into a Carriage in the Countryside.*

Le Chanteur Chenard en Sans-Culottes (detail), Louis Léopold Boilly (1792-1793), Carnavalet Museum, Paris.

From the Old Regime to the Revolution

"(If) A woman has the right to mount the gallows, (then) she must also have such to mount the rostrum." (Déclaration des Droits de la Femme et de la Citoyenne, Olympe de Gouges, 1792.)

The Triumph of the Sans-Culottes

A nglomania ruled, and in the eighteenth century, the horsewoman's outfit would become a must. This was thanks to certain relaxings — for example, the abolition of the use of whalebone stays to "lighten" the waist, worn under the shepherdess attire that Marie-Antoinette was quite fond of at

the Petit Trianon. Chic young people adopted the *chenille*, a style of pants that succeeded in leaving them exposed. Sheathed in their clothes, the "fine air featherbrains" promenaded through the Palais-Royal wearing white trousers that had no pockets and which were so tight, it was impossible to sit down.

With the "canary tail" or "sulfur" pants, with the *Incroyables* wearing ancient-style dresses, there is no question that never had the passion for one's appearance been so crystallized as it was at the end of the eighteenth century. In 1789, the Jacobins, in order to distinguish themselves from the aristocracy that sported French-style tight-fitting trousers that were held at the knee with garters, adopted the long twill pants of sailors, which they wore with a Phrygian cap and a short jacket called a *carmagnole*. These were the "sans-culottes" of the National Assembly.

1

From the Old Regime to the Revolution. The Triumph of the Sans-Culottes

Beyond the name, which marked a transformation in clothing, it was the overall look that changed, symbolizing a new attitude that corresponded with a new manner of presenting oneself — hair was natural, faces were powderless. The fops reacted against this "carelessness" by opting for an elegant tailcoat, white pants and hair coifed in the style of "dog ears".

The democratization of appearance did nothing to cast a shadow over the war of the sexes. Before the French Revolution, one could already read in *Le Magasin des Modes* (1787), "Today, with the exception of attire that still does not replace dresses, and trousers that still do not replace petticoats, women's attire is the same as men's, as much in their cut as in their colour". Louis Sébastien Mercier, in his *Tableau de Paris* (1781), went further. "Women are drawing closer, as much as they can, to our manners. They now wear men's clothing, triple-collared frock coats, hair tied at the neck with a bow, a switch in their hands, flat-heeled shoes, two watches and a short vest."

Horsewomen of Freedom

The Revolution parted the doors of utopia. For a female army known as the army corps of Fernigh, women devised a military uniform comprised of a large skirt-pants and a overshirt. But the dream of an "egalitarian"

1- Portrait of the Count of Provence in the grand attire of the Order of Saint Esprit presenting the *Privilèges de la Ville d'Angers*, François-Hubert Drouais, Museum of the Chateau, Versailles.

2- Equestrian portrait of Catherine II of Russia, Vigilius Erichsen, Museum of Fine Arts, Chartres.

3- "A citizen being stopped to put a national emblem on his hat," gouache by the Le Sueur brothers (18th century), Carnavalet Museum, Paris.

4- *I am Free,* the abolition of slavery, print.

5- *The Great Household Quarrel* (18th century).

outfit appears to have had its limits. Adventuresses like Olympe de Gouges, the author of *A Declaration of the Rights of Women and the [Lady] Citizen* (1792) and Théroigne de Méricourt, the *Belle Liégeoise* and founder of a patriotic society that called upon battalions of horse-women to save the new regime, were the first to set off an explosion. Upon meeting them, Fougeret, the Officer General of Finances declared in 1791, "Some public girls, such as Mademoiselle Théroigne, walk through the

HISTOIRE DES PIRATES.

A. Debelle del

MARIE READ.

Tuilleries gardens and the Palais-Royal dressed in horse-woman attire with pistols on their belts." Lashed naked by Jacobin ladies, this "Horsewoman of Freedom", "Martyr for the constitution" was confined to an asylum. Chaumette, the public prosecutor criticized a group of women who had come to the Commune council wearing Phrygian caps. "Imprudent women who want to become men, are you not sufficiently split? You dominate over all our senses; the legislator, the magistrate are at your feet [...]. Instead of envying us the perils of a stormy life, be content to absent them from the bosom of our families." Two sisters, Félicité and Théophile Fernig, sixteen and eighteen years old, disguised themselves as men and by their great exploits, asserted themselves as warriors of the Revolution. In Paris, the new horsewomen adopted a

From the Old Regime
to the Revolution.
The Triumph of the Sans-Culottes

white "à la constitution" outfit, with its blue and Bavarian red frock coat, a chiffon jabot, tight-fitting sleeves, a blue belt and with long tails ending in tassels. Two small pockets made it possible to carry two watches. Some women would go about with a walking stick, leaving the elegant men to sport tapered tailcoats with "the tail of a codfish" and tight-fitting trousers "à la horsewoman" that were attached to striped stockings with bows.

But combat was on all fronts. Female Republicans, in pants and with pistols had to confront the abuses of the fishwives at *Les Halles* who did not hesitate to attack them with whips. The Commune made inquiries, the Convention joined them, and on September 27, 1793 Fabre d'Églantine mounted an assault. "[If] today one demands the red cap, it will not end there, and soon one will demand a belt and pistol for [buying] bread in a manner that will perfectly match the troop maneuvers, and you will see lines of women going for bread like one does marching in the trenches." And to conclude, "These societies are not comprised of mothers of the family, nor girls of the family, nor sisters who look after their younger brothers and sisters, but of a species of adventuresses, of errant *chevaliers*, of emancipated girls, of female grenadiers."

Taken by the great ladies, the empresses and the emancipated queens, from Semiramis of Assyria to Hatshepsut of Egypt who had taken on the attributes of a pharaoh, from Elisabeth Petrowna to Catherine II of Russia, ("likeable woman, great man" as was written below one of her portraits), trousers attracted too many intolerable eccentricities. They almost became the symbol of the counter-revolution.

In November 1793, Olympe de Gouges, who had ironically called for Robespierre to commit suicide in order to deliver France from "its greatest scourge," was guillotined. Four days later, the Convention banned women from wearing uniforms and rendered suspect the wearing of pants. A Committee for Public Safety closed women's clubs and banned them from "exercising political rights and from taking an active part in affairs of government". Did not a fifteenth-century sermonist, atop his pulpit, hurl these terrifying threats? "They shall be punished, they shall be pursued by celestial lightning, those who shall dress in the attire of the opposite sex."

6- *Marie Reed, woman pirate* (18th century), print.

7- *Jacques Cathelineau, general from the Vendée,* Anne Louise Girodet de Roussy-Trioson, Art Museum, Cholet.

8- *The Waltz,* satirical engraving (1820).

8

George "Beau" Brummel (detail). Watercolor on paper by Robert Dighton (1805). Private collection.

Horsewomen, *Merveilleuses* and **Bloomerists**

"An elegant man's pants must be tight, but tight in such a way that he is unable to bend, without which elegance is not possible."
(Le Journal de Tailleurs, February 26, 1838.)

Heroes Afoot

2

I n the nineteenth century, the middle class imposed its values, laying down, through clothing, a social and moral order that reflected its taboos. Gone were the egalitarian noises of the Revolution, and the suit once again fell into the male domain. Formally adorned, its hierarchical and sumptuous finery drawn from the uniforms of the Old Guard, it sported embroidered bars, the white pants of constables and chamberlains, a three-cornered hat and the blue tailcoat and red belt of a "minister in his all his finery".

1

In its varying models, colours and fabrics, the tailcoat defined the ages and documented the power and the grandeur of the state, codified social status, set the look of older and younger women, distinguished the respectable lady from the prostitute, the Parisian woman from the country maid. With the transition of an aristocratic society into a middle-class one, the male role was no longer identified with the hero and the courtier, but rather as a member of society at large and whose purpose was to make a system based upon such fundamental values as work, the family and patriotism work. The

Horsewomen, *Merveilleuses* and Bloomerists.
Heroes Afoot

image of the responsible man was inseparable from the black tailcoat, the new uniform of the middle class, which vexed the eccentrics in their puckered, pleated *culottes à pont* that puffed out at the knees.

Students dared to wear big colourful plaids just to set

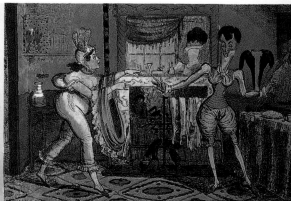

themselves apart from the uniformity. If "dandyism" were the "last heroic cry of decadence" as Baudelaire wrote, the intrusion of the state into all corners of private life must be thwarted. The aristocratic look of Brummel, typified very early on by the golden garter of his immaculate stockings, was in answer to the somewhat base caricature of Milord L'Arsouille, always in the

company of Chicard, with his feathered cap, leather trousers and rider's boots. The dandy's pants were extremists. The ultras preferred their pants tight-fitting and clinching at the waist. "I forewarn you, if I can get in them, I do not want them." (*La Mode*, August 18, 1839.) "Down to the heels (how hideous!) these pants go." So wrote Musset in his *Premières Poésies* (1830), referring to the finery of the dandies who were above all, eccentrics, as the elegant pants of Lord Petersham attest to. Punning

1- *Tableau de Paris*, "Aux Arts Réunis". Opitz (1831), Carnavalet Museum, Paris.

2- *Portrait of Louis-Philippe, the Duke of Orléans wearing the Colonel-General uniform of the Hussards with his sons the Duke of Chartres and the Duke of Némours*. Louis Hersent, after Gérard Baron François, Versailles Chateau.

3- *Des Anglomanes*, Private collection.

4- *The Duke of Medina*. Alvares de Toledo (1846), Quennieux Chateau, Amiens.

5- *The Hen-Pecked Dandy*. Robert Cruikshank, Towner Art Gallery, Eastbourne.

6- *Le Parisien anglaisé*. Caricature by Auger, engraving (c.1840).

7- *Le Coiffeur* (1800). Private collection.

in English, the were said to be Toulon (too long) and Toulouse (too loose). Occasionally, eccentricity cloaked itself in sobriety, as can be seen in the obsessional gray pants and blue tailcoat adopted by Brummel.

During these stylistic changes, middle-class conservatism returned in the form of etiquette, putting to rest the extravagances that had emerged at the height of the *Merveilleuses* and the *Incroyables*.

The 16th Brumaire of the year IX (November 7, 1800), a Napoleon decree, stated the dress code. "Considering that many women cross-dress, and of the belief that no one should abandon the dress of his sex for reasons of health […]. Considering that such authorization must be uniform and that to this date different allowances have been accorded by different authorities," the Dubois police ordain that "all women desiring to dress like men must present themselves to the police for such authorization".

The patriotic calls by the legions of horsewomen in 1789 seemed to have vanished in smoke. "It is not the fantasy of wearing uniforms that goes to our heads, but the desire

Horsewomen, *Merveilleuses* and Bloomerists.

Heroes Afoot

to bear the sword that we carry in our hearts!," as was written in *Les Étrennes Nationales de Dames.* While, under the influence of the Romantics and the fencing craze, men's pants became more and more slim-cut, fitting tight to the leg, women's pants became an underwear, relegated to the "boisterous," the "mysterious" and the "lionesses". Henceforth, a woman had to get permission "to cross-dress" and "dress like a man".

Lionesses and "Tank Tops"

In 1830, now more than ten years old, pants were deemed "unseemly" by *Le Journal des Desmoiselles.* The same year, one could witness the return of the corset. This inflicted a peculiar body movement, constraining the "woman of leisure" to the immobility it imposed. An ordinance dated May 31, 1833 authorized "cross-dressing [...] during carnival times," giving rise to Gavarni's engraved scenes of lady aristocrats dressed in pants act-

12

8- Permission to cross-dress (1806).
Museum of the Police Archives, Paris.

9 to 12- Engravings by Paul Gavarni (circa 1840),
Carnavalet Museum, Paris.

9- "Thank you, Monsieur le Marquis.
The champagne goes to my head."

10- "Thrown into jail like a nobody..."

11- "Tomorrow morning my dear husband will bellow."

12- "A young couple and love."

ing like children playing hooky. Wearing blouses the like of "tank tops," they were outspoken. "Come on, Landerneau, my good man, you have been drinking and you know get nasty after a taste." Quite colourful, these etchings depicted characters free to emancipate themselves on carnival day. Here, well-dressed women find themselves in prison — "To be thrown in jail like you're nothing! Two fine women, great God!" Here, they swear, "It'll be tomorrow morn when my dear husband bellows.

13

13- *"Les Parisiennes à Montmorency"*, Print.

14- *Le Café des Variétés*, Engraving (beginning 19ᵗʰ century), Carnavalet Museum, Paris.

15- *Woman lancer.* After an engraving from the Restoration.

16- *"Les Vésuviennes ou les Soldats pour rire"*, Édouard de Beaumont, *Le Charivari* (1848). "Ma'am Coquardeau, I forbid you to answer to military reserves... It's not a good idea leaving me like this with three kids in my arms and no pacifier!" Marguerite Durand Library, Paris.

Oh, but darn, tonight I'll damn the marriage and *vive* Chicard!" "And if Cornélie didn't find the carriage? We'd go by foot! Thank you. I'll be cheap about anything you might want, but I'm never a bad sort. Never!" The "Momignardes" freed themselves of conventions. "Have I the honor of dancing a gallop with Monsieur le Baron?!" The gallant press observed the "lionesses" of the Champs-de-Mars parading in their Tilbury outfits, who dared to wear pants under their dresses in the manner of Virginie Letellier, a dancer at the Opéra and mistress of the Duke of Berry. With cotton petticoats, scarves and ruffs, "winged pants, ample in the seat and narrowing at the cuff," so revealed the intimate and pastel universe of Madame Bovary, in which Flaubert described the "affairs of women".

Far from the provincial boudoirs, it was in the city that pants, having proved to be the fetish clothing of horsewomen and modeled upon the styles of the Anglomanics, were the first worn by daring men at dinners, balls and galas. The shock of the arrival of a young man dressed in baggy black Wellington-style pants into a salon on the Faubourg Saint-Germain disturbed the rules

Horsewomen, *Merveilleuses* and Bloomerists.
Heroes Afoot

15

A FEMALE LANCER.

of the chic Restauration which was subject to the "laws of the culottes".

"The culotte, for which during the past several years there has been a vain attempt to abolish, will undoubtedly persevere for a long time to come amongst better company," as was written in *Le Code de la Toilette* in 1828. "It is far more elegant and comfortable than the pants they are trying to replace it with. Even in

16

military attire, today it remains the culotte that is solely acceptable as full dress at receptions and balls."

But leaving these nostalgic ones to their fake calves and their padded stockings, the horsewomen opted for pants. It was these new women who drank flaming punch and frozen champagne, fenced with épées and shot pistols and smoked cigars. "Woman as man!" declared a chronicler in 1832. "It takes nothing more to make passersby turn around, to set the police off. But just as often, the police are privy and let it go by. No doubt when it is Mademoiselle Dejazet or some other star dressed like a man."

These arrivals, like Louise Aston the author of the 1846 *Meine Emancipation*, were already loved in Berlin. "The French still remember the impression made by a famous writer of our sex when she appeared amongst them dressed in such attire. In Germanic countries, such eccentricities are still far more difficult than they are in France, because the German police believe that they are not merely charged with the protection of government and property, but that it is their duty to make citizens observe Lutheran, Calvinist or Catholic morals, in accordance with the region" as was written at the time. In explanation of her "conduct" before a magistrate who asked, "Why then do you flaunt your disbelief in God?" the woman dressed in culottes responded, "Your Excellence, because I am not a hypocrite."

In the Time of the Vesuvians

The events of 1848 revived the utopias of the French Revolution when the Fernig citizens promised to "abandon the seduction of love until their co-citizens had walked off with the laurels of glory". Their uniform comprised a jacket, a white outfit culottes, a vest, stockings and linings of different colours depending upon the legion, breeches "cut à la Portuguese" and a bronze hel-

Chez Bauger, R. du Croissant, 16.

Chez Aubert, Pl. de la Bourse.

Imp. d'Aubert & Cie.

Si de Georges Sand ce portrait,
Laisse l'esprit un peu perplexe,
C'est que le Génie est abstrait,
Et comme on sait n'a pas de sexe.

George Sand: Culotte Memories

"I was no longer a lady, I was no longer a sir. I was a lost atom in that vast crowd" wrote the "fine lady from Nohan" born Aurore Dupin, the baroness of Dudevant. At the Opéra she was taken for a "boy hairdresser" and at restaurants as a "little pedantic boy" which qualified her as a "young man." Indeed, as a "street urchin." The French novelist George Sand (1804-1876) was the first to make pants her feminist civil uniform.

"I wear culottes and find this attire perfectly normal. The Creator gave us all two legs. I do not understand why women, particularly working women, would not be more comfortable and more properly suited having two separate legs to traipse through the mud and get into a carriage.

"Having dressed like a boy during my childhood, having then gone hunting in a smock and gaiters with Deschartres, I am not at all surprised once again to wear clothing that is not new to me," she wrote in Histoire de Ma Vie *(1855). During this period, style was singularly helpful for disguising. Men wore "long checkered frock coats, called "à la landlord," that reached just to the heels and that so little defined one's waist, that my brother, putting his on Nohant laughingly said to me, "It's very pretty, isn't it? It's the style, and doesn't bother me. The tailor took the measurements on a sentry box, and it will be the rave of all the regiment. [...]*

"So, I had a sentry frock coat made from a heavy gray cloth, pants and vest from the same. With a gray hat and a wide wool tie, I was all the little first-year schoolboy. I cannot tell you what pleasure my boots gave me. I would gladly have slept with them on, as my brother did when he was young and put on his first pair. With the little iron-tapped heels, I was solid on the sidewalk.

"I flitted about from one end of Paris to the other. I felt like I had gone 'round the world. And my clothes were sturdy. I ran around in all weather, I came home at any hour, I would go to the stalls of all the theaters. Nobody paid attention to me, nobody doubted my disguise. Aside from dressing comfortably, the absence of concern for stylishness in my dress and physique removed any question."

met. "To defeat the despots/Farewell, dear parents./We wear the culotte./It is today's woman" cried the battalions of horsewomen in their marching song. A convicted feminist, citizen Monsieur Borme proposed on March 1, 1848, to form a legion of 'Vesuvians' that would be comprised of single women aged fifteen to thirty years old." A chemical manufacturer, he did not hesitate to plaster all around Paris a yellow poster addressed "to [women] patriotic citizens, my sisters of the Republic". For months, such satiric journals of the day as *Le Pamphlet*, *Le Charivari*, *La Silhouette* and *Le Canard* needled these women citizens "of the barracks." Among them were Eugénie Niboyet, Elisa Lemonnier, Pauline Roland, Jeanne Deroin and Anna de Schnitzburg, the last two of whom, according to *Le Tintamarre*, were suffering from "demonstration mania" and whose motto was, "More confident love than obscure devotion."

In the name of the right "to come and go," the restyling of women's attire was a primary preoccupation. "Women must imperceptibly work to eradicate the differences that exist in men's and women's attire, without transgressing the limits of decency and the absurd, nor retreating from graceful lines and good taste. Moreover, it will be a change in which men, upon seeing their funerary dress, will not really have any reason to complain," declared the *Vesuvians*. Thus, the April 28, 1848 issue of *La Voix des*

Femmes advocated the masculinization of women's attire. *La République des Femmes* offered the horsewomen of 1848 a "feminist" *Marseillaise*. "Tremble, tyrants who wear culottes./Women, our day has come./Arise, Vesuvians, arise."

If some women called for obligatory service in the "women's corps," others demanded the right to serve the country as workers, cooks or ambulance drivers. Flattered and caricaturized, the Vesuvians, those "horsewomen of peace" according to *La Voix des Femmes*, demanded the right to divorce and mandatory marriage from which the "lame" and the "moronic" would be excluded. Borme,

who had been their defender, very quickly became their worst enemy, denouncing the private lives of the "princesses and marquises of the Boule Rouge and Breda quarter" in Paris. Under their influence, feminist clubs burgeoned, with some three hundred opening in the capital in March 1848. In the April 6, 1848 edition of *La Voix des Femmes*, Eugénie Niboyet called for the candidature of George Sand for the National Assembly. "Seamstresses have their apostles. Thinking workers, let us make a choice of our own. A representative who unifies our affinities. He. She. Male by virility. Female by divine intention. By poetry. We want to *man* George Sand [to the post]." This woman who "presents a man in spirit, but remains a woman in terms of the maternal" engendered both fascination and repulsion.

Stovepipe Hats

The actions of such feminists as Flora Tristan served as fodder for the cartoons of both French newspapers *(Le Charivari)*, as well as for their London and Berlin equivalents *(Der Kladderatatsch)*. Pamphlets deriding women in "stovepipe hats, neckties, frock coats and pants" multiplied. "Either they are inelegant, pretentious, frumpy, unclean blue-stockinged ones, or they are severely turned out, pinned and ironed like a Quaker lady," wrote F. Soulié in a *Physiologie du Bas-Blue.*

With a flower in his lapel, his white-gloved hands, a top-hat planted upon wavy his hair, the elegant gentleman jealously protected his dandyism, excluding the woman-man from his smoky coterie. In his book *La Femme en Coulotte* (1899), John Grand-Carteret devoted an entire chapter to "diverse individuals: women poets, great ladies, eccentric women, lady travelers, women of letters, women of politics, painters and actresses". Pants were to women what "inspired hairstyles" were to young writers walking the streets of 1848: a sign of style.

Horsewomen, *Merveilleuses* and Bloomerists.

Heroes Afoot

What remained was for pants to confront obstacles. In 1841 in the United States, the attempt by Amelia Bloomer to launch a jacket and pants outfit for women ended

as a failure. Born in 1818 and married to a Boston lawyer, Amelia Bloomer Jenks defended her ideas in *The Lily*, a journal that remained private. Here, she advocated the replacement of the petticoat by a culotte that went down to the knees. "Bloomerism" inspired cartoons, like the one that appeared in Vienna in 1851 showing two women in hat and tie, nastily smoking cigars and scornfully eyeing the dumbfounded children. The same year, the London magazine Punch portrayed a bloomerist, "a superior creature," kneeling at the feet of a man, asking for his hand in marriage. In the same issue, an illustrated panel entitle *Bloomeriana, A Dream* depicted a man reduced to the state of a bizarre, caged animal. Something like a bear from Mars. In 1866, Larousse described Amelia Bloomer as belonging to a time already past.

While the cadaver-like thinness became the prerogative of poets and the *exquisites*, it was for women of character to defend pants, both in dress and in literature, the legitimization of an intellectual authority, a true private hunting ground, according to some. "One woman who writes of two wrongs, she augments the number of books and lessens the number of women," declared the writer and journalist Alphonse Karr *(Les Femmes,* 1856). A quartet of women directed by Jenny d'Hericourt would nevertheless take up the pen and denounce this "cloud-like clothing" that Proudhon, Michelet and Auguste Comte wished to impose upon them.

The culotte question became a social battle. "Women's dress is the garb of servitude. It shows that we are a sex, not individuals," as Madeline Pelletier, a militant member of the French Socialist Party would proclaim. Questioned by John Grand-Carteret, some women "dressed in the classic bourgeois skirt" would answer, "In truth, dear Sir, as you well know, I wear a man's suit. But when spirited women do dumb things, they don't generally keep the proofs".

17- (preceding page) George Sand.
Satirical engraving by Lorentz (1842).
Le Miroir Drôlatique in *Le Charivari*.
"If the George Sand of this portrait/leaves the mind a bit perplexed/it's that the genius is abstract/and one doesn't know the sex."

18- *"Les Vésuviennes ou les Soldats pour rire",*
Édouard de Beaumont, *Le Charivari* (1848).
"Josephine Frenovillot takes advantage of her resemblance to Napoleon to make the troops believe that the emperor was not dead as the police had rumored."
Marguerite Durand Library, Paris.
(rights reserved)

19- *The Bloomer Polka,*
Portrait of Amelia Bloomer,
J. J. Blockley (circa 1850).

Blanche D'Antigny et Son Vélocipède,
by Bétinet (end of 19th century),
Museum of the Île-de-France, Sceaux.

Elegants, Suffragettes and Pedalers

*"I am before your question
as I am before women bicyclists,
only a passerby who steps aside,
but if their motive is to show their legs,
I prefer that it would a skirt riding
up, a feminine relic, not boyish pants."*
(Résponse à des Enquêtes…,
Mallarmé, 1896.)

Hygiene and Emancipation

"**A** woman was nothing. Today she wants to be everything. She aspires to employment that until now has been occupied by men, going into offices, receiving bachelor degrees, becoming doctors and lawyers, riding a bicycle, adopting men's clothing, smoking, taking on an casual air, speaking loudly, making decisions, adorning her blouse with the honorary violet ribbon that she obtains through her boldness, through judicial protections, and through others of equal weight, seeks to be as much as possible "a man." And it appears that these women, adorable women, but from the "outside" would be what one would call *hommes manqués*," wrote Auguste Reiser in the September 10, 1899 edition of the *Journal d'Asnières et de la Banlieue Ouest*.

Upon the background of the great discoveries, political scandals and the Industrial Revolution, pants found themselves split between the taboo and the erotic, between the functional and the sinful. They stood out with a suggestive rustling that would fascinate writers from Huysmans to Daudet. A character emblematic of the *demi-monde*, Nana emerged from the pens of Émile Zola, "so arched back over her toilette, that the white plumpness of her panties protruded and tightened with the little end of her blouse." Certain moralists nevertheless became indignant with the "infamy of her slit" for which the sado-masochistic scene in *L'Assommoir* (1877) by Zola sets the tempo. "Gervaise seized Virginie by the waist, bent her over, pressed her head against the tiles, her hips raised high in the air, and despite the jolts, she grandly lifted up her skirts. Underneath, she wore pants. She passed her hand in the slit, took them off, exposing all, naked thighs, naked buttocks…then, the thrasher raised, she submitted to the beating."

Rustling and Hygiene

Far from the boudoirs, women's pants were a protector of virtue. In 1877, Dr. Becquerel, in his *Traité élémentaire d'hygiène privée et publique* recommended, "the use of cloth leggings to protect those. organs exposed to dust and bad weather by petticoats and open, flouncy dresses."

The obsession with hygiene did not spare men's wardrobe, as the German doctor Hans Gustav Jaeger denounced pants for men whose tubes of fabric let pass currents of air that were noxious to the health, causing the stomach to blow up and "crow's feet."

While men's attire, with the birth of the suit (pant, jacket and vest cut from the same fabric) in 1875 became simplified, even codified according to the rules of the circumstances — from the "bowler" to the "eight tints for the evening" — women's attire became more complicated with an avalanche of laces, crinolines, turns, gigantic sleeves and tulip skirts. Made a fuss over by Montmartre's ladies of little virtue, pants gained ground, making their entry into middle-class life. Absent from the numerous types of trousseaus suggested by *Le Moniteur de la Mode* between 1845 and 1850, they made a timid appearance as part of a "mountain" theme.

Styles derived from the waltz and the polka provided another chance. It

was in 1867 that the "indispensable," presented adorned with lace, ribbons and embroidery, became the ideal accessory for dancing the "can-can" (the art of lifting up the skirt) and the "chahut" (the art of kicking up the legs). Pants, until then relegated to the snowy trousseaus of the demi-mondaines and the ladies of the Bal Bullier (Henriette Zou-Zou, Louise Voyageur and Pauline L'Arsouille, for example), henceforth would form a part of the mythology of love, as *L'Adorée*, a novel by René Maizeroy revealed. "Pants, which went no farther than the lace-garters, drive a lover wild better than immodest state of nudity." It was again in 1867 that the illustrated catalogue from Aristide Boucicaut's *Au Bon Marché* offered a wide choice of pants in "madapolam" (an Indian cotton), in brushed cotton and in percale, adorned or not.

But once again, emancipation was elsewhere, contrasting the sacred, perfumed image of the "Parisian lady" with the androgynous Anglo-Saxon. "True chic, when travelling, is comfort. The English have understood this and they are, in respect to this, our indisputable masters." So wrote *L'Illustration* in its May 22, 1890 issue. The wind was blowing from London, where in 1874, Alexandra, the Princess of Wales, was photographed in a "sailor's" outfit with a belted jacket. Appearing between 1885 and 1890, the suit was first reserved for the privileged classes.

Charles Poynter, a fabric merchant during the 1850s in Cowes, a seaside village on the Isle of Wight, opened a department for women's clothing. His suit was the ancestor of the women's pants suit. He opened a branch in London, then in 1881 another in Paris, and in 1885, he created the marriage trousseau for the Princess of Wales. "It is routing toward this uniformity of women's attire demanded in America and England. As for us, we see in

1- A tart in undergarments (1895). Private collection.

2- Open pants in percale.
Le Moniteur des Dames et des Demoiselles (1879).

3- *Battalion of volunteer riflewomen in England.*
Gustave Janet (1860).

4- *The Emancipation Suit (1875).*

3

it a serious danger for our Parisian *chiffoneuses*," the magazine *L'Art dans le costume* indignantly declared in December 1890.

Skirts were cut from the same fabrics as men's pants — wools and linens in neutral colours, brown, gray and dark blue for winter, and ivory or white for summer. "For some time, precious silly ladies and *femmes manquées* tried their best to introduce the fashion of the very wide sailor's pants that went all the way down to the boots, floating around hoop. What a cure for love!" wrote Alphonse Karr (*Les Femmes*, 1856).

English Creases and the Dinner Jacket

The tailored suit is a model of puritan severity and sobriety. "Religious morality defined an ethic of sober, sensible

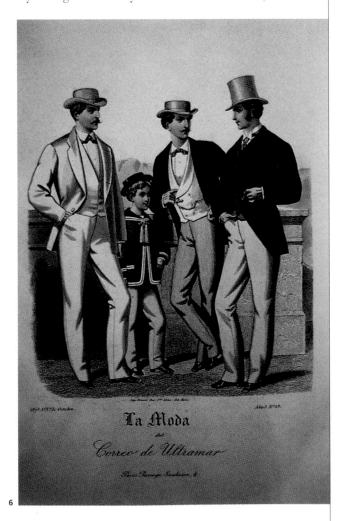

La Moda
del
Correo de Ultramar

clothing that was worn with modesty and adhered to three functions: it protects from inclement weather, it offers a barrier to pruriency and a guard to virtue [...], a suitable attire, indeed graceful is recommended. Beyond that, it denotes an exaggerated cult of the individual," wrote its advocates. During this period, the *Rational Dress Society* was founded in London and in 1894, it organized an exhibition that drew four million visitors. Under the exalted patronage of Queen Victoria, innovations in the women's lingerie such as the restrictive corset and the small crinoline petticoat were introduced.

At the same time, the dinner jacket became important with the English. Worn by men in clubs as well as at home, to escape the stiffness of the starched shirt, it became the symbol of a look. In 1895, the pants crease was made with an iron, the hem "reawakened" each morning. The French ironically remarked that "one "reawakens" his pants in Paris because it is raining in London." The grand ladies did not hesitate to petition for that would legalize the wearing of pants.

Without constraining it, the suit delineated the figure of the emancipated woman. A woman too free in her move-

Elegants, Suffragettes and Pedalers.
Hygiene and Emancipation

ments and who dared to go out alone would be dubbed "English." Colette would walk her small dogs in the Bois de Boulogne wearing a chestnut-coloured waterproof outfit with buttoned boots. She would ride horseback dressed in *amazone* along side Willy, wearing a large gray felt hat with broad feathers. The writer, who sat for the photographer Nader, loved the "rough woolens coming from England," cut her "too long hair," admired her friend Valentine in her "splendid tailored suit" of a "mousy gray" velvet "that hugged the wife from her neck to her feet."

Justified by sports and travel, the wearing of pants would remain for a long time limited to the elite and the new devotees of speed. Appearing in England in 1854, the bicycle did much to further the flight of pants. In a nutty homespun or a caramel scotch-cloth, worn with a striped

man's shirt with a regatta tie, pants clothed a new way of life. The bicycle would be the herald of this emerging generation about which Marcel Proust in *À la Recherche du Temps Perdu* would note "the air of fragility and guile." Albertine would speak of her bicycle as "my *bécane*" and would make fun of the little ladies of Ambresac who dress with a "city elegance, not for the beach" and who "golf in silk dresses."

Indignant voices rang out. "The fat and the thin seem to be competing for prizes for the Ridiculous and the Grotesque," wrote a certain Pierre Lafitte, taking part in the debate." The columnist responded, "Well, culottes were largely responsible. With them, the most suggestive forms became unseemly or... disheartening. The derriere vanished without warning and the stomach perpetually

7

5- **Members of the Jockey Club. Belgium (circa 1895). Collection of A. Vassiliev, Paris.**

6- *Corneo del Ultraman.* **Men's fashion in Madrid (1873). Biblioteca Nacionale, Santiago.**

7- *Les Sports Modernes.* **Watercolor. *L'Album des Sports* (August 1908).**

8- **Vacationers at the beginning of the 20th century.**

threatened its neighbour. The mystery of the legs became transformed into knock-knees or bow-legs, and the ankles work-a-day."

"And to say it took five years of struggling to arrive at making women understand that the pleasure they derive from dressing like men was not worth, ultimately, the ridicule that this craze earned them. Today, the proof is there. The skirt-culotte was the ambassador negotiating the peace between good taste on one side and women's independence on the other. Pants are no longer the priv-

Elegants, Suffragettes and Pedalers.

Hygiene and Emancipation

A History Afoot

ten meters of fabric to custom make a "bicyclist's outfit out of very tightly woven smooth English cloth of a neutral shade."

On July 1, 1893, *L'Illustration* devoted a page to the phenomenon. "The *Bois* is being invaded by indefatigable *velocewomen* who travel along the paths in all directions. [...] Nothing is more graceful than to see a pretty woman, well turned out, in a seductive bicycling outfit and a woman who is already experienced in this sport retains all her elegance. Her svelte and agile waist has here a very special opportunity to put itself in the fore, as can be read in the writings of Fanfreluche. The ques-

ilege of professionals and ladies who take to doing their hundred kilometers during the day at the price of God knows how much sweat! The culotte is dead! Long live the skirt!"

Victory of the Little Queen

In 1888, people spoke of the new "Olympism." In 1892, the bloomer revolution disturbed the minister of the Interior who regulated the wearing of pants by women and the boundaries of bicycling. But the irresistible call of fashion was there. The first bouffant culottes appeared on advertising posters such as "La Bacane, Quina of the Cyclists, Delicious Aperitifs." In 1893, on the eve of the inauguration of the Vélodrome d'Hiver on the Champs-de-Mars, the Louvre opened a "special bicyclist's counter for women." One could find there "tourist blouses," "zouave pants in jersey" and "bolero-style suits." It took

9- *Le Chalet du cycle au bois de Boulogne*,
   Jean Béraud (circa 1900). Carnavalet Museum,
   Paris.

10- *Le Courrier Français*. Drawing by Adolphe Willette
   (August 25, 1895). Carnavalet Museum, Paris.

11- Cover illustration of *La Femme en Culotte*.
   John Grand-Carteret (1899).

12- Men's bicycling fashion (circa 1890).
   Collection of A. Vassiliev, Paris.

tion of dress has always been a source of embarrassment for women the world over in respect to mounting a bicycle. Now, they can no longer use this as a pretext, as the

crown. Jean Cocteau described Colette in these terms: "thin, thin, a sort of small fox in a cycling outfit."

The opening of the Moulin-Rouge on October 6, 1889 was dedicated to the triumph of the Goulue, that "flower of the washbasin" according to Jean Lorrain, immortal-

ized by Toulouse-Lautrec with his pants open to the four winds, symbol of eroticism at the end of the nineteenth century. Defended by the grisettes and women workers, pants in another manner seduced the young airy lady aristo-

prettiest outfits are now designed especially for this endeavor."

Made of "glove leather" or of jersey and worn with gaiters buttoned up to the knees, the culotte was at the point of straddling the century.

The first bicycle salon was held at Wagram Hall in 1894. It marked the triumph of the "lady bicyclists" who appeared on the advertising posters for Gladiator and Liberator bicycles sheathed in straps and wearing a

crats. Thanks to the "little queen," the chloric young women of 1830 had "the longest arms and the most sup-

Elegants, Suffragettes
and Pedalers.
Hygiene and Emancipation

ple legs." The bicycle gave to those who mounted it the dignified appearance of an ancient goddess. "In an instant, the bicycle pitched, and the young body seemed to have been hoisted up by a sail, an immense wing; and soon we saw stretching out with all quickness, this young creature, half-human, half-winged, angle or peri, pursuing her journey." (Marcel Proust, *La Prisonnière*, 1932.) In her biography of Queen Victoria, Edith Sitwell evoked Paris at the end of the nineteenth century. "…we shall see the most feminine women wearing strange, amorphous masculine attire — with men's paletots, men's collars, men's cravats and walking sticks. Later in the evening some will flaunt military coats of yellow velvet covered with Chinese embroideries…"

Suffragettes on the Move

Soon, people no longer spoke of "culottes" but rather "bouffant pants" which illustrators enjoyed personalizing. The "sphynx" for enigmatic foreigners, the "otéroadeor" for spicy brunettes, the "collet monté" for lady teachers, the "tangara" for alert ladies, the "fatma" for nonchalant women and the "chérubin" with ribboned garters and long flowing lace was reserved for demimonde tarts. The skirt-culotte would become the accepted attire of the suffragettes. The Women's Social and Political Union (WSPU), a suffragist association, was founded in 1903 in Manchester by Emeline Pankhurst and her daughters Cristabel and Sylvia. Blouse knotted with a lavaliere tie, boots and a beret, these women advocated direct action.

13. Advertisement for Liberator bicycles, after Pal. Museum of the Île de France, Sceaux.

14. La Goulue at the Moulin-Rouge. Poster by Toulouse-Lautrec (circa 1892).

15. *Le Sceptre*. Drawing by Adolphe Willette (circa 1905).

16. English suffragettes Dove Wilcok, Dorothy Smith and Kathleen Paget (March 1913).

"The Workers' Party is not interested in women's political rights. Let us put the pressure on it!" In France, a woman in pants was still a strange animal. "I do not have a dress," answered a certain Madame Libert, director of a Right Bank press, to a judge who made her appear at the *Palais de Justice* in 1889. Leaving

16

Astié de Valsayre's Crusade

"In all the brawls on land and on sea, women, because of her clothing, is a victim predestined to die, and accidents on streetcars, for the same reason, occur daily." So wrote Astié de Valsayre to the French deputies on July 1, 1887. This reformer, who presented her lectures with Louise Michel, added, "Thinking of the unfortunate women who were thus impeded from fleeing the fire at the Opéra-Comique, it seems logical and humane to strike the common law that prohibits women from wearing men's garb that is utterly decent, and one might even say, above all, incontestably more hygienic. In the name of those who are not slaves of luxury, I thus, come, Sirs, to beseech you to greatly desire to decree the freedom of dress which, after all, can harm no one." Astié de Valsayre was the first to conceive of a "mixed suit," an idea presented to Worth who did not respond, but soon thereafter, in 1888, introduced a mountain outfit for tourists. One day, finding herself in her petticoats covered with mud, she made it known to the prefecture of police in Lozé that henceforth, she would dress as a man. "I did as I had said […] but the vexations were so unbearable that I had to totally renounce it."

Mᵐᵉ ASTIÉ DE VALSAYRE

Strasbourg, where she had abandoned her husband because of "incompatible spirit," Madame Libert arrived in Paris for the 1878 Exposition having joined her lover. No one, save for him, was aware of her false quality. On the eve of the twentieth century, women's pants horrified the police captains who issued fines. Two fines, levied in one year against the same person, were adjudicated by the correctional court which had to impose fines and sentences. In 1904, a bearded lady (it was twenty centimeters long) was accorded special authorization by Minister Émile Combes to wear this taboo attire. At the end of the nineteenth century, there still existed in Paris an "inspector of pants" at the Moulin-Rouge. The prefecture of police ordered him to prohibit the dancers from exposing "their natural charms and their too intimate undergarments."

17- Madame Astié de Valsayre. Caricature appearing in *Le Charivari* (September 28, 1889).

18- Marth Jane Burke, known as Calamity Jane.

Elegants, Suffragettes
and Pedalers.
Hygiene and Emancipation

A History Afoot

Calamity Jane, or Prudishness Unbuttoned

"Look, I wear men's pants and that let me move around when these females in petticoats had to ask for help," wrote Martha Jane Cannary Hickock around 1880 to her daughter Janey whom she had otherwise abandoned. "You must excuse your mother, Janey, she knows she's strange and badly raised. I'm going to see you soon, but now, I've got to join a poker game and win 20,000 dollars before I can come to you." Better known by the name Calamity Jane, this great horsewoman of the American West left these letters to her daughter, translated and published in French in 1998, stand in evidence of her rage and difference. "I still have never killed anyone, but I'd like to smash on the head some women from Deadwood," she admitted in her letters in a rare moment of intensity. "I can go into the Sioux and Apache camps where a man could not go without being killed. They think that I'm truly crazy."

Leaving her horse Satan at the door of a saloon, she did not hesitate to grab the pants of a "convenient nasty woman" where a gun had always been stashed. "I let them hide it in their underpants so that the men could have a good time. Then, I took the pants with their lace trimmings and knotted them around the neck of another woman who was hitting me on the head. When I saw her tongue hanging out, I was attacked by another woman."

(Calamity Jane, Letters to a Daughter.)

Nijinski in *Sheherazade* (1910), Bibliothèque Nationale de France, Paris.

Idols, Parisian Sultans and Odalisques

"Favoring freedom of movement, the pants-dress, if successful, will re-launch the natural suppleness that constraints had made it lose." (*L'Illustration*, February 11, 1911.)

Orientalism and Society Life

2

"**Y**ou run, you wander, you move about, you alight… there you go, so like a little bird that no one can lay a hand on," wrote Marie Viaud to her brother Louis, alias Pierre Loti, whose novels foreshadowed the great twentieth-century invitation to travel. In 1888, the author of *Aziyadé* (1879) had already decorated his house at Rochefort with a Turkish salon, an Arabic bedroom and a Japanese pagoda.

Within a dream of spices, bazaars and snake charmers, Orientalism was already reclining upon a silk pillow when the sixteen-volume French translation of *A Thousand and One Nights* by Doctor Joseph Charles Mardrus exploded like a bomb on the world of fashion, ballet and design.

The 1906 colonial Exposition at Marseilles, the publication of Pierre Loti's *Désenchantées* — a novel about Turkish harems — the same year, the first Russian ballets devoted to this phenomenon, once again extolled the wedding of society life with the exotic. Donning an egret-feathered turban, they smoked "pink-tipped Abdullas" in cigarette holders fifty centimeters long.

Harem Pants

After the "Mamluk" tunic, the "Sultan" dress and the so-called "harem" pants first appeared in 1910 in *Sheherazade*, a ballet choreographed by Michel Fokine. Bakst, the "Delacroix of fashion" created a signature finery that was expressive and colourful, that, under flaming billows of orange, indigo and fuchsia, hinted at a body in

1

1- **Zobéide, the favorite. Lithograph by Léon Bakst of the ballet costumes of Sheherazade presented by the Ballets Russes at the Théâtre du Châtelet, Paris (1910). Private collection.**

2- **Nijinski in Sheherazade. Gouache by Georges Lepape (1910). Private collection.**

3- **Drawing by Léon Bakst. Private collection.**

4- **Nijinski in *Afternoon of a Faun*. Costume and illustration by Léon Bakst (1912). Bibliothèque Nationale de France, Paris.**

5- **Valentina Kaschouba (a Diaghilev dancer) and Pierre Michalowski in Oriental costumes (1919), Paris. Collection of A. Vassiliev, Paris.**

Idols, Parisian Sultans
and Odalisques.
Orientalism and Society Life

smitten by "hilly expanses" and white minarets. "As to attire, there are baggy pants and an embroidered vest that goes down to the abdomen, while the pants, on the other hand, held up by an enormous cashmere belt that is folded over

motion, freed from all taboos and restrictions. Ida Rubinstein, the beautiful sultana drunk with passion, shone like the priestess of a new ideal, leaping and flying high. "We others, in our corsets, our tight shoes, our ridiculous girdles, elicit pity. Grace takes revenge on our science." So had Eugène Delacroix already written by 1832 in Tangier. The Oriental body had been an absolute revelation for researchers the likes of Gustave Flaubert,

many times, does not begin until way low down, so that all the stomach, the hips and the tops of the thighs are naked beneath a black gauze tight against the skin. […] It ripples on the haunches like a shadowy and transparent wave with every movement." (From a letter to Louis Bouillet, Cairo, January 15, 1850.)

At the beginning of the twentieth century, the so-called harem pants were highly paradoxical, revealing the nudity of the recluse in a dream of emancipation. Although "ungainly," the Zouave culotte was a "necessary form of transition in the evolution of women's clothes that succeeded thanks to the bicycle," wrote the chronicler Lip Tay in

6

1899 in response to Monsieur Cassio, editor of the *Droits de L'Homme* regarding his article *"Le Procès du Pantalon"*. The stranglehold eased. Since 1909, the wearing of pants by a woman was no longer considered a crime, as long as she grasped a bicycle handlebar or the reins of a horse.

Paul Poiret's Seraglio

Paris fell under the spell — beginning with the couturier Paul Poiret who just then was "doing battle" with the corset. His perfumes with names like *Minaret*, *Aladin* and *Antinéa* enveloped elegant women transformed into odalisques who made up their eyes with Ouled Naïl kohl. The boudoirs and drawing rooms of the fine neighbourhoods were adorned in mysterious and sensual fabrics, crêpe de Chine and crêpe de Maroc, complementing an array of damasks, ottomans and Smyrna brocades. On June 24, 1911, at his townhouse on Avenue d'Antain, Paul Poiret, the caliph of the hem, presented his celebrated Persian ball "The Thousand and Second Night" and dressed like a sultan, he received some three hundred guests, ranging from the princess Lucien Murat who,

6- Mikhsz Mordkine (a Bolshoi dancer) in *La Bayadère* (1916). Collection of A. Vassiliev, Paris.

7- *Smoking Dress* (c. 1910), England.

8- *Memento from the Thousand and Two Nights,* the famous Persian ball presented in Paris by Pierre Poiret. Gouache b Georges Lepape (1911). Private collection.

9- *Those of Tomorrow.* Four dress-pants from *Les Choses de Paul Poiret Vues par Georges Lepape* (1911). Collection of C. Lepape.

Idols, Parisian Sultans
and Odalisques.
Orientalism and Society Life

9

60-61

according to Lucie Delarue-Mardrus, was disguised like a "Turkish marquise" to Madame Paul Reboux "turbaned and culotted in green silks". Emirs plated in gold held on their arms elegant ladies wearing babouches.

That day, Madame Poiret, making her entrance in a golden cage from which she was released, presented the colours of the new style. She wore those celebrated bouffant pants that allowed one to partake in the latest dance vogue — the tango. In Great Britain, this attire was reserved for the masked ball, whereas in the United States, a certain Mrs. Powell, trying to launch the "pants-dress", met with failure. In Spain, the police intervened. In Paris, when such eccentric women as Louisa de Mornand dared to wear the pants-dress at the reopening of Auteuil, the debate took hold dividing partisans of the "tight-fitting dress" from those of the "masculine dress". "Here's how they intend to deck us out. Clinching Zouave pants, tight at the calves with Russian socks," as it was indignantly stated in *Femina* in February 1911. "Is this not rather close to what this supposed *artistic* creation amounts to? And what a graceful silhouette! Proposed are the luxurious fabrics that will be used to make this innovation, the gallant and unfettered look that quickly will take on the audacious women who will launch it. This shall seduce the truly elegant women, converting them to the planned style. Illusions, illusions!" Jean Worth, interviewed by the Parisian correspondent of *Vogue USA* declared, "It's vulgar, horrible. Madame, the world has gone crazy! No one talks about art, literature or public affairs! Conversations are about nothing more than this detestable garb!"

Sultan Skirts and Bouffant Pants

The man of the world had to confront these dilemmas. To get rid of or not to get rid of his lapels, which were still called *retroussis* (lips). And when it made its presence in

his circle, to adopt or not to adopt the silk stripe down the pants of his tuxedo. The black attire reached its heights, even if some dreaded being mistaken for their valets.

Worn under a flared skirt made of a golden fabric,

11

La Mode Nouvelle. · **Les Jupes-Pantalons**
Au Bois · Avenue des Acacias

Création Labor...

Madame Poiret's chiffon pants, also used as costumes in Jacques Richepin's play *Le Minaret* (1911), let loose a wave of madness. The same year, the newspaper *Les Modes* devoted several pages to this new "skirt-pants". "A separation of the skirt into two parts" capable of "saving proprieties". Long folds, or more often an apron-like look, and long overblouses of silk chiffon "detailed at the bottom with an almost opaque embroidery, heavy tight fringe, or a simple cuffed hem".

Idols, Parisian Sultans
and Odalisques.
Orientalism and Society Life

Always very critical, the *Femina*'s tone took itself to be more qualified. Didn't the Béchoff-David house register patents for a few types of skirt-culottes in June 1910? If Paul Poiret made his "sultan skirts" the style most popular at dinners and evening affairs, Béchoff-David, on the other hand, specialized in skirt-culottes designed for the "promenade". And as *L'Illustration* confirmed, Doucet, Redfern and Drecoll "are prepared to make for their clients bouffant or straight pants as they should desire". The pleat took hold. "Despite all predictions, the dress-pants has exited the realm of fantasy and has entered reality. These past days, one has seen young women walking along the avenues in the park, and even venturing upon the boulevards dressed in this neo-Oriental garb." as one could read in the March 1911 edition of *L'Illustration* where various styles were shown either worn with a bolero or a chiffon overblouse. "These amusing photographs show that the dress-pants, different from the restrictions, allow women to get into carriages, to step down from the curb and retie a rebellious lace on her shoe."

Whether dress-pants *à la Turque* in charming "antique blue" or rose-petal pink silk chiffon, or Zouave culottes in Peking silks, silhouettes were elongated, like the necks of carafes coloured by "those mysterious and reprehensible drinks" served at Paul Poiret's Persian ball. Some journals, such as *Women's Wear Daily*, became roused by the idea that this "caprice" should not become "a popular vogue". The success would be limited to a new monied elite dethroning a decadent aristocracy on its own territory and which longed for the age of waltzes and conversation.

10- **Caricatures of Maurice Rostand and the Count Boni de Castellane.** *Fantasio* (February 15, 1922 and October 15, 1906).

11- **The first skirt-pants in the Bois de Boulogne (1911).**

12- **A Zouave with wide checks, created by the house of Béchoff-David (February 1911).**

12

Pants, A History Afoot

Paul Poiret, whose illustrated designs by Lepape appeared in *Art et Décoration*, was able to launch them to Americans. "When it first came out in America the skirt-culotte took the form of pajamas. Now, you can wear them to lunch, and further variations of the theme even to dinner. The skirt-culotte is inescapable". His winter collection presented on July 22, 1912 would prove a memorable success for him, with orders surpassing thirteen million francs. A record never before attained by a couturier, and where the dress-pants with broad lapels, appearing in *Les Choses* under the title "Those of Tomorrow" foreshadowed the baggy pants of the *rappers*. *La Vie Parisienne*, which was never kind to Poiret, proposed bestowing an award upon him, the first to present his "living dresses" in Frankfurt, Berlin, Warsaw, Moscow, Saint Petersburg, Budapest, Vienna and Munich, which he did with the assistance of nine new models. Adopted by such actresses as Mademoiselle Yane and by several women pioneers who endured "courageously Parisian gawkers and cocky kids" and even had to ask for police protection, the *divided skirt*, as it was called by the English, was scandalous across the Channel. In Paris, Colette, eschewed by the Paris chic because of her divorce from Willy in 1910, did not hide her irritation. "The skirt, yes! The culotte, yes! The skirt-culotte, no!" she declared, glaring with an air mocking Valentine who "perfumes himself with rose and jasmine, swearing by Tehran and Esfahan." She pose for the photographer Henri Manuel in his studio wearing a three-piece suit, her hair cut short and with a cigarette in her hand.

The Pants of the Emancipated

Horsewomen like Colette and Renée Vivien, who signed her love letters to Nathalie Barney "Ton boy" (your boy), preferred a man's wardrobe emphasizing pants to the "sultan" finery. This was also true for Louise Delarue-

Mardrus who chose "for the country" riding pants worn with leather leggings. But pants, such as men reserved for women, remained an undergarment, whether open or closed, subdued or saucy, as the vast production of illustrated cards depicting "assault" pants, "ballerina" pants and "debutante's" pants proved. One had to wait for the end of the tyrannical hold of the corset, which came about in 1915, for pants to no longer be associated with lingerie. "Pants are useful! I, sir, find a woman who does not dress in pants, is no longer a woman," So one could read in *Leurs Pantalons*, a work by Jacques Mauvin, the author of a very important opinion poll. In *Suzette veut me lâch-*

423
ПРЕОБРАЖЕНСКАЯ

er (1908), a novel Willy published "solo," the first chapter opens with a break-up scene. "'Why, Countess, do you put your pants back on?' our unavoidable Henri Maugis asked courteously from the depths of his auspicious easy chair, impressive in his brick-red pajamas. 'Because it is over between us, my friend.' 'You have done well, little girl,' he said, 'to put your pants back on before making such a great renunciation.'"

13- Colette with a cigarette (1910s).

14- Olga Preobrajenska, star dancer
   from Saint Petersburg, in a sailor's suit
   (circa 1905). Collection of A. Vassiliev, Paris.

15- Colette in a sailor's suit at the age of 23
   (circa 1896).

15

Hélène Dutrieu in an aviator suit
designed by Bernard (1914).
Bibliothèque Nationale de France, Paris.

Munitionnettes, Garçonnes and Montparnos*

The Avant-garde and Liberation

(*Munition Ladies, Boy-Ladies and the Montparnasse Crowd)

"My wife is free. Must I beat her?" asked Louis Couriau who was excluded from the Lyon chapter of a writers' organization for having let his wife work as a typist. This affair, that came to a head one day in 1913, reveals the tensions of a time that was caught between the traditions of yesterday and the beginning of a new century. Pants instead of culottes, the body as opposed to the corset, the naked hand rather than the politeness of the glove, manifestos against the tail-coated duel.

"In the end, you're weary of the old world," wrote Guillaume Appolinaire in *Zone*. Pants became the witness to a new generation: with men, pants became less stiff, the image of a figure freed from its shackles — the horse-drawn carriage, the breeches, the fob watch hanging over a huge belly; and with women, it stood out as the arbiter of emancipation (alas, brought about by the war), the realization of an ever-more androgynous figure that became less distinct under the "barrel-dresses" and pajamas, clothing that until then was reserved for men.

Times were no longer for puckering of the lips or scornful petticoated criticisms worthy of *Femina* which stated in January 1911, "Amusing cross-dressing, perhaps too amusing for a serious woman academic" read the blurb of a Préjean drawing, ridiculed for having dared to imagine a pants suit for a female member of the Académie Française. Far from the "voluminous paunches" that Stefan Zweig spoke of, or the hourglass female figure, relics of the nineteenth century, the sports vogue would prove to be a great contributor in refining the new image and in creating a new more striding gait. It was the foreigners in Paris who were the first to set this style. Some, like Paul Morand, sneered at the new blue-stockings of the cosmopolitan capital, where upon seeing these Americans, he commented [that they were] "a kind of cowboy with short hair and flat feet." But a page had been turned. Artists were the first to straddle the ages of their time. Young men preferred hunting pants, sweaters and heavy shoes — ideal for forging the century divide — to city dress. Picabia, Modigliani, Van Dongen, wearing linen pants and sandals with leather straps over bare feet, set the tone.

Futurism and "Tuta"

The Futurists, like Giacomo Balla, included functionalism in their priorities. The manifesto called for clothes "cut in such a way as to let all the pores breathe easily." Art and life started out nude, ready to give birth to the long-awaited century. "Painting is the tie over a gentleman's starched shirt and the pink corset compressing the bloated stomach of a flabby woman… There was no realism in painting that formed its own end, there was no creation," wrote Kazimir Malevitch in *Du Cubisme au Suprématisme* (1915). The "Tuta" which was a shirt and pants of linen that was conceived by Ernesto Thayaht, a sort of uniform for the new man that Farid Chenoune spoke about in his *Des Modes et Des Hommes* (1993)

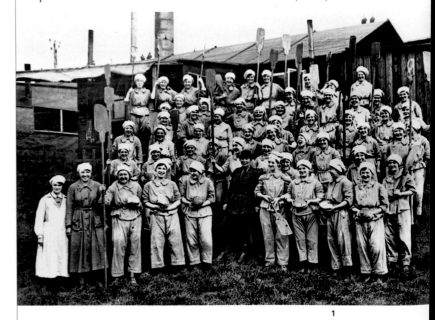

1

Munitionnettes, Garçonnes and Montparnos.
The Avant-Garde and Liberation

defined this dream of the absolute. "The Tuta is supposed to be very short. Without question, it was one of the first well-thought out attempts to make work clothing, a multi-purpose civilian attire without passing through the classic intermediary stage of leisure attire."

As far as women were concerned, this dream of physical ease would find its legitimacy in political and ideological struggles, where the wearing pants would become a by-product. Style became militant. It was in Great Britain where it took off, as Aquascutum's advertising slogan recalls: *Coats for women leading to votes for women.* When on December 15, 1913, feminists, supported by the League of the Rights of Man gathered more than a thousand people, a page had already been turned. The death of Emily Davidson, a militant and martyr for the cause of suffragettes, at forty-one suddenly dramatized these claims. *Deeds, not words* is written on her gravestone. Pants accompanied this on-going revolution. On August 1, 1914, the men left just as the harvest season began. Shells had to be manufactured even though the workers were now at the front or singing in the trenches "When Madelon comes to serve us something to drink…"

The *Munitionnettes*

On August 7, 1914, René Viviani launched an appeal to women farmers to harvest the fields in place of men. In munitions factories, women nicknamed *munitionnettes* were taken on, and thus, it was a tragic phenomenon, namely the war, that permitted women to replace men in the workforce.

Through new activities and new habits, women not only conquered economic and cultural bastions, but that of clothing, as well — pants, the clear symbol of work, being emblematic. With the need of uniforms for the soldiers,

1- Bakers of the auxiliary army working for English troops on the French front during the War of 1914-1918.

2- Serbian soldier during the War of 1914-1918. Collection of A. Vassiliev, Paris.

3- French worker checking the wheel of a car as it leaves the factory (circa 1912).

came the first law that set a minimum salary for work done in the home. In addition, women became mayors, blacksmiths and joined the rural police force. In France, great resistance was felt, but the state was hesitant to suspend the obligation of the "marital" signature for most acts of daily life.

In 1916, the Ministry of Work empowered a committee for women's work with the condition of women in factories. *La Française aujourd'hui*, a feminist monthly that began publication in October 1915, depicted daily life. "The women break off as if they were a bit touched, with an air of having passed some invisible limit and crossing into the other side of life," wrote Colette in *Les heures longues* (1917). Bourgeois and aristocrat women, among them Edith Wharton, Gertrude Stein, Alice B. Toklas, organized the workplace and became nurses, or transformed their properties into hospitals and their cars into ambulances. Sarah Bernhardt went to the front to raise morale among the troops. Marguerite Durand launched patriotic appeals. During the elections of 1916, a group of women marched along the boulevards decrying, "Women must have the vote! She submits to the law, she pays taxes. We want universal voting, not unisex voting." A referendum of women was conducted by the daily newspaper *Le Journal* in 1914 which drew five hundred thousand positive responses.

Famous feminists, the likes of Marguerite Durand and Jane Dieulafoy, proposed that women be admitted into all the auxiliary forces as replacements for the men. The idea, which was set forth at the feminist congress of 1908 and then again in 1913 saw absolutely no success in public opinion. For years hence, Jane Dieulafoy endured sarcastic barbs. "A complex nature, double personality, a woman forgetting her sex without having disavowed it" and according to F. Loliée *(La Revue Bleue*, 1896), she wore a black outfit with a confidence that exasperated the

detractors of the "emancipated." She shared with Rosa Bonheur the office authorization to wear men's attire. Writer, wife of the renowned archaeologist Marcel Dieulafoy who notably discovered the ruins of the Persian palaces at Darius and Artaxeres, Jane, who accompanied her husband on his trips, began wearing men's clothing in September 1870 on the banks of the Loire. As the army admitted women in its ranks only if they wore the garb of canteen workers or in disguise, Jane opted to take on the uniform of the irregulars — a grey blouse and grey pants. Decorated by President Carnot with the Cross of the Legion of Honour in 1886, she remained a model for many who envied her way of dress. "The sombre and simple black velvet outfit, with its high-button mandarin collar." *(La Vraie Mode*, May 28, 1903.) First adopted at the beginning of the century by the artistic and literary elite, pants became the uniform of women workers, tram

Munitionnettes, Garçonnes and Montparnos.
The Avant-Garde and Liberation

conductors, electricians and "machinists drilling in the steel holes" as was stated in the March 25, 1917 edition of *Le Miroir*. They were some five hundred thousand who, as the song said, breathed "ether, alcohol and benzine." The same journal announced that "enthralled with the greatest patriotism, Canadian women had decided, wherever possible, to replace the men who had gone off to war, and they have adopted a sort of masculine uniform." In July 1917, women in France represented 40% of the total working population, which represented a 25% increase over the figures of 1914.

Pants, Defiance and Uniform

Outside the context of the war industry, no change. In May 1918, the suffragette movement came to Paris. But the end of the war also sounded a return to order and the end of utopian thoughts. "Women, back to the house!" "We need some French kids," declared *Le Figaro* on

5

January 9, 1919. Now, women's pants ostensibly displayed a refusal of the official ideal. In 1918, as the right to vote had been accorded the women of Great Britain, short hair, an unsheathed body, the wearing of sport pants (riding breeches, fishing and ski pants) became a

defiance of the moral order. "We want short hair, dresses that do not bother us, and we want to have an occupation," declared the lawyer Maria Vérone. Hélène Brion, a teacher, was judged before the War Council on March 25, 1918 and the army reproached her for her "pacifism" and because of her short hair and that she sometimes wore cycling pants, tried to have her stated a deviant. Sentenced to a six-month suspended prison sentence, she was dismissed from her post and not reinstated until 1925. Other sisters of the cause were Julie Bertrand, Marie Mayoux and Lucie Coliard.

But four years of pain and hardships would also open the door to an irreversible freedom which evinced itself in higher salaries, the result of strikes and job actions. "Equal work! Equal pay!"

With the war, the mythology of female heroism was refreshed by several great figures, of whom Jane Dieulafoy upholds the memory of the likes of Isabella la Católica, the woman captain and Catalina de Erauso (1592-1635), known as "la monja-alferez, the Spanish nun flag-bearer who obtained the authorization from Pope Urbain VIII himself to wear men's clothing. Placed in a Dominican convent from which she fled at age fifteen, for her acts of heroism, she received a pension from King Felipe IV as thanks for her services to the crown. She then became Antonio de Erauso.

During this period of war, with such spectacular films as *Joan the Woman* (1917) by Nino Oxilia which appeared ten years before the introduction of Fancinetti in Carl Dryer's *The Passion of Joan of Arc* (1927), Joan of Arc stoked the flames of patriotism. Canonized in 1920, Joan,

4- **Workers and their babies in a nursery annexed to a war factory (January 13, 1917).**

5- **Oyster fisherwomen of Marennes (1922).**

sex by cutting her hair and dressing like a man — in 1929, she inspired a legendary postage stamp, the first with the image of a real woman, as opposed to an allegorical figure.

On a poster depicting the first battalion of women volunteers in Russia (1917), the caption read: "They who set an example for the men." And the women posed, wearing caps and pants. A line is crossed. "Fairy tales are too fan-

the "older sister of *Poilus*," was honoured by numerous monuments before being declared in 1922 the "secondary patron of France." Guilty of "one of the most abominable crimes before God" — wanting to escape her

6- Miss Fanny Harley, traveller and publicist. New York (1919).

7- Loretta Rhodes in golf pants, the "latest thing in women's fashion" (circa 1920).

8- Silk pajamas by Marie Nowitsky. Paris (1927). Collection of A. Vassiliev, Paris.

9- Outfit for air travel, by Madeleine Vionnet (1922).

Munitionnettes, Garçonnes and Montparnos.
The Avant-Garde and Liberation

.THAYAHT. 2 2

tastic to move us," wrote Raymond Radiguet in *La Gazette du Bon Ton* (1921). In the same issue, appeared an article entitle "Unheeded Advice to a Proud *Warrior* Regarding Her Dress." "A woman's dressing will either be autonomous or not. [...] What gracious attention toward us, what nice flattery as that which consists of imitating thus us in every way. Because, as need not be said, to be in the thick of it, you must be masculine from gloves to hat, from handkerchief to under to fabric."

Pants in the Time of Ragtime

In the crazy years that moved to the beat of ragtime, the story picked up pace, thrusting the pioneers into a bygone past. The black suit with satin lapels came naturally to Duke Ellington, Louis Armstrong, Fats Waller and in a different realm, Maurice Chevallier. The new Eve of the tennis court, golf green and dance hall, wore Charleston dresses that showed the leg and matched her outfit to her luggage when travelling to the Riviera. Sarah Bernhardt, who was quite the thing when she cross-dressed in *L'Aiglon* (1900), died in 1922. The heavenly ones went away and language became embittered. "The *garçonne* (lady-boy)? A slim figure without a defined waistline. [...] A hairstyle that flaunts virility under a silly hat — silly and more silly." Shrouded in mystery, emancipation could once again rhyme with seduction. The house of

Madeleine et Madeleine opened shop on Paris' Champs-Élysées in 1921 and drew in elegant women, particularly in 1926 with a novel outfit that would became famous: the evening tuxedo. Eccentrics like the Englishwoman Nancy Cunard was among the first to adopt the "evening pajama."

10- Jeanne Lanvin's 1921 winter collection. Gouache, House of Lanvin, Paris. (rights reserved)

11- "Eccentric" model. Jeanne Lanvin's *Paris Plage* collection 1925-1927. Gouache, House of Lanvin, Paris. (rights reserved)

12- Jeanne Lanvin's 1928 winter sports collection. Gouache, House of Lanvin, Paris. (rights reserved)

13- Nancy Cunard and Tristan Tzara. Photograph, Man Ray (1924).

12

Munitionnettes, Garçonnes
and Montparnos.
The Avant-Garde and Liberation

The Garçonne *According to Chanel*

Nothing forthcoming, Chanel cultivated the pre-war days, desiccating Worth and Paquin. She was a shepherdess, who knew well the training trail, the leather boot, the haymaking season, dung, undergrowth and saddle soap," wrote Paul Morand about the woman to whom he was a friend and confidante. The first to wear jodhpurs the model for which (furnished by a stable groom) was copied by a tailor of the Croix de Saint-Ouen, she posed in 1918 wearing a white pajama identical to the one worn by Henri Bernstein at her side. "Hiker of a style never seen," according to Edmonde Charles-Roux (Le Temps Chanel), in her way, Gabrielle Chanel hijacked men's fabrics like the jersey and with a bow to Colette, from 1917 she proved herself to be partisan to "subversion with short hair." Paul Morand remarked in his Journal that it was at this point that Coco "decided to become a personality."

While in 1922, Paul Marguerite published La Garçonne, *Chanel observed the amazones who wore beach pajamas, which was rather intuitive to create a style and "launch" it with a rare sense of media. When going fishing for salmon with the Englishwoman Vera Bates, she did not hesitate to borrow the Duke of Westminster's jacket, sweater and pants. "It is clear that in 1929, the wearing of pants is a freedom that only wealthy women are able to appropriate, revealed Edmonde Charles-Roux. But the corner had been turned and the era of leisure had arrived, as had the standardization of clothing, so that the Chanel style would no longer descend into the street where the wearing of pants would win by a landslide chosen by thousands of women."*

14

As Gabrielle Reval, a member of the *Vie Heureuse* jury (a prize that predated the *Prix Femina)* wrote in her memoir *La Chaîne des Dames* (1924) it is no longer the time of "those women of letters [who] in remembrance of George Sand, decked out in *boursingot*, believed they had to call attention to themselves with their attire." Deceased in 1916, Jane Dieulafoy had fallen over in the dust of time. "In those times, one could see […] on the Passy hillside, the wisest and most reasonable of lady-explorers sporting a top-hat, morning coat and pants!"

14- *Les "Montparnos"*. **Illustration for Bars et Cabarets de Paris by Sem (1929).**

15- **Gabrielle Chanel and her friend Vera Bates posing in the clothes of the Duke of Westminster (1928). Private collection.**

Munitionnettes, Garçonnes
and Montparnos.
The Avant-Garde and Liberation

Fashion for the Beach, *Femina*
(July 1932)

Beach Pajamas, Knickerbockers and Norwegian Pants

"Pajamas with red and white polka dots, neither too Gavarnesque, nor too Mexican, nor too this, nor too that, completed with a wide-brimmed hat that might call to mind Martinique, without seeming exotic, at once both naïve and extreme."
(*Femme de France*, August 1, 1931)

Sports and Holidays

From enclosed lawn courts to greens at the beach, the "1930s" pants hung loosely in the crazy years, during those first "neo-classical" years of this decade that brought back importance to the cut and averted a crisis thanks to luxuriously functional clothes. These heralded the coming of the unisex suit and an androgynous generation which would lead Klaus Mann to write in his autobiography *Le Tournant* (1942), "It's odd. If you were a boy, one would certainly say that you were extremely beautiful." Symbol of sports attire, pants were the essential new classical wardrobe of men and women.

After having flirted for a long time within the confines of eccentricity and the *boyish look*, pants became a style dominating the fashion that elongated the figure of the bathing beauties and other *sportsmen* who frequented the seaside resorts of Trouville, Juan-les-Pins (nicknamed "Pyjamapolis") and Cannes, where in 1932 a *Gala des Pyjamas* was held. In these edens of elegance of cosmopolitan spas, the new naiads knew well to show off their legs that their wide, flouncy pants hinted at.

"Once the first moment of surprise had passed, you couldn't remain insensitive to the grace of its harmonious line, its shimmering vibrant colours and the inexhaustible ingenuity of its harmonization," as Robert de Beauplan wrote with great emotion in the August 22, 1931 edition of *L'Illustration*. "The pajama gives women a novel look, a freer, smarter one whose casualness always remains in good taste. It emphasizes a sveltness and often corrects the disgraces that a short skirt did not save us from enough. The width of its bellbottoms (the knee-length pajama is a much rarer eccentricity), along with the huge straw hat that the "elegants" wore as an accessory, contributed to refining the figure and shape, and created a decorative ensemble that hardly seemed like masculine with all its many versions." The same month, the magazine *Femina* devoted its cover to the pajama. "Where do you not see the pajama? Its modern grace, moreover, lends itself to quite well to all settings, and this one, which was so exemplary at an evening party at the Impérial d'Annecy, is ravishing in the beautiful lakeside setting," the monthly had already pronounced in September 1930.

Pyjamapolis at Juan-les-Pins

Princes of the Riviera and the heavenly ones on holiday became initiated in the joys of water sports. Just as with dances, all swimming strokes — the over-arm, the crawl and the trudgeon — were new. The first to dare to wear beach pants were the Americans and such Parisians in

1

1- **Elegance in pajamas at Juan-les-Pins (1931).**
Private collection.

2- **Gabrielle Chanel and Serge Lifar on the Côte d'Azur.**
Photograph by Jean Morin.

Beach Pajamas, Knickerbockers
and Norwegian Pants.
Sports and Holidays

3

Beach Pajamas, Knickerbockers
and Norwegian Pants.
Sports and Holidays

the artistic circles as Gabrielle Chanel who, on the boardwalks of Deauville, on the arm of Serge Lifar, wore white linen *slacks* with her sweater and pearls. Marie Laure de Noailles, a patron of Buñuel, Dali and many others, took to wearing the pajama aboard her boat in Paris which had been decorated by Jean Michel Frank. As pants became the vogue, fashion houses, having first launched their lines as "special editions," began to project commercial plans. If Jacques Heim were the first to introduce the pareo (Biarritz, summer 1934), Jean Patou was one of the pioneers of sportswear when he opened a "sports corner" his Deauville boutique in 1924. "This year, I present a complete sport collection where it will be as possible for a Parisian woman to find the outfit she needs for her favourite sport, as for that charming sport of doing nothing," he said in *Femina* in 1926. The phenomenon exceeded its own reach when in 1932 the *Femme de France* pattern store offered for 6.75 francs pajama patterns to whomever wanted, accompanied with the slogan "the indispensable attire for the beach." Jeanne Lanvin's *Paris-Plage* collection presented styles named *Matelot*, *You-You* and *Algue*, and in 1929, she opened a "Sport" boutique in Cannes.

Transatlantic Luxury

"Sporting fashion, backed-up by the medical profession, recommends sun-bathing," announced Pierre de Tréviers in *Comment s'habiller* (1929). The Riviera was still a "club" frequented by women in woollen *simplicités* and yachtsmen in white pants and Eton jackets with broad lapels and white corozo buttons. A "celebrated couturière" (as *Vogue* still referred to Chanel), Russian princes, young women from the Île-de-France, grand ladies and rich Americans chose this "country dear to the Gods." The beauty of the sky, the mild weather, the ongoing social festivities, the glamorous parties all conspired to endow the outfits with a special tone. In October 1933, transatlantic luxury broadened its hori-

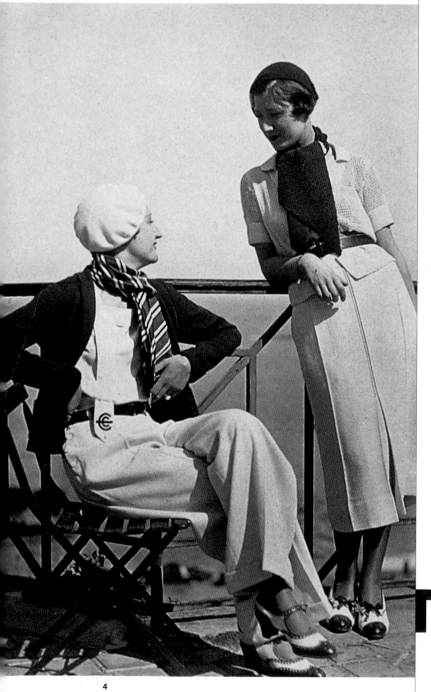

3- (left page): Renée on the beach (August 1930). Photograph by Jacques-Henri Lartigue.

4- Two elegant women on the pier dressed in the Patou collection.

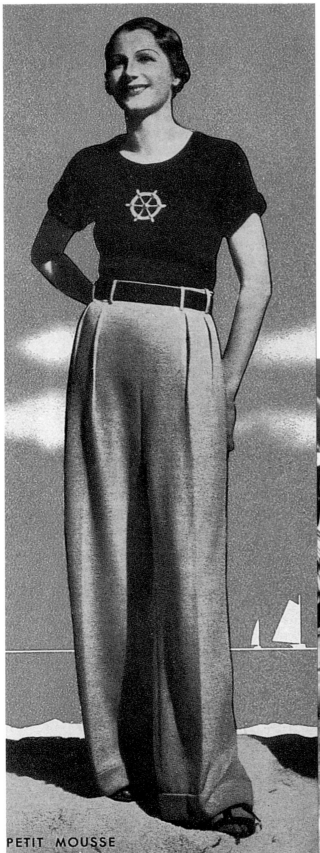

PETIT MOUSSE

zons aboard the Normandie, and the sailor fashion was born.

Some people were quick to wear their ink-blue jersey pants with a red woollen cap, borrowed from Catalan fishermen by the designer Rosine Paris.

At the Eden Roc in Garoupe, women's pants henceforth were a part of the "beach ensemble" that comprised a "swimsuit very low-cut at the closure and under the arms" and a "pajama" which might be worn under a wide-brimmed horsehair hat. A look ideal for exposing tanned shoulders in the evening that gently brushed against a crêpe de chine dress. Certainly, women's pants were restricted to a very precise sphere: the seaside, where they were intended for all hours of the day — a

Beach Pajamas, Knickerbockers
and Norwegian Pants.
Sports and Holidays

blue jersey for mornings and a silkier fabric for afternoons, tea-time, dances and cocktails. From afar, worn at the baccarat tables and in the casino drawing rooms, one could mistake her version of the evening pajama with its wide gores for an actual dress, provided a quick foxtrot did not reveal its true identity. "The evening divided skirt had a growing number of devotees. Today, one must be very diligent to tell the difference between a pajama and a divided evening dress," as *Harper's Bazaar* stated in April 1931.

At the beginning of the 1930s, the magazine Heim conducted a survey of several personalities regarding the pajama. Monsieur Chiappe, the Paris chief of police who was known for his conservative opinions, declared that if

5- The "Petit Mousse" outfit from Hermès (1933).

6- Marlene Dietrich during the filming of *Morocco* (1937).

7- Two men wearing summer attire and smoking (Lithuania, 1933). Collection of A. Vassailiev, Paris.

8- Greta Garbo (circa 1927).

a woman committed the crazy act of walking in the street wear a beach pajama, the crowd would see to returning her to reason. "Under no pretext would there be a question of me arresting her, as the pajama could not be considered men's attire."

Sweater Lady's Shorts

The extravagance of the 1920s with its garçonnes in pleated pants and shirt and tie, became blurred. In 1933, Marlene Dietrich moved into the Trianon Palace Hotel at Versailles where she could come and go dressed in pants. Nor was she prevented from wearing certain elements of her favourite look when she ventured into the capital. "On days when she comes to Paris, she wears […] collar, tie, boy's jacket from the young-girls' department of Lucien Lelong, man's hat from the matrons' *rayon* at Rose Descat," wrote Janet Flanner in *Paris Was Yesterday* 1925-1939.

Monseigneur Baudrillart confirmed that, if it were up to him, it would be forbidden for women wearing pajamas ("more ridiculous than improper") to enter a church. Nevertheless, on the terrace of the Hermitage at La Baule, just as on the beaches from Palm Beach to Monte Carlo and at the Miramar bar in Cannes, the pajama — in all sorts of materials: tussanam (Marcel Rochas), green Peking silk (Worth), black tussinya (Schiaparelli) and more simply, white wool (Hermès) — strutted about. Outrage was heralded. For, two years later, it was not the pajama that caused an uproar as in 1934, it was hardly any longer worn, save in Venice by men "of the sort found on the banks of the Adriatic where you sometimes had the impression of being in the middle of a group of people who just got out of bed." *(L'Illustration*, September 15, 1934.)* The Mediterranean coast had succumbed to a new wave: shorts. Jacqueline Delubac "the applauded partner of Sacha Guitry" posed in them for *Femina*, her eyes

LE PYLA

closed because of the sun. Her hair short and black, the new Sweater Lady took to the joys of swimming. Tennis required skirt-culottes, the most up-to-date were to be bought in the sports department of the fashion house Yvonne May, where the tennis star Suzanne Lenglen had become the director of the boutique.

Shorts were worn with a blouse "a large piece of clothing like a handkerchief that left the back nude down to the

Beach Pajamas, Knickerbockers
and Norwegian Pants.
Sports and Holidays

hips," according to *L'Illustration* (September 15, 1934). "Shorts are walking about the city as naturally as tailored suits in the streets of Paris. They go into the casinos, taking their chances at roulette. At cocktail hour, their hordes occupy the terraces of the bars. They dance to the sounds of jazz, they stay out late at the nightclubs." The episcopate could, nevertheless, be reassured. "Do not be in a hurry however to see in shorts an indication of a dubious freedom of styles or morals; irreproachable mothers walk their children and do their shopping in stores wearing shorts." Clearly, it was important to accompany shorts with wearing light make-up, some dark brown cream or powder, a trace of red on the lips, and above all, nothing on the eyes.

11

Blankenberghe Latest Fashion.

Jodhpurs and Knickerbockers

An aristocratic bastion, horseback riding still kept as women's attire skirts made of a sombre material, even if influenced by such pioneers as the duchess of Uzès, the most emancipated preferred the culotte in "Saumur beige or ochre" which was worn with yellow boots, a somewhat long riding jacket and a soft felt hat. For, as was noted in the May 5, 1933 issue of *Femme de France*, "some sportswomen prefer the riding saddle and have adopted the men's culotte." A tone that had already been sounded ten years earlier in February 1922 with *Vogue*'s assertion, "Women should not ride astride because most of them are not built for that." Or again through the art of dissimulation advocated by *Femina* in July 1924: "For doing sports, a 'woman taking her paces' would be authorized to wear culottes. She would hide them under a skirt, buttoned up the side. Cycling stockings would complete the outfit."

9- The "Plya" shorts from Hermès, 1937 summer collection.

10- General Larminat and General Leclerc in Al Kufrah, Libya.

11- Jersey pants on the Belgian coast in Blankenberghe (1932). Collection of A. Vassiliev, Paris.

10

For the "morning ride" Pierre de Trévières recommended jodhpurs for men, as "these pants are rather wide in the seat and tight at the knees as to appear tight along the length of the leg and are held with inside buttonholes and under-straps. [...] It is the attire that officers in the Indies play polo in when the temperature rises." A soft short, a regatta tie, a Panama hat an red leather gloves with decorative stitching complete the outfit.

"A pair of pants for every occasion" could have been the motto of this decade of great metamorphoses where, as international tensions mounted, elegance took root,

according each hour a new idea, from the knickerbockers for hunting migratory birds to the dinners at the Casino. In between, the "severe mourning" and the "elegant mourning" which required a dinner jacket. This fashion became rather widespread during the decade, largely due to the illustrations in *Adam* and *Monsieur*. As regards the five-piece for travelling, it comprised a pair of pants and a culotte which would match the fabric of the cap.

The invention of the "city-country" look was not unknown, according to Farid Chenoune, at the time of the appearance of the *culotte-sac* (also called plus fours) which was cut from one of several rustic/chic fabrics — Shetland, tweed, Saxony, Donegal, "thorn-proofs" and homespuns — and in colours of the lochs and heaths. Fabrics that British gentlemen such as the Duke of Windsor, a great lover of golf, made their choice material.

Bermudas and the Modern Life

This softening of the look, with its liberated look permeating the world of design, had already been addressed in Great Britain by the Men's Dress Reform Party (1929-1937) which was formed to permit men to "better their

Beach Pajamas, Knickerbockers
and Norwegian Pants.
Sports and Holidays

health and their appearance, as had come to happen for women" (A. C. Jordan in a letter to the *London Times*, June 17, 1929). Members of this party called for the abolition of pants, ties, suspenders and the hat in exchange for velour overshirts, blouses, culottes and shorts. But if women were able to free themselves through fashion from taboos, men, despite themselves, quickly fell from conformity to rebellion. Thus, in the final of the first football World Cup held in Uruguay (1930), the Uruguayans and the Argentines, who had opted to wear calf-length Bermuda shorts, were forced by the Belgian referee, a certain Monsieur Langenus, to replace them with the regulation tie and outfit. In 1927, S. Wood, a fifteen year-old student, caused a sensation at Wimbledon when he appeared on centre court in knickerbockers. In 1933, standing up against the Oxford bag style of very wide

cream-coloured flannel or woollen pants, Bunny Austin was the first tennis player to wear shorts at Wimbledon, a revolution as important as the one provoked by Suzan Lenglen (1920), who was chastised by some people for

12- **The Prince of Wales, future Edward VIII, at the Royal Golf Club, St. Andrews, Scotland.**

13- **Bunny Austin in a training match during the Davis Cup (1935).**

14- **Cecil Beaton on a suspension bridge during the 1930s. Photograph by Cecil Beaton.**

15- **Yellow taffeta Pagliacci pants. Photograph by Man Ray, *Harper's Bazaar* (January 1937).**

pants for all occasions — travel, city, evening, sports — that were less voluminous than the pajama, more refined that the skirt-culotte. What she created in 1933, "a dress that was no more for day than for evening" made pants an element of her realm: the night. In what was certainly an homage to Poiret, at the 1933 Oriental Ball presented by Mrs. Reginald Fellows, Schiaparelli made her entry in a *persane*, a zouave silk culotte that heralded the beginning of the eccentricities of the surrealists.

This attitude contrasted with the darkening of a Europe that was at the depths of an economic crisis and marching to the sound army boots. In 1935, Mussolini forbid the wearing of long pants by women because of the amount of fabric it required. In its place, fascist fashion promoted skirts.

shortening her skirt a little bit for each tournament.

A symbol of modernity linked to the development of sports and travel, during the 1930s pants were to the world of fashion what the Empire State Building, erected in 1931, was to New York: a stroke in space, an absolute line that marked this "vertical city" dear to Paul Morand. Elsa Schiaparelli, who presented a jump-suit in her February 1932 collection, nevertheless proposed skirt-

16- August Sander, the wife of the painter Peter Abelen (c. 1927-1928). August Sander Archive, Cologne.

17- Skiers wearing the Allard collection. At right: Hilaire Morand (1930).

18 & 19- Ski outfits by Jean Patou (1930s).

20- Hermès' 1926 winter sports look.

17

Beach Pajamas, Knickerbockers
and Norwegian Pants.
Sports and Holidays

Culottes on the Peaks

"As regards winter sports, they were all the rage. All the same, knowing how to ski or skate well is unimportant," confirmed Femina in January 1924. "The essential thing is to wear a pullover sweater, culottes, heavy boots and tutti quanti well." A Zermatt cloth or a whipcord? Culottes or pants? Ten years later, the debate was still on, as leisure activities at altitude calmed the "excessive nervousness of the overly civilized" (according to Pierre de Trévières), and guaranteed the success of such spots as Gstaad, Davos, Font-Romeu and Saint-Moritz, where Chanel offered luge outings to the likes of the Duchess of Gramont and the Count and Countess of Beaumont.

"The culotte will be preferred for skating, hiking and excursions. Pants, even for women, will be the choice for skiing and for luge and bobsledding." Winter sports will be the making of the Norwegian pants, which retain a certain width at the calves by a knitted band. "These pants, tucked into heavy woollen socks, are perhaps less stylish, but they are absolutely more convenient, more practical," as could be read in the January 1930 issue of Art-Goût-Beauté. The fabric used for these pants is a "tight weave" that keeps the snow out. For example, the "policeman blue" gabardine from Burberry's, that came before the first stretch ski pants in tricotine, sewn by Alphonse Allard, a tailor at Megève. Allard had created his first version in 1930 for Hilaire Morand, the uncle of Émile Allais who was an instructor at Megève and one of the best skiers of the time.

The technical feats of the decade concurred with the golden age of idleness. Certain elegant ladies in Patou dressed like the champion skier Hilda Sturm, nonchalantly keeping pants for sleigh rides. In January 1933, Femina organized a contest for elegant ski-wear during the afternoon tea-dance at St. Moritz. And what about the rather sassy Maria Paradis who, in 1808, dressed in a skirt and hood, scaled the 4807 meters of Mont Blanc?

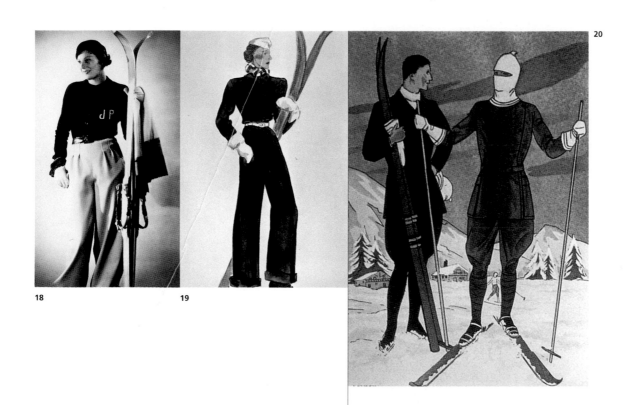

18   19   20

Katharine Hepburn: the star in men's pants and buckled moccasins

Stars, Zazous and Enlisted Women

The Fabric
of the
Incorruptible

"**W**hen I would do my shopping, I would dress like a skier" *(Marie Claire,* February 15, 1941). Hooded coats made of a heavy cloth, clodhoppers and pants — World War II made men's wardrobe available to women who, in defiance of shortages, mounted their bicycles, at a time and place when overcoats were accounted for with ration tickets. "Make new with the old" as the British ministry of commerce slogan said, while in France couturiers the likes of Elsa Schiaparelli and Robert Piguet were pushing extravagance to the point of proposing a "shelter" fashion that included multipocketed jumpsuits

2

to do away with the encumbrance of handbags during air-raid alerts, while providing a place for one's papers, silver and jewels. Knizé and O'Rossen presented pants suits to be "worn on the boat" and an assortment of skirt-culottes "for going on land." The wives of prisoners did not wait for fashion to dictate wearing pants. "These women, promoted to head of the family," wrote Bruno Du Roselle in 1940, "consciously obeyed a reflex of simplicity and resourcefulness, but unconsciously one of emancipation. Since circumstances imposed upon them a role of responsibility, in adopting pants, they expressed the new role of head of family that made them equal to men." In Great Britain, women enlisted in the Women's Royal Naval

1

Stars, Zazous and Enlisted Women.
The Fabric of the Incorruptible

Service left with a uniform comprised of an overcoat, three white shirts, two pairs of shoes and three navy blue knickers called *black-outs.* Women in the rural army marched in bouffant culottes.

In France, the last fine days faded away, leaving behind them the colours of hot sand, white pants, bouffant shorts and role games. "For summer fashion, women have borrowed men's pants" as was declared in the September 2, 1939 issue of *L'Illustration* under the title *Pantalonnades.* "They said they found them quite to their liking and deemed them more practical than a skirt, too short for the

movements of a semi-sportive life, as well as for the freedom of rural and seaside strolls."

But times were no longer hazy or subtle. The *culottin,* the old-time cyclist's culotte brought back into fashion by the couturiers in 1939, in a longer style became prominent and was worn with a "black market" jacket, when with the absence of cars, eleven million bicycles were sold in 1941. A contest of "bicycle elegance" was even organized in June at the Pavillon d'Armenonville. *Marie Claire* took care to inscribe in the ten commandments of the Parisian woman: "thou shall only wear culottes on a bicycle." Thus, styles on offer had footstraps and were made of a bonded fiber, while others, that opened in the front, could be worn "in the city." And the black curtain came crashing down on "liberation clothing." And the pants? Even Colette, who wrote blurbs for the magazine's fashion

1- **Woman working in a factory during World War II (1942).**

2- **Outfit for an air-raid shelter created by Robert Piguet (1939).**

3- **British postwoman during World War II.**

4- **The Republican side during the Spanish Civil War; Valencia (1936).**

"They live in slacks there, and they've got the knack of wearing them" declared *Harper's Bazaar* (March 1939) a magazine that featured such Hollywood stars as Joan Bennet posing in pants. Munkacsi caught the movement from behind his lens. Teachers and cowgirls, smiling women dressed in pants posing in natural settings from an aerodrome to a ranch, when artists weren't sketching them leaning on a bar. In the United States, Schiarparelli's *abris pants* were presented as *après-ski* attire. These were harem pants in a royal violet silk jersey that, when worn sprawled out on the carpet, were a great success.

The French critics were disturbed. As to pants, it was in America "where you could really see them everywhere" from the "hotel thief" and the "faker disguised as a priest"

drawings, seemed to have rejected them. "Neither one nor the other. These women don't wear them with great ease" *(Marie Claire,* May 24, 1940).

The debate was elsewhere. Replete with outrageous extravagances, French haute couture maintained the confusion between sophistication and frivolity, elegance and idleness. A more modern trend was developing in the United States where fashion was always more pragmatic.

Stars, Zazous and Enlisted Women.
The Fabric of the Incorruptible

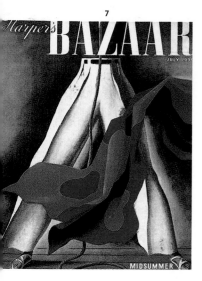

for the evening, to the woman skier racing in her car, where they were really rooted. "Those poor Hollywood stars. They are far, so far from Paris fashion that they sometimes forget what taste is. They are beautiful. All their disguises serve them well. [...] The pajama pants have been adopted by all of California as comfortable sports clothing. Now you see them all hours of the day." Murderous captions detailed the image of a crêpe negligee. "In Hollywood, they believe you have to dress to seduce a sultan" (*Marie Claire*, January 26, 1940). In this time of privations, women's magazines preferred more to advise their readers about household tasks, like the making of soap from beef bile or sewing gros-grain ribbon on the inside of their *monsieur's* pants to mend worn out spots. In France,

women's pants were relegated to gardening, when not being worn to restock at the farm. At the same time, however, in the United States, the young women featured in Coca-Cola advertisements were "very with it."

For or Against the *Pantalonnées*

A hood made of codfish skin, a dress cut from a bedspread – during a time of making do when a painted leg was better than a leg hidden under androgynous clothes. "A woman, even a ravishing American one, is she permitted to consider this extravagant cross-dressing and that rag knotted on the head as 'fine dinner attire?'" further emoted *Marie Claire* in its October 11, 1941 issue. As according to the Vichy government, the family was the "essential cell of society" and the return to a typical French style that extolled the woman as mother and wife was, in the Pétainist doctrine, a rejection of American influences, notably shorts, a symbol of moral decadence.

For Dominique Veillon, author of the important work *La Mode sous l'Occupation* (1990), "In truth, a form of women's emancipation was set. Many people deem pants responsible for the edging toward an 'equality of the sexes'. Tolerated for bicycling and working in the fields, this attire was strongly ill-advised for public places." On February 7, 1942, the newspaper *L'Œuvre* made a show of opening the debate under the title "For or Against *Pantalonnées*" by welcoming Arletty, an actress then in vogue, onto their pages. "For women who have the means to treat themselves to boots and an overcoat, it is inexcus-

5- Contest of "bicycle elegance" (June 1942).

6- *Abri pants*. Photograph by Munkasci, *Harper's Bazaar* (February 1940).

7- *Harper's Bazaar* cover (July 1939).

8- American elegance at the beginning of the 1940s.

96-97

able to wear pants. They shock no one, and this lack of dignity is simply proof of their bad taste." Marcelle Dormoy, former head seamstress with Madeleine Vionnet, who opened her shop in 1933, said, "I am against pants, which are not at all feminine. They do not leave a woman her natural charm. I would allow the pajama. In any case, you can be sure that the couturiers will never offer pants. We have too much concern for the elegance of the French woman. Her sister colleague Germaine Lecomte went fur-

9- Beach party in the United States (1940).

10- Marlene Dietrich upon her arrival to Paris (1940).

11- Claire McCardell's leotards on the cover of *Life* (September 1941).

12- Lauren Bacall.

13- Ginger Rogers and Alfred Gwynne Vanderbilt at the Culver City rollerdrome. Hollywood (1937).

10

ther. "It is a real joy for me no longer to dress boys manqué. Today, intimate life is reawakening."

Thus, a young woman's figure, seen as a "beautiful healthy fruit" according to the magazine *Femmes dans la France Nouvelle* (1940) must replace the androgynous

Stars, Zazous and Enlisted Women.
The Fabric of the Incorruptible

image of the starlet with plucked eyebrows, a regular of the artificial shadows that bathe her, and at the edges of homosexuality and perversion. In the May 1941 edition of *Votre Beauté*, Lucien François saluted the advent of a new feminine image in ankle socks and a short skirt "healthy, without physical flaws, as capable of stamina as of exertion." This explained why in Hollywood "where losing weight remains the great concern" *(Marie Claire*, March 15, 1941) stars took on wearing pants. These stars created their own style: Lauren Bacall, Ginger Rogers (who, photographed on her own ranch in Oregon, made *Life* magazine's cover in 1942), Bette Davis and Katharine Hepburn. Hepburn unquestionably was the great ambassador of pants which she made into an art. On screen as in life, she incarnated the image of the absolute individual, an aviator, single and amorous.

Celebrated in the United States for its practical aspects, in France, pants seemed to challenge the interests of corporatists. This utilitarian clothing, diverted by both men's and military wardrobe, drew a line of demarcation between the impersonal, subject to the risks of privation, cold and fear, and the privileged elite of *Paris bei Nacht*, for whom "the elegance of good tone [is] the only that suits today. A hat, gloves and a dress form an indivisible trilogy" *(Journal de la ganterie française*, September-October 1941).

Gabrielle Chanel, who was having a relationship with a German diplomat while living in Switzerland, was no longer there to defend this attire that she had made a symbol of emancipation. She, riding a horse in Capri in 1939, wore it with jersey slacks, a sailor's pullover, her necklaces of Indian stones and a white linen beret.

Swing and Baggy Pants

In the face of this return to traditional values, and in an act of provocation, the *Swings* and the *Zazous* (the name coming from the chorus of a 1938 Johnny Hess song), drew attention to themselves with their eccentric clothing. "Hair in a tall brush, brow low, eyes vague, a fine mus-

tache," according to *L'Œuvre* (March 4, 1942), they adopted pants that were "short, narrow at the bottom, swimming at the knee, with wide cuffs" that were worn with "white socks and thick-soled suede shoes."

After the bellbottom *culbutants* adopted by the "bad boys" of the 1930s, the punks around the Bastille and the Paris street kids, the wide X found a new home. The Zazous with their "pink cheeks, bowler hats and baggy pants" as Boris Vian wrote gently responding to the U1-A11 and U2-A3 decisions of the General Committee of the *Organisation de l'Industrie Textile* which, in April 1942, regulated the manufacture of men's clothes with an eye for economizing fabric. "Swing who can." In a jungle born of defeat, these small "shifty cats" these toughs in short pants and long jackets, these *incroyables* as they were called in slang were only "dangerous in the way lice are [...]. They itch, they annoy." *(La Gerbe*, June 11,

1942.) Presented as a Gaullist henchman, a Jew and a black marketeer, according to Dominique Veillon, Zazous were subjected to the humiliations of collaborators. Singers like René Paul ironically said, "Ever since I put on my fine suit, my tailor would say to me, 'Monsieur, I have over there some drapes that come from the factories at Baden-Baden, the latest thing in modern industry... From plants. Only poplars, pure fiber! There's not an ounce of wool in it. One drawback, moisture destroys it. You go out in long pants, a good downpour, you return in shorts."

The United States was free to the flow. Well-cut tail coats and *Punjab* pants, enormous, that were held up with patterned suspenders, the Harlem jazzman lent his tone and look to this fashion. Humphrey Bogart's "square" pants became a classic, with a sweater replacing the shirt and tie and of course, complemented by the trench coat. In 1946, during the filming of *Martin Roumagnac*, Jean Gabin was

photographed in jeans as he accompanied Marlene Dietrich to Orly airport. The brand wars had begun: Levi's declared that Gabin was wearing their chinos. Lee said that "Grandpa Moko" sported a *boss of the road* that he had bought in Los Angeles. The post-war period gave women's pants a role for the American star. Along with the wavy hair of Lauren Bacall, elegant women adopted the *après-ski* look. André Ledoux was one of the stars of this

new urban sports fashion. The Vera Borea couturier, which had opened in Paris in 1934, matched an "amusing" velvet chestnut-coloured suit with large *mécano* pockets to its brown suede low-cut boots. Deposed by Christian Dior's *New Look* which, on February 12, 1947, re-established the *femme fleur* over the bicyclist with "boxer's shoulders," women's pants became the stakes of the commercial and social competitions that went on in interposing realms: the Triangle and Seventh Avenue, Paris and New York, haute couture and ready-to-wear. When Christian Dior's *jupes-corolles* set Avenue Montaigne spinning, brands like Sacony offered the "coordinated look": lipstick and a cigarette in hand, a blond woman in a pants suit. The American power look was already set.

Pants, however, would not make their mark for another generation. With the duffle coat borrowed from New World fishermen, pants would triumph after the war, leaving behind a camouflage look for a completely free one, emblematic of youth and a quest for the ideal.

14- Bette Davis (left), accompanied by her hairdresser at a Hollywood studio.

15- Gene Kelly.

16- The zoot style of the 1940s.

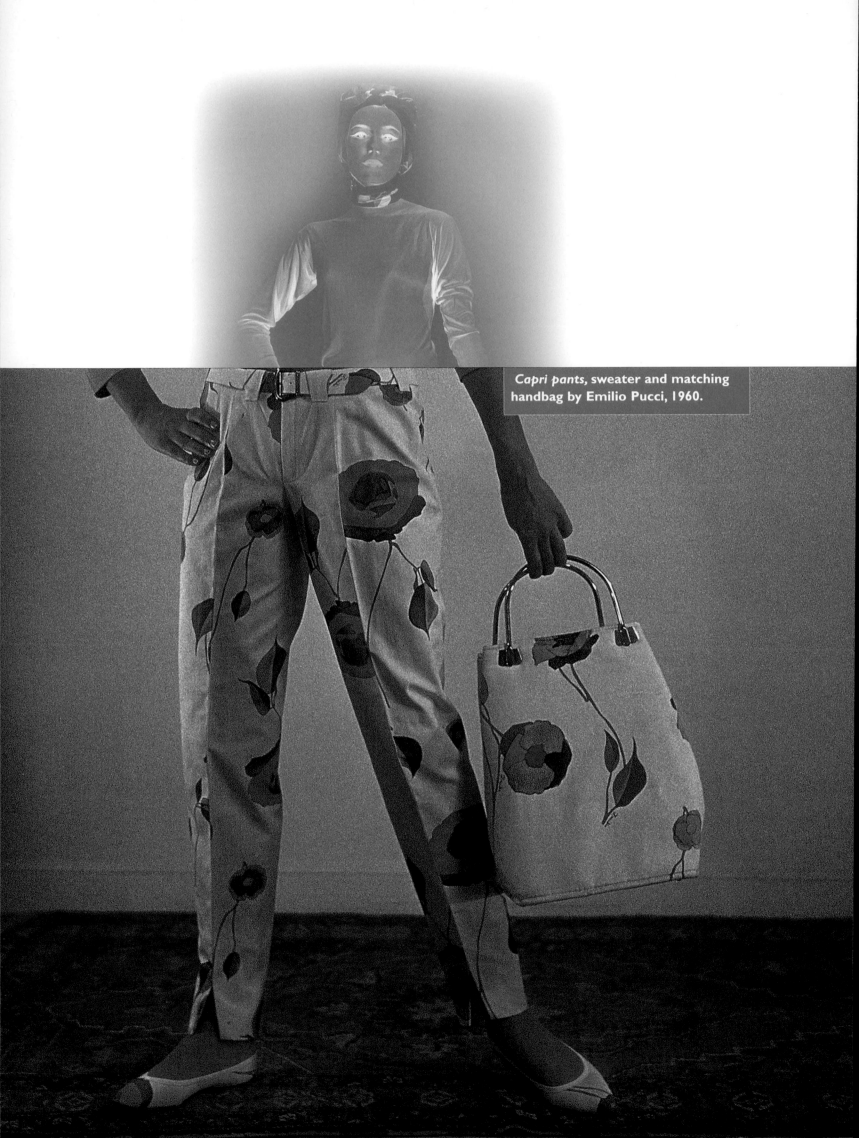

Capri pants, sweater and matching handbag by Emilio Pucci, 1960.

Stretch Pants, Corsair Pants and Teddy Boys

The Beautiful Getaways

From 1942, on the refound Côte d'Azur, the figure once again emerged, impertinent, under the stroke of René Gruau in *Elle*. "To get dressed, women put on culottes, to undress, less than nothing." Barefoot in soft moccasins, the new heroine walks about without a handbag, keeping one pocket of her blue linen slacks for "cigarettes, one for a handkerchief, one for money, one for make-up…" In 1954, the five hundredth four-horsepower car left the Renault factory. In a dream of escape and sun, the auto-

1

a style the *Capri pirate* pants, which in 1954 would win him the Oscar of the fashion world awarded by the great Neiman Marcus store. All the post-war café society came

2

mobile, the "grand duchess of machines" according to Roger Nimier, led everyone to other places. Cannes, but also Capri, where Emilio Pucci, having opened his shop *Canzone del Mare* (Song of the Sea) in 1950, introduced

1- Hitchhikers on the vacation route, 1954.

2- Emilio Pucci's *capri pants* with a silk blouse, 1959.

3- Françoise Sagan in Saint-Tropez (1956).
Photograph by David Seymour.

4- Slim Keith, symbol of the *California girl*.
Photograph by J. Engstead.

Stretch Pants, Corsair Pants
and Teddy Boys.
The Beautiful Getaways

and danced a tarantella and drank Americanos before mixing with the riff-raff at Quisiana. Sweaters were adorned with coral or pearl necklaces.

Pants of the 1950s were mascara for the legs, elongating the figure. The *ragazzi* of Rome rode around on their Vespas, their skin-tight pants slim and hitched up, corsair pants on the rocks and stretch pants on the ski slopes. For manufacturers specializing in them, these pants opened a

standing before a white wall that reflected the light. As of 1947, cotton country clothes made their entry into the American fashion museums, while in 1948, in *Vogue* magazine, a woman mounted upon her steed ensured publicity for Wrangler's *Authentics* under the title *Fashion in Action.* For the first time, the flies on women's pants were not on the side, but rather in front like men's. An innovation deemed scandalous by some. Sex entered upon the scene.

market of millions of Americans who lined the mountains at Yosemite, Sugar Bowl and Mineral King. At the same time, an elite tanned themselves in Nassau and Hawaii. The American ready-to-wear brands emphasized "sea legs" with fisherman pants in a Pacific blue twill that were rolled up at the knees. When sold to the French, they of course became Mediterranean blue. And their pants, as the "amusing bodysuit" attested to, brought attention to Elsa Schiaparelli's single shoulder model that *Femina* in 1952 suggested "for fishing." Pants were a sign of style, confronting the hot sand with a turquoise crêpe (Christian Dior) and the picturesque villages with a red-checked poplin (Jacques Fath). "Pants are a part of relaxing; there's no summer without a good pair of pants." *(Femina, July-August 1954.)*

In the United Sates, pants were the classic attire for weekends. The large American store Saks sold denim ensembles. In *Vogue*, Cecil Beaton posed his beauties in shorts,

Stretch Pants, Corsair Pants and Teddy Boys.
The Beautiful Getaways

Taboo Breakers

Far from the troubadours of swing, the last curly-haired poets, two new images of virility put themselves tight on the scene. The first was the "creaseless" man in tight pants with no pleats, spearhead of the functional and perfect decade where any illusions of renewal rhymed with nylons, Bic ballpoint pens, the transistor radio, the LP record, the mixer, dried soup, Tergal permanent creases and plastic containers. "It's pants that depress me most. I find them far too tight, even though they swore to me that skin-tight is in style. On the other hand, the fabric is seductive — it doesn't crease." (Henri Calet, *L'Italie à la Paresseuse, Journal de Voyage.)*

The other symbol of virility was the cowboy in his blue jeans and leather chaps, a natural armour to confront the great plains where he would sleep under the stars. His belt, with its heavy etched buckle, freed him from wearing suspenders. It was as indispensable to his outfit as was his bandanna and his boots, which made up the modern Adam, immortalized by John Wayne in *The Fighting Kentuckian* (1949) and Gary Cooper in *Shane* (1953).

5- **Henri Salvador and Mimi Brilli, dancer in a Parisian cabaret, giving a demonstration of rock and roll on the streets of Paris (beginning of the 1950s).**

6- **Grace Kelly during the Cannes Film Festival (1954).**

7- **Marilyn Monroe in jeans, working out with free weights in Hollywood. Photograph by Philippe Halsman.**

8- **Doris Day playing with a lasso.**

The " Rodeo Wars" started between the jeans makers. On October 22, 1951, the 5,200,000 readers of *Life* discovered Casey Tibbs, the world rodeo champion, posing in a shirt and jeans by Lee. He followed Jim Shoulders, who had been chosen by Wrangler two years earlier. In 1956,

9- **The doe-eyed Audrey Hepburn in stretch pants and flats.**

10- **Jacques Tati photographed by Philippe Halsman (1954).**

11- **A leaping acrobat in Allard stretch pants (1948).**

12- **Jacques Charrier and Brigitte Bardot in Saint-Tropez (June 21, 1959).**

J. P. Logan's film *Bus Stop* with Marilyn Monroe was underwritten by the Lee company.

Pants were the symbol of a textile industry in full expansion which registered 5 million dollars in sales for ready-to-wear women's and children's clothes in 1950, compared to the 1.3 million in 1931. A phenomenon gone crazy with the advent of sportswear, Claire McCardell being its pioneer, defined the *American Look*, a style first mentioned in the May 2, 1955 issue of *Time*. It was in 1942 that McCardell presented her first denim hostess dresses, which were followed in 1943 by her "leotards," forebears of the bodysuit which came back in the 1980s with the aerobics craze. As an alternative to the neo-*Belle Époque* style of the Paris haute couture, she proposed a less formal wardrobe, permanently veering in the direction of an active, sportive life. "Sportswear has changed our lives. Perhaps more than anything else, they have made us into independent women." Born in 1905 in Frederick, Maryland, she discovered Paris in 1925 during the era of the *garçonnes*, and starting in 1934, began offering separates (jersey tops and pants) to the large stores for travel wear, as well as for morning and evening dress.

A breaker of taboos, pants enabled magazine cover shots previously unpublished, such as a model lying in the grass flat on her stomach. Or in the movie studios where

Stretch Pants, Corsair Pants and Teddy Boys.
The Beautiful Getaways

Lana Turner, during the filming of *Diane de Poitiers* (1955), appeared seated upon a platform, her hugging her knees. On her feet, she wore the ballet slippers that Claire McCardell introduced in 1942. Rid of its pleats, pants revealed more of the body than it hid. Madame of the well-shaped legs met her rival: the young lady with a charm more ravishing than the American *bloomer girl*. She was named Brigitte Bardot, Dany Robin, Cécile Aubry, Dominique Blanchar and Anouk Aimée. On April 19, 1956, Grace Kelly became princess of Monaco. The doe-eyed Sabrina became the new idol, and it was the Parisian couturier Hubert de Givenchy who dressed her.

Crêpe Suzette Pants

Previously a designer with Schiaparelli, Hubert de Givenchy, who founded his own house in 1952, eased traditions with his blouses made of shirting, an inexpensive crease-resistant fabric that from the summer of 1952 complemented those vacation pants that came down just to the calf, and were belted with a scarf that set off his wasp-waisted styles. Its driving force was Bettina, a legendary Russian posing at the Bar des Théâtres with a

cigarette in her hand. "During this period, collections passed through the couture salons day and night. It was like going to the theatre. There were many lunches, many balls at the home of the Noailles and the Rothschilds. I didn't go to them. I preferred to dress in my own things – ballet slippers, cotton or gabardine frontier pants, long skirts and blouses. My life, was photograph studios."

To the readers of the American magazine *Seventeen*, French couturiers offered slacks and a matching black shirt. American critics had a great time with this style, a sort of corsair pants in lace that they dubbed *crêpe suzette pants*. Countesses crazy for yachting and swimming started wearing pants in Biarritz. Shorts made a comeback for lunchtime on the beach, complemented by a summer wardrobe complete with rompers, bathing suits and white print dresses.

"This summer, women will have a hundred ways to abandon the skirt" announced *Femina* in its special edition Summer 1946 issue. "Will they gain in authority?... Certainly not. In grace? All depends on their figure. And this is why, I think, couturiers have saved a choice for them, one that ranges from shorts, very short shorts, I would say almost a loincloth, to the bouffant culotte of the lady cyclist." In a role game, the golf culotte became the holiday look for women while on the eighteen hole green, golfers have replaced them with pants like the dancer Gene Kelly wore with a sweater.

The movement inspired new materials: the ski pants introduced by Armand Allard in 1930 appeared in 1952 in a stretch version. Signed Henri Ours, Carven in a grey alternatively called "iron" and "lead," worn with an anorak or an after-ski jacket, the prewar "tumbler's pants" entered into the realm of sports chic with the help of *Liaisons Dangereuses* (1959) that Roger Vadim had filmed in a snowy setting. If Audrey Hepburn, alias Sabrina, set the image of the ideal young woman, Françoise Sagan, who tooled about in jeans and barefoot in her Aston-Martin, incarnated all the values of non-submission and amorality that "the odour of the night, the taste of encounters, of discoveries, of everything, of politics, of follies to be committed." The author-star of *Bonjour Tristesse* (1954) treated herself, on April 15, 1957 along the National 7 highway, to the most media-covered crash of the decade. "Just as she reunited play and risk, speed reunited with the joy of living and by consequence a confused death wish that always lies within the so-called joy of living. Speed is neither a sign, nor a proof , nor a provocation, nor a challenge, but rather the spirit of joy." *(Avec Mon Meilleur Souvenir,* 1984.)

13

13- **"Midnight leotard as an evening gown."**
A Pierre Cardin bodysuit in a white latex
seersucker weighing 100 grams (1958).

14- **Marlon Brando in *The Wild One* (1954).**

Stretch Pants, Corsair Pants
and Teddy Boys.
The Beautiful Getaways

The Jeans of Heroes

Jeans, in blue denim disembarked with the GIs during Liberation and became a Hollywood star. Bought rough, washed in courtyards beaten with a broom, they trailed behind them an illicit air — the exportation having been

15- Elvis Presley live in the United States (1957).

16- Yves Matthieu-Saint Laurent in the studios of Christian Dior (1955).

17- Jean-Paul Belmondo and Jean Seberg in *À Bout de Souffle* by Jean-Luc Goddard (1959).

strongly set to quotas, the first devotees went looking for them in army surplus shops and in the hangars where imported second-hand clothes, authorized under the Marshall Plan, were sold. In Saint-Germain-des-Prés, they wore jeans and a trucker's pullover sweater with a rolled existentialist collar. In Great Britain, *teddy boys* and black jackets were gotten in trade for their "drain pipe" pants and marked the advent of a uniform of social revolt. With James Dean wearing Levi's in *Giant* (1956), Joan Crawford in jeans *Johnny Guitar* (1954) and Marlon Brando wearing them *The Wild One* (1954), jeans created their aura. On July 4, 1954, American Independence Day, the release of *The Wild One* put the

Stretch Pants, Corsair Pants and Teddy Boys.
The Beautiful Getaways

Biker Look on the map. The black Schott jacket and Levi's 501 jeans formed the outfit of rebellion that would move to the first beats of rock and roll and the hum of a Harley-Davidson. High school principals pulled out their hair. In their jeans stained with grease, rockers declared war on ice cream-coloured fashion, permanent-pleated pants and Clarks on the feet. The bomb was about to drop. On September 7, 1957, America discovered Elvis Presley in *Loving You*. A true living advertisement for Levi's, he played an ex-truck driver turned rock 'n roll star loyal to the 507 jacket and famous 501 jeans, the precise outfit that would be taken up a few years later by Johnny Hallyday. Elvis was sacred in his jeans, an ever-growing legend. "It's all leg movements, I don't do nothin' with my body."

17

Pants, A History Afoot

The first tuxedo by Yves Saint Laurent, haute couture, 1966-1967.

**Béguines,
Trendies
and Taboos**

The Unisex Generation

What did the *drain pipe pants* of Gene Vincent, the jeans of Joan Baez and the bodysuit of Barbarella have in common? Perhaps nothing other than the energy of the decade, the baby-boomer decade, entering into a con-

sumer society as if into a new supermarket of appearances. Faced with the school kid's uniform, dad's pants held up with suspenders and mom's "house" pants, a generation defined its codes under the influence of pop music (110 million Beatles records were

sold in 1964), and by the needs of a body nourished on fresh milk. In 1964, Mary Quant's mini-skirt come upon the scene like a provocation. "I find it dirty, without any decency. Who is supposed to like it? It is pretentious. Showing the knees, that ages a woman," declared Mademoiselle Chanel.

If England set off bombs, then France confirmed in Yves Saint Laurent and in a more exclusive manner, a style, a way of life that did not lock the knees. Symbol of the ready-to-wear clothes inspired by the new American

Béguines, Trendies and Taboos.
The Unisex Generation

scene, pants would become more than an article of cloth-ing. Rather, an attitude, a standard of liberation that con-curred with the liberalization of the pill in 1967 and the feminisation of the workforce. Between 1962 and 1985, women's participation went from 40 to 66%.

In 1965, almost 10% of the world population was under 20 years old. The haute couture that dressed the café society in vogue since after the war seemed to be beyond

1- Dorothy with a camel at Baalbek.
   Photograph by William Klein (1961).

2- Jacqueline Kennedy, illustration by Edith Head.

3- Robert Kennedy at his home in Washington, DC.
   Photograph by Burt Glinn (1968).

4- André Courrèges' *moon girl*.
   Photograph by Willy Rizzo, *Marie Claire*, 1965.

5- Courrèges ensemble, summer 1965.

7

1964, large, sportive, tanned, behind her groovy slit glasses, Courrèges' moon girl appeared in the pages of *Vogue* wearing white pants signed by William Klein. From hereon, there would be the mother's fashion, immortalized by *Jolie Madame* in the 1950s, and the daughter's fashion, incarnated by Twiggy who took off on roller-skates across the Paris Trocadero esplanade. Yves Saint Laurent was interested in the twenty-five- to thirty-year-old woman, who would come to make him the head designer of a generation and its emancipation. The "Beatle" of rue Spontini were more inspired by the amazones of the 1920s and the smoke of their cigarettes than by the readers of *Mademoiselle Âge Tendre* brought up on canned soup.

In his inaugural collection of 1962, Yves Saint Laurent presented pants with a three-quarter woollen coat with gold buttons, a style implanted itself as the heir of Chanel. While in 1967 Lanvin introduced his "zouave pants" in crêpe and Nina Ricci a "dress culotte," Saint Laurent was the first of the haute couture stylists to take up again of the techniques of the menswear tailors, adapting them to his ready-to-wear Rive Gauche line introduced in 1966.

The blank page of the year 2000 lay in contrast to the eternity of the *Soleil Noir* that Barbara sung about in 1968. At the cusp of a time of innocence and the first surprise parties, a scent of seduction floated in the air. "I love it in the city and all day long. Not all women can wear them, but all women can no longer wear dresses," declared Yves Saint Laurent defending the ambiguity of pants.

age. "The *lady look* is ten years old," as *Vogue* put it when the 'Courrèges bomb' crashed upon the world." Women took off into pace and pants gave them wings. In 1964, one year after the Soviet "seagull" Valentina Terechkova took flight, André Courrèges' first collection, which was defined by the colour white, a symbol of light, glorified the new woman made for surveying the moon in ankle boots.

Breaking with the goddesses of Hollywood, like Marilyn Monroe who sometimes had to be sewn into her clinging dresses, unisex was born. Monroe's death in 1962 marked the end of the mythic woman and the advent of the woman "friend" obsessed with thinness and youth. In

6- Françoise Hardy in a metal bodysuit (16 kilos) signed by Paco Rabanne.
Photograph by Jean-Marie Périer (1968).

7- Men of the future in Pierre Cardin's zippered ensembles. Photograph by Yoshi Takat, 1966.

The Rive Gauche Style According to YSL

In 1968, Yves Saint Laurent's pants-suit, worn with a transparent blouse, consecrated the height of the "II" style. "I want to find for women an equivalent to the men's suit." Pants, which the post-war years had reserved for leisure activities, was making its entry into the city. They necessitated new movements, a new attitude, a confidence in one's body which although hiding the legs freed the spirit. With Yves Saint Laurent, pants became a classic part of women's wardrobe, the cult-clothing of liberated women as attested the heroine of Doris Lessing's Golden Notebooks (1936) Anna Wulf , who in revolt against marriage, ended by submitting to fickle men who "measured their emotions as one weighs vegetables." Pants were the accomplice of the safari jacket and the three-quarter

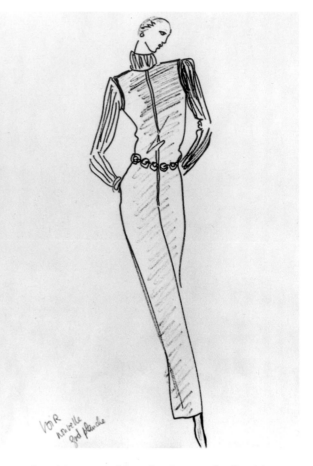

coat that thirty-somethings fought over the flagship store on rue de Touron.

There where Mary Quant's mini-skirt maintained the myth of the woman-child, the Rive Gauche pants disrupted in a more ambiguous way, braving the puritanical codes. Yves Saint Laurent's pants did not exactly dress juniors. "A twenty-year-old girl doesn't need anything more than a T-shirt and jeans. It's from thirty that she begins to become interesting."

The tunic-pants suit arrived at the Côte Basque restaurant in New York. Nan Kempner, an haute couture client of Yves Saint Laurent, was barred from entering because she was wearing pants. "I took them off," she remembered. "I wore the tunic as a dress. I couldn't bend down, as the waiter had taken my pants away. I had to sit with a napkin on my knees. 'Do you find this better?' I asked them."

10

Béguines, Trendies
and Taboos.
The Unisex Generation

8- Françoise Hardy dressed in the first Yves Saint
Laurent Rive Gauche tuxedo, winter 1966-1967.

9- Knit pants ensemble. Yves Saint Laurent
haute couture, summer 1969.

10- Black velvet tuxedo, white cotton blouse
with a lace jabot. Yves Saint Laurent haute couture,
winter 1966-1967. Photograph by Kazan/*Marie Claire*.

11- The first Yves Saint Laurent haute couture jumpsuit,
winter 1968-1969.

12- Pants and sailor top. Yves Saint Laurent
haute couture, spring-summer 1966.
Photograph by Marc Hispard/*Marie Claire*.

13- Hunting outfit with a heavy cardigan of glossy oilskin,
studded suede tunic and crocodile thigh boots.

14- Somali panther coat and beige crêpe pants.
Yves Saint Laurent haute couture, summer 1969.

15- Short, black sequined jumpsuit with gauze blouse.
Yves Saint Laurent haute couture,
spring-summer 1968.

16- Drawing board of the first Yves Saint Laurent
Rive Gauche collection, summer 1966.
(Archives Yves Saint Laurent, rights reserved.)

15

*"It was with the ready-to-wear
that I realized men were much
more free in their movement
and much less preoccupied
with their clothing. Because
his clothing was always the
same and it gave him confidence. A confidence superior to
a woman's as each year she
had to address problems like, 'what am I going to put
on?'. Little by little, I created a wardrobe that was cal-
culated on men's attire. In any case, for me nothing is
more beautiful than a woman dressed as a man! Because
all her feminity is put at stake. A woman does not
become part of men's clothing, she must fight against it,
and her feminity expresses itself that much more."*
(Yves Saint Laurent.)

16

Béguines, Trendies and Taboos.
The Unisex Generation

Sonia Rykiel, who complemented her short black sweater with pants remembers, "A woman wearing pants in a restaurant was like a man without a tie. In London, I was not allowed in a restaurant. My mother-in-law had to say

that I was a great creator." In 1968, she opened her first store in Saint-Germain, making her mark as the liberated woman in a knit pants-suit.

The polar opposite of the body "in an amphora" of the Christian Dior years, the androgynous body came out of the shadows, narrow hips, the bust of an ephebe, matchstick legs made to be set ablaze. At the time when feminists were burning their bras, pants, which had been prohibited for women working in companies all the way up to 1968, would progressively make their appearance and win acclaim with styles in fine wool, cashmere and flannel. Directors such as Francine Gomez, also known as *Madame Waterman*, the most famous businesswoman of the era, would wear pants at administrative meetings. Beneath judges' robes and the white lab coats of medical workers, two black pants legs would been seen. But scandal was abreast. In 1966, the six-foot Betty Catroux, first to adopt Saint Laurent's tuxedo which she wore over bare skin, was booed as she entered the Opéra. Jane Birkin was the first to go out at night wearing jeans and using a straw shopping bag as a pocketbook.

Garçonnes 1968

Starting in 1965, more pants than skirts were manufactured in France each year. In Tecryl, in Elastiss velvet and in Courtelle netting the challenge was set. Peroche also introduced its *Faraman* pants made of a heavy unbleached linen, with the zipper, equipped with a huge ring, placed on the side, and with no gusset, giving great ease of movement. Artal placed the zipper horizontally. A

17- Yves Saint Laurent and his sister Brigitte.
Photograph by Helmut Newton, 1968.

18- Sonia Rykiel in one of her jersey ensembles, 1968.

19- Glossy jacket and pants ensemble.
Hermès sport, spring-summer 1968.

ray of sunlight, and the pants got short. In the United States, teenagers with their hair combed back were crazy about the Pantino, skin-tight pants with an invisible zipper that were sold at Lord & Taylor and Marshall Field. Experimentation multiplied, taboos remained. In 1965, although for the first time as many girls as boys had passed the high school exams, girls were still prohibited from wearing pants except on extremely cold days. The emancipation of pants reflected the paradoxes of a country where husbands still remained the sole person authorized to manage household affairs, but however, where a

woman could finally work without producing permission from her husband. In a question written to the Conseil de Paris, a certain Doctor Bernard Lafay, recalling the ordinance of 16th Brumaire in the IX year implored, " the Parisian spirit" of the prefect. "This requirement is certainly no longer current, but it remains the jurisprudence and [thus] its obsolescence cannot substitute for a formal text abrogating a legislative or regulatory measure […]." A threat would continue to weigh upon many women. The response of the prefect, which appeared on June 29, 1969 in the *Bulletin Municipal Officiel*, gave women wanting to wear pants a real headache. "The Prefect of police considers it wise not to change the laws due to any foreseeable and unforeseeable variation in fashion that could at any moment come into being…"

But once again, sports gave the momentum. In 1968 at the winter Olympics held in Grenoble, the official outfit of the French team, which was the same for both men and women, consisted of a two-coloured tunic and pants by Ruben Torres. Saint Laurent made the greatest fortune of all the designers, ranging from Harry Lans, who sold 20,000 pairs of pants during the 1968 winter season, to Birgit, who made 10,000 pairs a month for Morbihan. There was also Arvel, whose famous *androgynous* pants sold at La Gaminerie, had the same cut, the same fly, the same legs for men as for women. Cut from a jersey or caviar black fabric, they went through five hundred pairs a day.

The Two-Faced Venus

Male-female. A new style was born, a confirmation of a contemporary look. "The new you," according to the American *Vogue*. "Yves Saint Laurent, style direct," for *Marie Claire*. "The two-faced Venus," according to *L'Express*. "In all women, there sleeps an actress who dreams of playing both Juliet and Messaline, to be at once

**Béguines, Trendies and Taboos.
The Unisex Generation**

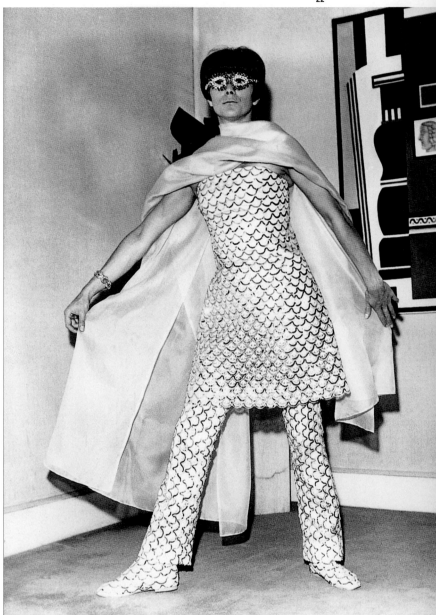

both the young romantic girl, the seductress, the intoxicating, androgynous, equivocal, *inaccessible grande dame.*" The repertoire would be infinite: alpaca bermuda shorts, but then also the black velvet knickers *à la Lorenzaccio.* This romantic look modelled by Jean Shrimpton was photographed in 1966 by Guy Bourdin. The dandy-look came to the cities, thanks largely to two women whose role in the world of fashion would grow: Maïme Arnodin, editor-in-chief of *Jardin des Modes,* the first to endorse ready-to-wear clothes in France, and her accomplice Denise Fayolle, then in the style department of Prisunic (a mid-level chain of department stores).

Maïme Arnodin, who had just brought out her line of pants made by an army tailor, was also one of the first women in Paris to wear an YSL pants suit. Madame

20- Demonstration in Paris, May 1968.
   Photograph by Henri Cartier-Bresson.

21- Printed leopard ensemble.
   Valentino haute couture, winter 1966-1967.

22- Evening tunic and pants ensemble in lace sequins.
   Jacques Esterel fall-winter 1965-1966 collection.

Lazareff, who had until just then prohibited her women editors from wearing pants, would devote an editorial to the phenomenon. "Saint Laurent at the head. The youngest of couturiers, has set the tone, the momentum and the shape of the new fashion. We believe that his city and evening pants suits can be worn by the great majority of women, regardless of their age or their figure. The answer to any woman's unease is the belted jersey tunic with its silk fringe that gives a comforting note of feminity. We believe that this variation is as important as Balenciaga's sack dress or Dior's 1947 *New Look*." So wrote *Elle* in its August 26, 1968 issue.

In the autumn, a thirty-year-old Yves Saint Laurent, dressed in a Renoma jacket, Tillbury shoes, custom-made tortoise shell glasses by Gualdoni, inaugurated his first transatlantic Rive Gauche store in New York. "Yves' name is magic," declared *Time* magazine on September 27, reporting $25,000 in the first day of sales. The best seller? The *City Pants*, which sold for between $145 and $175. "When it's pants, it's Yves," declared Lauren Bacall, cutting as she was in the style the most suited to the new Fifth Avenue *pompadours* who dressed in top-of-the-line Chanel suits.

In October 1968, the Saint Laurent store on rue de Tournon sold one hundred and fifty suits in less than fifteen days. Among its clients were, Elsa Martinelli, Stéphane Audran, Mireille Darc and Anne-Marie Malle, then wife of the filmmaker. They all wore the suit with a white silk blouse, highly polished flat shoes with a metal buckle and a gold chain. Everything was in the detail. The cuffs of the pants had to go way down, almost touching the floor, as far as the heels would allow, so the pants could be as long as possible. "Everything the same, each different." A headline in *Marie Claire*, December 1968. For Christmas night, the elegant Hélène Rochas asked her guests to wear pants. "Pants, they've won!" as a

headline declared in *Le Figaro* of May 8, 1969. "Pants triumph. In six months, they have effectively moved from the street into the offices, where they shock no one. The most recalcitrant will be able to follow in the footsteps of the young women pilots who have, without fear, have drawn the curiosity of men." Whether in a ribbed jersey, a white gabardine, a pink silk or the beige tussor of Turlututu, pants were associated with three major venues: the city, the evening and sports. Dressed in pants, when questioned by the same newspaper, students declared they'd end the year "in beauty." One of them, Suzanne, an "eccentric anti-woman," chose pants in a purple acetate jersey.

The Drugstore Lions

From London to Paris, colours exploded like butterflies. Wanting to copy Mick Jagger, with his skintight hip-huggers, some teenagers were temporarily suspended from their high schools. The Peacock Revolution was in full swing on Carnaby Street, with the first low-waisted pants and Shetland sweaters on offer, and on weekends, the "hippest" girls and boys, those who liked eggs and bacon, tooled around in Asten Martins and preferred vodka to whiskey. Pillars of the Bunny Club, Parisian trendies were fond of Marina's pants that broadened a bit at the cuff, heralding the bell-bottoms of the 1970s. Marriage, on the boulevard Rochechouart, offered the "transfosmoking" – sold with its sating lapels, with one simple snip of the scissors, it became the suit of the city.

But the sixteenth arrondissement address of the lion cult was Renoma (the Castel of the ready-to-wear), a label introduced in 1959 and set aloft by the yéyé culture. Because at "the international market of *in*, Antoine is

23- Johnny Hallyday in a dandy outfit. Photograph by Jean-Marie Périer, September 1968.

king" *(Paris Jour*, June 10, 1966), Johnny Hallyday, Serge Gainsbourg, Alain Delon and François Mitterand all crossed paths at the store on rue de la Pompe, a veritable HQ of waisted suits, jacquard pullover sweaters, corduroy pants, linen madras and seersucker were fought over like cookies. "The Renoma Brothers were the only ones to have their clients wear black shirts under club ties with deep purple or sky blue velvet blazers." *(Journal de*

Textile, January 1965.) Here, tuxedos in satin inspired, with their tight waists delineating the torso.

The number of men's stores devoted to this new "English" unisex style multiplied. The style would be the

24- The Rolling Stones at the London Airport, April 1966.

25- Audrey Hepburn in Paris, 1967.

25

glory of the Carnaby store on rue de Longchamp, and even more so the New Man store with their fine-striped, low-waisted brightly-coloured pants. In 1968, Renoma presented their Lénine suit with gigantic loops allowing for the inevitable belt. "Following the material used, the Lénine suit became the weekend outfit or the tuxedo of the avant-garde," advocated Jacques Chancel in the October 1, 1968 issue of *Paris Jour*. Jean-Paul Belmondo would be one of the first clients. Idols had renounced the tie, taking on the Mao jacket sold at Mayfair's a former butchery where Jean Bouquin, the future dresser of the bohemian Left Bank, officiated.

The revolution of appearance was consummated. In 1969, sales figures at Renoma reached twenty million francs. That year, Yves Saint Laurent opened his first Left Bank store for men. "I address myself to free men. What I am offering them is not a new line, a new constraint, but rather a new freedom. Virility is no more linked to grey flannel and broad shoulders than a woman is to chiffon and high bust lines. I think that the time of lady dolls and dominant men is past. Girls no longer need to simper, or prattle or show their legs to show that they are women. Boys do not need to slap one another on the shoulders nor twirl their moustaches to prove they are men."

He Creates Tuxedos For Her

"Black, I only like it for slimming. A girl in a tuxedo jacket, a long black jersey dress with embroider and sequins. It's overdressed," explained Yves Saint Laurent to *Elle* on March 7, 1968. With him, the dinner jacket, its origins harkening back to 1880 but which was prohibited from being worn in public up until the death of Edward VII in 1910, became an evening classic. Initially, men only wore them when they met in a smoking room. (In French, a tuxedo is called *un smoking*.) By making the tuxedo an

evening attire for women, Yves Saint Laurent found, in the wake of Marlene Dietrich, an evocative and scandalous scent. Far, very far from those "nice audacities of fashion" which Jean Cocteau spoke of. "That good taste that placed the bad taste of yesterday on a pedestal, projecting around it neither any mystery nor significance." The tuxedo is like a familiar intruder into the wardrobe, a faceted accomplice who sends invitations all over the world. The Sevillan tuxedo (1968), the long skirt-tuxedo (1969), the "Blue Angel" tuxedo, the short version in a fine woven wool with satin lapels. The tuxedo dressed the metamorphoses of the decade and established itself as a classic, and since 1966, it played all the roles — in turn, a dress, a coat, a jacket, a suit — without losing itself. It is the black stroke on the white page, the obsession incarnate. "If I had to chose one style among all of the ones I've presented, without the slightest doubt, it would be the tuxedo."

**26- Twiggy in an "Al Capone" pinstripe suit.
Yves Saint Laurent haute couture, summer 1967.**

**27- Hippie-chic. Twiggy and her manager Justin
de Villeneuve in London, October 1967.**

Mick Jagger live wearing low-waisted pants with a raised motif.

Hippies, Overalls and Bellbottoms

"Karting pants are surprisingly supple and comfortable. Karting, the pants without a fly, flattens the stomach and refines the haunches. What's more, Kartings don't get baggy at the knees and the permanent crease means no ironing after washing." (Karting advertisement, 1974.)

The Hippy Generation and Low-Waisted Pants

Tents, camp fires, beards like a Greek priest and Swedish sandals. In September 1969, the route that led to White Lake, in the way to Woodstock, heralded the great upheaval of the 1970s. Sixty kilometers from New York City times were changing and the trip had begun. From Hyde Park in London, where the Rolling Stones gave a free concert, to Katmandu where jeans

were worn with bare feet and Indian tunics, *Flower Power* established its anti-establishment attire.

The first anarchist felt-tip signs, the first frayed clothing, the first tie-dyed. In 1969, the "erotic year" according to Serge Gainsbourg, everything got longer, everything came down a notch: bangs, hair, armpit hair, belts, charms. Waistlines were lowered and the future was patchwork. Chairs disappeared from living rooms and were replaced with soft chairs filled with marbles and gigantic cushions. Women became pals with men, sitting down like them. The "cross-legged" skirt appeared in history. They no longer talked, they chatted. About the pill, drugs, everything. The natural wanted to triumph over the artificial. Dyed, embroidered with flowers and rainbows, pants were like a flying carpet. With them, you could travel around the

1- **Hippies at a festival in Bath, England, June 1970.**

2- **Blue jeans with a peace symbol, New York. Photograph by René Burri.**

3- **Serge Gainsbourg and Jane Birkin. Photograph by Oliviero Toscani, *L'Uomo Vogue*, 1972.**

1

Hippies, Overalls
and Bellbottoms.
The Hippy Generation and Low-Waisted Pants

dom, and freedom of movement stimulates that of the mind." At the same time, Pierre Cardin emphasized the body of his male models, whose skintight pants, worn with zippered jackets thrusted the rock star with the wild hair into the towns of the glorious future.

Folklore and Home-Made

But the times were a changin'. Brigitte Bardot could take off her outerspace bodysuit. The new, however, was the old. Yves Saint Laurent set off his "retro" bomb in January 1971. Flea markets were in vogue. Surplus stores styled upon *Baba'z* started in Avignon and then spread throughout the south of France; secondhand clothes were making their way into the city. Studded, pearled, patched

world from a pop China in the far west to the jungles of the Steppes. Kenzo's China blues were popular, as were grandfather's shirts, flannelettes and stoneware dishes. In Paris, the new stores were called Jean Bouquin, Gudule, Zozo, Anastasia and La Gaminerie, with its troglodyte setting. You rode a bicycle because "cars stink and pollute."

In 1968, Courrèges presented the first "pantacourt," a name the couturier from the French Pyrenees city of Pau coined, but never trademarked. Then came the second-skin tights, overalls, and mini-overalls. "I want everyone to find his free-

4- Marithé and François Girbaud, 1967-1968.

5- Levi's patchwork jeans.

6- Unisex outfit for a couple.
Jacques Esterel, fall-winter 1971-1972.

7- Marithé and François Girbaud's *boutonneux* with its 50 buttons, 1970.

Hippies, Overalls
and Bellbottoms.
The Hippy Generation and Low-Waisted Pants

or fraying, jeans, along with Indian jewelry, wicker baskets and tooled leather cigarette lighter cases, comprised the indispensable of a new daily life where everything was made by hand – the knitted sweater, the hammered jewelry, the string belts with pebbles. "The mood is for savings, the fashion is for crafts," confirmed the January 26, 1970 edition of *Elle.* At the top-speed ski resorts, tight ski pants and anoraks were replaced by Cossack pants, Afghan fur vests and ponchos. "Cut, knit, lengthen, puff up," pronounced *Elle* on October 5, 1970. Pants have not escaped the '100 ideas' generation. Golf or muzhik version, they wore dyed velvet vest and dog collars, and with giants steps, gained their independence in the city, free from the taboos that kept them at home. Jeans became coats, shorts, even shoulder bags. Short-circuiting the debate over mini-midi-maxi that plunged sales into a torpor (one billion francs of unsold ready-to-wear in France in 1970), pants was making its way. Dropped waist,

flared legs, they flourished on advertising posters and were unbuttoned in sex-shop windows, symbolic of all freedoms. Specialized brands began to emerge, from Lothar (pastel jeans cut from Tuareg cotton fabrics), to Sym (who in the beginning of the 1970s sold a million pants per year and exported 20% of its production), to Philippe Salvet (whose pants laced in the back and were all the rage in Saint-Tropez).

The Unisex Style

In 1971, for the first time in France, more girls than boys passed the high schools exams and went on to university. Pants became dominant in offices as well as in high schools, evidence of the "woman's revolution" that Françoise Giroud, who would become Secretary of State for Women's Affairs in 1974, spoke about. Yves Saint Laurent gave birth to an entire wardrobe born of "hijackings": men's shirts, men's fabrics (flannels, tweeds and hounds-tooth) which reconciled the androgynous ideal and a nostalgia for the 1930s. In 1974, one woman in five wore pants. Nathalie Mont-Servan, a columnist for *Le Monde*, assessed the situation. "Following their youngest children, women no longer so young begin to appreciate the comfort of pants. They can been seen, particularly in the morning, doing the shopping or walking about in outfits that resemble someone taking a cure [at a spa]." (July 1, 1972.)

With pants, unisex fashion gained ground. In January 1970, Jacques Esterel and Ted Lapidus presented haute couture styles for men and women. Bell-bottom pants, which reached their widest in 1972, became the uniform of both sexes, complemented with a waisted jacket. Jeans (or the denim fabric) also was sold by the metre, and in

June 1975 Bouchara sold some two hundred metres a day! It was the real American denim washed fourteen times in an indigo bath that was truly appreciated. Softened, but not faded, Levis could be worn with sneakers or high heels. In Saint-Germain-des-Prés as in Saint-Tropez, they were rolled up to the ankles, hitched up to mid-calf and readily made way with riding boots and cowboy boots. When in 1975 co-education became compulsory for all schooling, woman's pants made their dif-

ference known in a game of varying lengths and shapes. The pantacourt from Courrèges, which introduced the style in 1968; the cigarette pants worn with a "centimeter-belt" for the "ultra-thin junior"; and the masculine, for the more built body. Progress obliged and the permanent crease became truly permanent – *pantawool*, a 60% wool/40% polyester mixture was machine washable. In this first year of the woman (1975), came the Karting: the pants "without the fly," that didn't need ironing and that "follows your moves without discomfort or constraint." Created in 1972 by André Faller and his wife Lou, the Karting pants would see its sales curve stretch with 90,000 items sold in 1975. Brigitte Bardot herself became (in the time of the commercial) an ambassador for the brand. Indeed, heaven on earth was sold indis-

Hippies, Overalls
and Bellbottoms.
The Hippy Generation and Low-Waisted Pants

criminately. "At the edge of the earth… or at the edge of your garden, what do you need to feel good? A good pair of jeans and a shirt to go with it!" declared an advertisement for New Man.

Hijackings

"Fashions no longer follow one another, they're knocking into themselves, contradicting themselves," Claude Berthod, the editor-in chief of *Elle*, wrote in 1973. Razors were throwaway and love was consummated on the ground. The past and nostalgia became confused. New cities would soon be sprouting up like mushrooms. Polo neck jerseys in Dropnyl Hélanca and stretch velvet pants bought at the Pantashop, real estate agents were to be

seeing a bright future. But the "op and pop" decade would waste away in disillusion. "We have matured a little, and we are a little freer and all that, but it's still the same game, nothing has really changed," explained John Lennon in *Rolling Stone Magazine* (January 1971). "The dream is over [...]. It's always the same, but I'm thirty and a lot of people have long hair, that's all." In a room

8- Gabardine pants suit and beige chiffon blouse. Yves Saint Laurent haute couture, summer 1971.

9- Jersey pants and angora wool sweaters. Sonia Rykiel, spring-summer 1972.

10- Outfit in "Mahé" lambskin. Hermès Sport, spring-summer 1973. Photograph by Jack Peg.

11- Jeans and shorts, sneakers and platform sandals. London, 1970.

12- Psychodelic print outfit. Emilio Pucci, 1970.

with burlap hangings, an Olivetti red plastic "Valentine" typewriter awaited the student dressed in brown corduroy pants and Clarks, soiled from the petrol of his Moped.

It was around 1974, the first oil crisis had come to pass, that old-fashioned clothes became the fashion with a high-jacking of military and professional garb, like the colonial beige shorts of the "army of the Indies," the butcher's hounds tooth pants, overalls and the painter's pants sold at Agnès B. It was during these years that she opened her first store on rue du Jour in the heart of Les Halles quarter of Paris. She would be one of the first to introduce a petrol attendant jumpsuit, which she offered in a fine cotton and a variety of colours. The originals, signed by Adolphe Lafont, were on sale at BHV, while UPLA sold the legendary Smith's American carpenter pants with tool pockets. After Charlie Chaplin's cane, Maurice Chevalier's hat, Coluche's striped overalls made their spot on

the scene. "Pockets, pockets everywhere" wrote *Elle*, suggesting its readers wear a butcher's blouse in combed cotton and grandfather's *peau de diable* cotton pants available at the Marché des Halles for 49 francs.

Suspenders were making a return. "The new way to wear pants: a little too big, high-waisted and tightly belted at the waist, in a style borrowed from pastry chefs." *(Elle, March 17, 1975.)* Of course, the coalman's cotton shirt was also then worn with suspenders, a style immortalized by Diane Keaton in the absolute image of the liberated woman and brainchild of the New York independent filmmaker, Woody Allen.

Hippies, Overalls and Bellbottoms.
The Hippy Generation and Low-Waisted Pants

Two clashing trends yielded evidence of the gap between authentic American style (Western House, Façonnable and soon Ralph Lauren) and the camp style of the Argentines living in Paris and all the new Left Bank bohemians. Brainchild of Yves Saint Laurent, Loulou de la Falaise made satin shorts and pants for YSL that electrified each of his appearances at Sept, which had been opened by the dandy Fabrice Emaer. The new romantics made declarations to the press. "Me, disguised? Look at the street. It's gray and ugly […]. If I happened to have clothes made of gold, I'd wear them. I'd be a true sun." Some treated them like fools: "Those are men? They're girls!" Or: "Oh yes, the beautiful *Mardi Gras*, the clowns, they make fun of the world."

16

17

18

13- Yves Saint Laurent and Betty Catroux. Photograph by Henry Clarke (1973).

14- Men's styles. Yves Saint Laurent Rive Gauche collection, fall-winter 1971.

15- Jersey pants suits on "rollerskates". Pierre Cardin, 1971.

16- Karting pants. Catalogue 1973.

17- Sonia Rykiel's velvet terry jogging suit, 1974. Musée de la Mode, Marseilles.

18- Drawing by Gotlib for Marithé and François Girbaud (1970s).

Sequins, Colours and Glam Rock

From Robert Plant, the legendary leader of Led Zeppelin with his bare chest and bellbottoms, to Angus Young, the AC/DC guitarist in shorts, singers and musicians would be the first to relieve fashion of its guilt. A liberated body

made for a peacock on stage, in all extravagance. Led Zeppelin, Elton John, James Brown, the Jackson Five, David Bowie (glam rock's sequined idol) and more modestly, Giorgio Moroder, who stomped in his Knights in White Satin (1976) and Cerrone (two million eight hundred thousand albums sold). But the slim hips and the agile knees of John Travolta would set the standards for disco fashion, the new "ready-to-dance" cut by the Bee

19

Hippies, Overalls and Bellbottoms.
The Hippy Generation and Low-Waisted Pants

(1976), unleashed, during the depths of an economic crisis, the rage of a generation. *No Future in England For You*. The manager of the group was none other than Malcolm MacLaren who, with his partner Vivienne Westwood, opened a store on King's Road in 1971. *Let It Rock*, became *To Fast To Live, Too Young To Die*, and then was re-baptized Sex at the end of 1975. Johnny Rotten became the anti-hero of *Bromley Contingent* (whose first fans came from the outskirts of London) and propagated the aesthetic of destruction and confinement: ripped T-shirts, safety pins and soon, pants attached with a belt around the knees, that restricted walking and prohibited running.

Rastas and heavy metal. Boom boom disco and trash culture. Creators and couturiers. Tracksuits and golden lambskin sandals. The podiums started to crackle. Canvas and lamé. Mink jogging suits. Everyone, male or female, was a diva. In this end of the 1970s, upon a background of insane decibels, all influences clashed, in the rhythm of an irresistible desire to dance under a shower of golden rain and illusions. If "a jogging suit is the clothing for the track," "Mister Jean [...] emerged victorious from every battle," returning "enshrouded in a brilliant array: paste, pearls, turquoise and lace." *(Elle*, July 31, 1978.)

Far from the beatniks of the west coast, the chic came back to New York and Paris, where the young lions of fashion and advertising, which was no longer called publicity nor communication, heralded the war of the look.

Gees, the band that exploded to the top of the hit parade with the original soundtrack from the film *Saturday Night Fever* (1977).

Whereas disco fashion had the body flashing in a trance and a white suit, punk style cast a spell over its demons. While Iggy Pop brought ripped jeans, a T-shirt and sneakers to the fore, and Lou Reed the same for the total black look, the first Sex Pistols record *Anarchy in the UK*

19- Elton John in mink and denim overalls.

20- David Bowie live, wearing uni-leg pants (1970).

21- Iggy Pop bare-chested and in silvered leather. London, 1972.

"The ones made by Levi Strauss are the best-cut, best-looking pair of pants that have ever been designed by anybody. Nobody will ever top the original bluejeans. They can't be bought old, they have to be bought new and they have to be worn in by the person. To get that look. And they can't be phoney bleached or phoney anything. You know that little pocket? It's so crazy to have that little pocket, like for a twenty-dollar gold piece." (Andy Warhol, *The Philosophy of Andy Warhol (From A to B and Back Again)*, 1975.)

22- John Travolta in *Saturday Night Fever* (1975).

Hippies, Overalls
and Bellbottoms.
The Hippy Generation and Low-Waisted Pants

The liberation of pants according to Agnès B

"There was Mary Quant, Levi's and the flea markets. Jeans and the mini-skirt. There was Jim Morrison, so sensual, who influenced everyone with his low-waisted pants. His belt was part of The Doors show. If there is a single article of clothing of the century, it is pants. They revolutionized a lot things. I remember Marilyn in The Misfits. *Jeans were the first article of clothing for both sexes. My first pair of jeans, I bought them in a surplus store. And I kept them a very long time. I grew up in a world where, at school, it had to be below 15° C to wear a pair... and then, with a skirt over it. No doubt, that's why I don't get cold easily.*

Since I came to Elle, *I started going to see the* films noirs *at the Mac-Mahon, I went to the flea markets, I bought men's undershirts and wore them as T-shirts. I remember May 1968. All of a sudden, you saw women fashion editors, who had always worn skirts and high heels, arriving in jeans and sneakers. My children were at home, playing cops and robbers. I was in the streets. We rode motorcycles, sat on the ground, the girls dressed like boys. A Christian education, then leftism, then the hippies, it went without saying. At concerts, everything was blue. Jeans were work pants that became everyday pants. A classic. In blue, in black, in leather, I wear them with a T-shirt or a blouse.*

I always wear pants. Overalls, I remember wearing them when I was pregnant, at a time when you hid any roundness. You had fun at every turn, like the painter pants I cut better because they came up too high. I dyed them all colors. On rue du Jour, sometimes they were still wet when you bought them."

  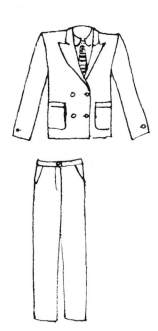

Marc Audibet's double-stretch velvet tights, winter 1985-1986.

Leggings,
Punks and
the Baggy Look

"*Flies could be worn open or closed. Something of a provocative gesture [...], for me, it's like winking at certain rites of propriety and good taste.*" (Jean Paul Gaultier, speaking about his summer 1980 collection Homme Fatal, in *Les Années '80*, Christian Schlatter, 1984.)

The Stretch Decade

1

Devoured by its ambitions, the decade of the 1980s cultivated the religion of extremes: from the black pants of Yohji Yamamoto to "snow" jeans, from skin-tight leggings, to the baggy look, from the torn jeans of the punks, to Ralph Lauren's chic jeans, from the "timeless" style (jodhpurs) to seasonal comets (the sarouels) – summer 1981, knickers – winter 1981, stretch ski pants – winter 1984), each new style was like a bomb exploding on a world of chimeras and mirrors where everyone had to permanently invent for himself an ephemeral identity that would make a thousand and one looks. Crowds in black invaded Iran. The West, with neither god nor master, flaunted itself as a society of leisure amid a proliferation of signs, codes, cathode images, video ads, logos on parade, electrifying the influences of new wave, raï, reggae and hip-hop. In 1981, Vivienne Westwood, who introduced the Collection Pirate, succumbed to the charms of the new "romantics". Casuals, a gothic precursor to the vampire look was smitten by The Cure. Fetishists in leather bodysuits, acid-rockers in Adidas *Gazelles*, beach boys, ravers all fought over an identity that the music of the street and the clubs fashioned in their image.

Pants, that had sheltered the opposition of the sexes, from here on claimed its tribes, isolating by interposed cities, the traditional and the future, the avant-garde and the conservative. It was no longer pants *per se*, but more its style that codified a genre and defined belonging. The XXL of rappers against the well-pressed jeans of yuppies, the ghetto-blaster against the walkman. The punks in London took the waistband down to the knees, and pants became the symbol of a rock attitude whose ambassador was Malcolm MacLaren, the mentor of The Sex Pistols, before being industrially manufactured by and becoming, via Vivienne Westwood in London and

2

Leggings, Punks
and the Baggy Look
The Stretch Decade

Steven Sprouse in New York, the uniform of the Haradjuka (the HQ of the Tokyo fashion world) fashion victims. The first rips, the first rejections, marking the end of the previous thirty glorious years. The three Ds of John Richmond and Maria Cornejo (Destroy, Disorder, Disorientate) defined a new culture that was boiling over, and that made music like street fashion – a scream.

Break Dancers and World Sound

With the Sugar Hill Band, a group created in 1979 in Bronx, New York, pants became looser to allow for dancing, and set the scene for new figures that started with the *break dance* look which, as of 1985, took on a worldwide influence: Adidas sweat pants, a cap with a long visor and Nike sneakers. These were the ones who, on the fringes of the "trash" look, became the new agents for brand names, cherishing their logos. Sportswear had an influence over the cities to the point that tracksuits, whether they were terry (Sonia Rykiel) or grey flannel (Hanes), became a

daily response. What was used for roller-skating or going out at night. Listening to the world sound, designers who were triumphant on the Paris stage, from Jean-Paul Gaultier to Claude Montana and Thierry Mugler actively took part at this festival of appearances where Hollywood rubbed shoulders with the city outskirts — the *divine* of the 1950s and the proud punk, the skirt for men and the duds of businesswomen. "With Gaultier, it's as if I were dressing in my man's suits," declared the actress Anémone in the weekly *Elle*. "I love thus androgynous side, a wink at modern times. I love the guy's style." Designer France Andrevie introduced the "anti-theft" pants-jacket.

Time of the Superwoman

Sharp shoulders, femininity outrageously dressed up, showed its claws. When in 1986 a published notice in the *Journal Officiel* defined the new rules regarding "the feminization of work titles," men's pants were being worn with silk blouses and pearls. Dressed in pants by Yves Saint Laurent, Helmut Newton's superwomen were a triumph in *Vogue*. After Vivienne Westwood put a bra over a sweatshirt, Chantal Thomass married a corset with a pair of pants (in champagne satin). Decked out in prostheses, the shouldered body, reinforced, magnified the woman under pressure who

1- Johnny Rotten, leader of The Sex Pistols.

2- Punks in London at the beginning of the 1980s.

3- In the outskirts south of London, rappers in Chipie jeans. Photograph by Richard Croft, *The Face* (March 1991).

4- Vivienne Westwood's pants with strapped legs, 1985.

played her career on a black and white chessboard between astral bodysuits and armed with shadows. Pants during the 1980s, in order to cope with the return of fine lingerie (Chantal Thomass), had to bow to the demands of a body sculpted by aerobics. Pants would become footless leggings in vivid colours, and when worn by the likes of Véronique and Davina in France and Jane Fonda in the United States, were the classic image of fitness.

"I hate jeans that are very tight, skin-tight, that are sometimes embroidered and worn with high heels," explained the Japanese couturier Yohji Yamamoto who, in the space left between the body and the clothes found the place for another direction, another truth other than the gloss and sequins

of the disco years. Inspired by the "working men" of the photographer August Sander, Yamamoto would make black a new colour, stripping it, dramatizing it with a softness and bringing a rhythm to the pace of the streets of the new Metropolises. Pants, which were a manifesto of the 1970s, became the signature look of the 1980s. Now stronger, women began to get rid of the terribly square shoulders and the overly rigid lines. As it had all been stolen from men, women would reconquer what they had lost: their difference. Tyrannical to *the look*, women preferred the softness, the nuances. Pants started to define the waistline, and with cer-

5- Pointed shoulders, men's pants and a chiffon blouse — the suit according to Yves Saint Laurent (1978).

6- Marithé and François Girbaud's Pedal Pusher. Sculpture, 1984.

7- Leather suit by Claude Montana.

8- Yasmine Lebon wearing an Azzedine Alaia outfit. Photograph by Peter Lindbergh, 1985.

Leggings, Punks
and the Baggy Look
The Stretch Decade

tain new details such as tortoiseshell buttons, Jean-Paul Gaultier's gold lamé vests and Yves Saint Laurent's chiffon blouses, came to the fore. By gently draping them, by using extremely flowing fabrics and an extraordinary grey monochrome with a 1930s nostalgia, Giorgio Armani feminized pants. "My ideal pants are those that ameliorate an individual's aesthetic, whether a man or a woman. If they're not flattering, if they're not glamorous to the body, if they don't respect or express the personality of the person wearing them, they can be very beautiful, but not ideal."

Couture Leggings and Exercises in Style

Sports entered the arena of couture, lending itself to a veritable exercise of styles. With Sonia Rykiel, the jogging outfit, in a jersey version, paced the streets of the cities.

With Azzedine Alaia and Marc Audibet, yesterday's leggings and those of times stretched over bodies of endless legs, jettisoned by the power of new techniques. In the

9- Drawing by Gianni Versace, 1980s.

10- Sonia Rykiel's 1980-1981 winter collection.

11- From Yohji Yamamoto's winter 1984-1985 catalogue. Photograph by Max Vadukul, New York.

Leggings, Punks
and the Baggy Look
The Stretch Decade

spirit of couture, Lycra was blended with materials like wool, cotton, silk and even mink. In Paris, at Azzedine Alaia's tiny *cabinette*, the new conquerors, still shy behind their flaming red lipstick, took flight in an assault of camera flashes. Stephanie Seymour, Naomi Campbell, Linda Evangelista, et al.

The machine-body of the 1980s armoured itself to win. Coming straight from the United States where, through Jennifer Beals it was triumphant in the 1982 film *Flashdance*, aerobics, introduced by Dr. Kenneth Cooper, dominated in France via Véronique and Davina under a florescent rainbow. Rolled up in the backpack of the woman on the run, the leotard became an indispensable accessory in the muscle factories that first spread over Paris and throughout France. Repetto, a brand bought

back in 1987 by Esmark Corporation, which already manufactured and distributed two brands of dance clothing — the industry leader Danskin (which comprised 60% of the American market) and Dance France, put itself on the map and sponsored French aerobics and fitness champions. Following Saint Laurent in 1970 and Calvin Klein in 1976, the arrival of designer jeans contributed greatly to the feminization of the market which fell in love with the new stretch cotton blends, as if as tes-

Leggings, Punks
and the Baggy Look
The Stretch Decade

fashion industry, ready-to-wear clothing with a neo-colonial look that took on a true value. By offering chic denims to the American consumer, Ralph Lauren sold them a dream of distinction with the Safari shorts like Robert Redford wore in *Out of Africa*, or the crinkled linen pants and a blazer with an insignia for watching a polo match in Palm Beach. The king of American sportswear confirmed a return to an authentic based upon the myths satirized by Tom Wolfe, the author of *The Bonfire of the Vanities* (1987), treating his expensive suits to a British inspiration, a kind of "pseudo-Savile" suit. In the mid-1980s, through an annual investment of seventeen million dollars for advertising, Ralph Lauren set the image for yuppies (young urban professionals) whose identification with an aristocratic world culminated in the outrageously powerful catch phrase by Calvin Klein who, in 1978, had Brooke Shields say, "Do you know what's between me and my Calvin's? Nothing."

Forever dressed in faded Levi's, a cotton shirt and cowboy boots, Ralph Lauren, who did not hesitate to open one of his first *megastores* in a townhouse on New York's Madison Avenue, rooted his "folk-chic" style in an infinitely deteriorating universe. Along with tweed jackets, pin-striped suits and patterned fabrics in cashmere, for a second time, jeans created their myth. In 1986, sales were four times greater than they were in 1981. *Time* magazine put Lauren on the cover of their

tament to the success of Cimarron and his stretch jeans. The pants of the 1980s either clung to the body or were unstuck to the extreme with the Pariente Brothers' extra-large bodysuit. In 1983, Naf-Naf would sell some three million of them, cut from a cotton canvas and stamped with its famous logo of a truck and the company's telephone number — a "really tough look." One last gimmick before the avalanche of the casual look.

A system was set in motion that produced, throughout the

12- Jean Paul Gaultier's *petit marquis*, borrowed from the 18th century, worn with jogging pants. Winter 1984-1985.

13- Jennifer Beals, the heroine of *Flashdance* (1983).

14- White blouses and black pants from Comme des Garçons. Photograph by Peter Lindbergh (1987).

September 1, 1986 issue, a privilege granted to the likes of Maria Callas, Nelson Rockefeller, Theodore Roosevelt and Queen Elizabeth.

The Temptation of History

Georges Marciano, who created the brand Guess in 1982, would come to ignite the dreams of a history of another

America with his black and white ad campaign and products like stone washed jeans, which would become the symbol of a "wild West" style. The first video advertisement, shown in 1985, began like a documentary on the West. In reviving original denims, the four Marciano brothers — Georges, Armand, Paul and Maurice — originally from Marseilles and transplanted to Los Angeles in 1981, would create an image authenticating the renewal of the California look. Whereas Ralph Lauren's jeans were worn on weekends with a Boston tweed blazer, Guess jeans, made glossy through new techniques, surfed the waves of fashion and sex appeal.

The 1980s would prove a period of veritable brand wars, fought upon a field of catch phrases which would bring pants out of the closet and off the cowboy ranches and into the realm of love. With Levi's, jeans would take the floor, becoming the living symbol of whomever wore them. "My Levi's, they're me." With Creek sneakers and a Hervé Chapelier backpack, 501s would authenticate a new style dominated by a search for "true values" that could not be reduced by the capricious hiccups of fashion. With each of their product lines, the large stores promoted a proliferation of private labels that championed a certain life style, and it was the Jodhpurs from Les Galleries Lafayette (1989) that were cut from a fabric between a terry and a Shetland in autumn shades which would signal a return to roots. "Beautiful, rich, true materials, in simple, classic styles that would never go out of fashion gave these clothes the discreet charm of authenticity. Worn over a long period of time, they will become more beautiful and more personal by the day."

At the end of the 1980s, a growing interest in History and a mania for museums contributed to making the "legend" into a new advertising and marketing ploy, and to setting a product into a context of adventure and conquest, as well as linking it to heroes of the 1930s and 1940s. This

15

Leggings, Punks
and the Baggy Look
The Stretch Decade

line of attack was promoted by French brands like Chipie, Bensimon and Chevignon, the last of which revitalized the taste for duffle coats and aviator jackets, anticipating Dockers' chinos that would appear in 1986. The market became international. With fabrics henceforth being made in Japan (like the Denim Double Ring)

15- The dandy look with trumpet bottoms, Martine Sitbon. Photograph by Javier Vallhonrat (1987).

16- Marithé and François Girbaud's *sirène métamorphojean*. Photograph by William Laxton (1989).

17- Alaia creation for men. Photograph by Bruce Weber (1991).

and products manufactured in Italy, Replay succeeded in selling a million jeans in 1990. Marithé et François Girbaud began importing American cowboy outfits in 1964 for Western House, the first "Western-style" clothing store in Paris, and in 1967, they started fading jeans. During the 1980s, they would expand their activities and under the brand name Closed (introduced in 1976), they would offer pants in all its forms, making them wider, shrinking them, shifting their defining lines to raise the waist, to lengthen the crotch, with a mind toward "returning," "transforming," "flipping over," "livening up" and "inciting other shapes." Pockets sculpted from denim and morphological cuts were the signs of the "métamorphojean" (1988), extolling an idea of comfort pushed to the extreme by the African West Line (1985), which let you stick your hands into the X-shaped pockets as far as the seam. *Cupro* denim was a sensation in the United States. In 1984, the year *destroyed* jeans were introduced, the American license belonging to Puritan was resold to Blue Bell (Wrangler). At the end of the 1980s, Marithé Girbaud, which comprised twelve lines of men's and women's products (Compagnie des Montagnes et des Fôrets, Métamorphojean, Maillaparty, etc.) would be represented by three thousand five hundred sales outlets in throughout the world. The seven hundred styles per season and the seven million articles sold established the fame of a couple who, in order to promote their jeans, did not hesitate to call upon Jean-Luc Goddard (1987-1988).

From Perverts to Grunge, the Urban Tribes

Like art, pants changed the streets. When graffiti artists abandoned the streets and subways for the temptations of the art market, the most rebellious clothing of the twentieth century in turn became bourgeois, embroidered and adorned with pearls, it paraded down the runways of haute couture Paris. In the style supermarket, the pants of the 1980s became a standard, the label of a look, membership of a tribe. Whether it was the urbane black architect pants (Yohji Yamamoto), the *ragamuffin* look with the hot pants of the Kingston beauties, the hyper-techno, the *"perv"* in a latex jumpsuit or the hip-hop look with its track suit and competition running shoes that the break dancers at New York's Roxy Club sported.

Never would a decade prove to have so many ruptures, so many clans, so many takes of itself and a war of looks contrasting rockers with skinheads and gothics and punks. Skin-tight or baggy, slashed or with cuffs, pants in the 1980s defined social spheres. To the rhythm of *acid house*, a generation would go from rediscovering materials to a joyous revolution under the influence. Thirty years after rock and roll stars were moulded into their jeans, twenty years after hippies in terrycloth, ravers dominated 1980s culture with the widest jeans coming from England, manufactured by Joe Bloggs in Manchester, worn with Puma running shoes and Adidas jackets. The final leaps of colour before styles became more uniform and the great unveiling of *grunge*, a gigantic machine to wash out the styles of past decades. The mother-daughter duo epitomizes this century torn between two extremes: the first moulded in "silhouette" pants could remind the world that she was still young, the second, dressed in pants four times too large, sets the image of a generation without shape and a little adrift.

18- Azzedine Alaia's pinned leggings.
Photograph by Jean-Baptiste Mondino (1987).

Leggings According to Azzedine Alaia

Born in Tunis, arrived in Paris in 1957, after a spell studying sculpture at the École des Beaux-Arts, Azzedine Alaia made his debut in Paris where he designed clothes for a private clientele, as well as for friends such as Arletty, whom he noted always wore Repetto leggings under her pants. A sculptor, a couturier surgeon, this master of women's curves hollows out the waist, stretches the limbs, turns in an obsessive manner around the loins, brings new life to the buttocks, straightens the back, all to make the figure of his clients more flattering.

At the beginning of the 1980s, which marked the "Jacques Lang decade" the explosion of designers into the media frenzy of fashion, Azzedine Alaia is one of the rare few who placed himself on both banks — that of the great French tradition, the school of proper presentation, of pleats and of the cut, and that of movement, of cross-breeding, of visual shocks, inspired by a generation boiling over, from Jean Paul Gaultier to Thierry Mugler, and that coincides with a new way of living, of moving, of running, an affirmation of the body. "Fashion is what you observe, and what comes from women." With Azzedine Alaia, the back, the plunging neckline, the haunches came out from the shadows. If Marc Audibet asserted himself as a pioneer in the development of stretch fabrics, beginning first in Italy and then in Japan in 1982, Azzedine Alaia was in the forefront of working with knitwear using the techniques of haute couture, as all the pins necessary to construct a pair of leggings testify. "First, pieces are knit and the material is tested. Depending upon the results, it is made more or less tight as the tension of the knit dictates. The derriere is capital, it must be made round. With the cut, the buttock can be pushed up."

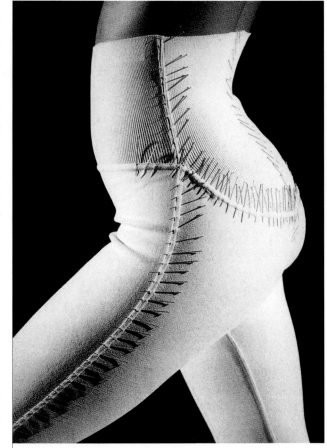

Invariably dressed in a black Chinese pants suit (he owns almost a hundred), Azzedine Alaia remembers his first attempts. "A catastrophe! The threads pulled, the fabric didn't hold. It took three years to find the solution, thanks to stretchable threads that would adhere to wool." It was on rue Bellechasse in Paris that Azzedine Alaia organized his first runway show letting his long-legged beauties Farida and Zuleika embrace the fashion world. "At that time, everything was large and flowing. I wanted to give women their bodies back." This was an adventure linked to the enthusiasm of such Italian mill owners and manufacturers as Miles in Vicenza. Although leggings may have become commonplace, their influence remains. "Leggings were a jolt. Women assumed their shapes and were liberated. They wore leggings when they were pregnant. Prior, a woman hid her roundness." In 1999, leggings became a classic. "They are like jeans. Some come out better than others. It is all in the cut. The worst, are the ones that bag at the knees, have a crotch that crimps and thighs that stretch out."

Dark wool and silk jacket over draped pants in a pearl grey silk. Giorgio Armani campaign advertisement, summer 1993.

Androgens, Hip-Chic, Techno

"*A white blouse, not too long. Straight pants, preferably the pantacourt version. And to go out, a simple small overcoat.*" (*La Redoute* catalogue, fall-winter 1999-2000.)

The Reign and the Passing

S kin-tight or baggy, fluorescent, black or white-blue "snow," pants in the 1980s would stand as evidence of all the whims of a decade braving contradictory trends that pulsed to a frenetic rhythm and where the sweat pants and leggings of the cities would be the stars. At the beginning of the 1990s, Iraq's invasion of Kuwait and the financial crash in the United States put an end to these incessant somersaults that a sacrificed generation did not have the time to appreciate.

There was no way out: to the west, the ruin of the American empire, to the east, disillusionment, mounting nationalism and everywhere AIDS, a new plague that condemned all the freedoms of the body acquired twenty years earlier. Time breaks down as retrospectives multiply. Thus, zazous, punks and the princes of hip-hop were brought to London's famous Victoria and Albert Museum under the tutelage of Ted Polhemus, an archaeologist of street styles.

While the street had made them common (one million one hundred thousand articles sold in France by Cimarron in 1992, representing 80% of its European sales), jeans found refuge in its own cult. Entering into the history books, immortalized by the first specialized auction sale, on September 7, 1992 at Drouot's in Paris, Levi's restored the prestige of heroes whose image had been greatly spoiled. For the conquering cowboy is out of work and the wide open spaces have shrunken to the size of a cathode box twelve hours a day. The punks' *no future*

Androgens,
Hip-Chic, Techno.
The Reign and the Passing

1

2

declaration was more of a statement filled with hope, but at the beginning of the 1990s, it coagulated in the return of me, the triumph of individualism and cocooning.

Grunge and Street People

As body-building machines went out of fashion, replaced by the pleasures of stretching which united body and spirit, pants would become softer thanks to stretchable fabrics, and would come down to the plat-form-soled moccasins, extending the period when you had to lie on the bed to zip up your jeans. Those worn by the very young would fall down on, "throwing up" so to speak, on Nike sneakers or Caterpillar work shoes. Farewell to the well-pressed cuffs of the prep-pies, grunge was parading over Paris. Labelled by the Belgian avant-garde, starting with Martin Margiela

who recycled clothing he hunted out at flea markets and organized his anti-shows on wastelands and at the Salvation Army.

While the poufs of the charities deflated, verdigris invaded the school yards and to "No more dance, no more tears, no more fears," the refrain from Marianne Faithfull's *The Boulevard of Broken Dreams*, models strutted across the Paris runways. Rich and golden, the 1980s gave way to the black eye of guilt and to lessons of ethics. Inspired by the pants of American convicts, the baggy sliding down the hips (worn as it was without sus-penders or a belt) became a uniform, at the same time that combat clothes became the uniform of youngsters. This, even though fashion heads no longer swore by "the street".

Manufacturers and designers competed to gain influ-ence. Using press reports printed on recycled cardboard, grey and neutrals dominated as starring colours. In the fear of too much, pleats tightened, straight creases returned, drawing a line on everything that moved. The boxy jersey pants worn by receptionists in the 1970s clothed the new fashion victims from Prada to Guewisold (a Paris store specializing in second-hand clothes). Not to forget the fine Deschiens team whose fashion show held at the Fondation Cartier in 1996 cel-

1- "Andy Warhol's Marilyn" leggings. Versace Studios, winter collection 1990-1991. Photograph by Tyen.

2- Grunge pants of the British "new age traveler." Victoria and Albert Museum, London.

3- Two young Koreans in Seoul. Photograph by Ling Fei (1995).

4- Jean Paul Gaultier's baggies for men. Spring-summer collection 1993.

ebrated the clothing of the anti-heroes — too fat, too small, in Bavarian lederhaussen or in crumpled pants under a hardware dealer's shirt.

Straight Legs and Politically Correct Pleats

Apart from these notes of derision, good conscience became the rule, and pants the basics of a wardrobe lacking in classics, that dressed a colourless, untouchable body, one with no wrinkles and above reproach, a body mad about itself, that clothing, when making contact with it, seemed to have lost its essential function — to adorn, to give cause to love. Heels came crashing down. The sexes became uniform. "Make sure that everything is clean, that the people are nice and do not have blue or

purple hair, make sure the women do not compete to be stylish, and as a result, creating the impression that they are inferior to our visitors," declared Michael Eisner, CEO

5- Pleated pants by Yohji Yamamoto, spring-summer 1994.

6- Inspired by "Savile Row" Alexander McQueen's pants for Givenchy. Ready-to-wear fall-winter 1998-1999.

7- Jil Sander pants, winter 1997-1998.

8- Androgynous-glamour satin pants signed by Tom Ford for Gucci. Winter 1997-1998.

9- The "skate." One of the key models by Ann Demeulemeester, spring-summer 1997.

10- Baggy low-waisted pants with a high belt. Tom Ford for Gucci, winter 1998-1999.

11- Design by Emporio Armani (Naples, 1994). Photograph by Ferdinando Scianna.

of the Walt Disney Company (*Le Monde*, April 15, 1992). With the *femme fatale* of the 1980s, the straight skirt, the high heels, the huge padded shoulders, a mixed style prevailed on the runways and in the catalogues. The final role games were played by Madonna who wore a pink satin corset under a Gaultier man's suit. But outfits were becoming uniform. Gilded buttons disappeared and the man's jacket with natural shoulders became inseparable from the pants. *Harper's Bazaar* defined it as "a hybrid of the 1970s and the high-tech comfort of the 1990s [...]. Wear them with high heels and you will give the appearance of being ten centimetres taller and five kilos lighter." "Pants could very easily be replaced by skirts, but they must have the right proportions," explained Miucca Prada, again in *Harper's Bazaar*. "Straight legs and flat in front, they must be very long." The new kings of the pants were Helmut Lang, Joseph, who added two pants shops to his empire (both in New York — one on

Madison Avenue, the other on Greene Street), as well as Jean Touitou, the guru of APC *(Atelier de Production et de Création)*. This brand, introduced in 1987, offered through its mail-order catalogue its "permanents" in minimalist and unisex terms. "Men's cut chino pants, one ticket pocket, two side pockets, two back pockets with piping, bottom width: 22cm, colour: grey. Size: 36, 38, 40, 42."

A new target for designers: the American woman executive. Between twenty and thirty years old, she persevered despite the pockets of resistance that remained in the United States, from Wall Street to the South, and across the Midwest. With the 1990s, came a relaxing of the dress code in the US senate, where one could see women like Carol Moseley-Braun and Barbara Mikulski wearing pants without breaking any taboos. The first lady Hillary Rodham-Clinton would be the first wife of an American President to make speeches and numerous public appear-

11

cotton-lycra blend and the most classic, the *Polo*, the inescapable cigarette pants without pleats, without cuffs and worn with a frock coat or a long pullover sweater. While the product had become standardized, new, more personal criteria that was more intimately linked to comfort rather than to appearance, would justify buying a new pair of pants. In the wake of the Bob Shop, a specialized store in Saint-Germain-des-Prés, signs went up and stores like Honest opened, offering custom-made pants, sewn from a selection of fabrics in an array of styles ranging from the classic cigarette to the low-waisted trumpet.

In men's fashion, new computer-assisted manufacturing methods enabled the development of reliable industrial measurement, of which the Bernard Zins company was in the forefront. In women's fashion, the new designers were the first to wear their own creations, an efficient selling point before a clientele ever in a rush and lacking basics. One could cite Régina Rubens in Paris and Daryl Kerrigan in New York, whose guest list filled up during the decade with many names of *cool girls* from the actress Gwyneth Paltrow to the Icelandic pop star Björk. Having made her debut at a small store in the East Village, Daryl Kerrigan would be the first Irish

14

Androgens,
Hip-Chic, Techno.
The Reign and the Passing

in April 1999. "Since 1987, I have worn a skirt suit or a dress and a jacket every day to work, like many women. The good news is that pants are making a comeback in the fall, and I will be one person happy again." The desire for comfort and well-being

woman who would dare to sell sexy-cut jeans that harkened back to a *vintage* style to Americans. A successful operation, by 1996, five years after its debut, the brand was being sold in three hundred venues throughout the world.

The *Casual* Machine

Pants refound its long, lofty legs at the house of Gucci with Tom Ford who, with abandon, drew from his inspirations at the house of Saint Laurent dating from the beginning of the 1970s. In August 1996, *Harper's Bazaar* went so far as devoting an entire special issue to the theme *all about pants*. "I am ready to admit it. I am very happy to wear pants… The problem is choosing a top and jacket to go with them," explained Liz Tilberis, editor-in-chief of the magazine, in an editorial. She died

14- Lilac woolen pants adorned with baubles and sequins by Tom Ford for Gucci, summer 1999. Photograph by G. Yarhi.

15- *Corsaire* pants in beige leather, Ashes by Claude Zana, summer 1999. Photograph by Marcus Mâm.

16- Tank top and sports *corsaire* in terry. The Gap, summer 1999.

17- *Corsaire* in stone chambray with a jersey T-shirt. Christian Lacroix's spring-summer collection 1999. Photograph by Marcus Mâm.

inspired more rigorous quality controls and ready-to-wear clothes more adapted to individual needs, such as the waistline and the length of the legs. Thus, "measurement cards" were given out by distributors such as Célio which, in 1996, opened a "jeans space" in an aesthetically correct setting: white wood, metal posts and light wood furnishings. Faced with a new, more constrained economic reality, designers absorbed the excesses of past years by signing licenses for jeans, thus ensuring their royalties. Initiated by *world brands*, the vast casual machine was set up and, in fish tank-style shops, pants became a generic product based on the American standard of The Gap and Esprit. The Italian and Spanish industry developed their own tools for production, from Max Mara to Zara, as well as the Saze Merino group, whose annual production rate during the 1990s reached twenty-nine million square meters of fabric and more than three million articles of clothing, most of which were sportswear pants and jeans.

Italian brands like Trussardi saw 30% of their sales figures attributed to jeans. The *new establishment* had as its guru the Viennese designer Helmut Lang, for whom "clothing is a language. And you can either tell the truth, or lie". It was in 1994 that Lang signed a substantial manufacturing contract with the Japanese giant Onward Kashiyama, accepting only two hundred hand-picked guests at his runway shows. They had come to

18- **Glimpse of the 1970s through Dolce e Gabbana patchwork pants. Spring-summer 1993.**

19- **Flowers of paradise and micro leather jacket. Hip-chic style by Tom Ford for Gucci, summer 1999.**

20- **Men's pants by Martin Margiela for Hermès, summer 1999. Photograph by Ling Fei.**

Androgens,
Hip-Chic, Techno.
The Reign and the Passing

admire his imperturbable house classics: men's pants, a cotton tank-top, a white shirt for men and women. Less was more. Fantasy and extravagance took refuge in the juniors' market.

Designer Jeans

Christian Lacroix put the accent back on "real denim" to which he added black lace for the "Faubourg Saint-Honoré look" and blurred the runways with a rash of colours like violet, pink and jade and an array of abstract and neo-Provençal prints. "This collection blends the chintz and striped fabrics of the nineteenth century with material techniques that reflect light. The Camargue (France's Far West!) right along side Hawaiian flowers and Mexican embroideries, the structures of eighteenth-century clothing merged with those of today's sportswear or work clothes," explained the couturier who introduced his line "Jeans" in 1996. It was when a Puritan revolution took sway in the West making pants the habit of function for the nuns of style that Asia opened up to new influences. Agnès B., who created her first store "Homme" in Paris in 1981, became the leader of the Neo-Modern school. Black and white defined an urban look that the *chapatsu* were wild about. Those young people with dyed hair who paraded along Omotesando, the Champs-Élysées of Tokyo, where, during the 1980s, Parisian-style cafés with terraces would be opened.

With pants having lost their "rebel-lious" connotation, wearing them became generally more accepted. In Indonesia, women teachers began wearing them with natural ease following a 1996 memorandum from the Ministry of Education that authorized the wearing of pants. Codes became more and more subtle, and in Indonesian newspapers care was taken to distinguish between *lady pants*, slacks, linen pants and jeans, which were reserved for extra-professional activities.

Hipsters and Neo-Punks

It was in London that the end to political correctness shot up. The *bumsters* by the "pitbull of fashion" Alexander McQueen were pants with a waist so low that they unveiled a good part of the behind, revealing to the world the advent of a new avant-garde that the *Sensation* exhibition presented in London in 1997 set into motion on a foundation of realism and provocation.

Having cut his teeth with the Savile Row tailors, Alexander McQueen applied the straight thread technique with a very acute sense of line and volume, carving a triangle on the stomach, hollowing out the fullness and elongating the line. On the fringe of the New York-Milan axis, London, Los Angeles and Tokyo became dominant as the capitals attracted to the new extravagance under the influence. Tokyo became the hub for *vintage* fashions, with surplus stores lining the Harajuku. On the 1,300 tons of clothing imported from the United

21

22

23

21- Kuwabara Keisuke, Tokyo. "Kokeshi Dolls"
1999 catalogue. Concept and photograph
by Olivero Toscani for United Colours of Benetton.

22- Kageyama Jun, Tokyo. "Kokeshi Dolls" 1999
catalogue. Concept and photograph by
Olivero Toscani for United Colours of Benetton.

23- "Utility" pants with pockets and a hooded
sweatshirt. The Gap, summer 1999.

States in 1991, Mister Taurus claimed 20%. The pros knew that they had to demand the "Big E", and went as far as spending 15,000 francs for a pair of Levi's that had been worn during the construction of the Santa Fe railroad. At the Banana Boat, each pair of jeans went for about 18,000 francs.

Other more wild styles appeared, along with a return to punk came big-checked pants that were belted around the knees. While girls dreamed only of money to buy their total Gucci or Prada look, the nice bad boys had returned. "Done is the basketball look, and charging in from England is the college boy style with its false air of first communion," announced *Libération* on March 30, 1997. On the front page was the short culottes in "its quaint elegance" that the leader of the group AC/DC wore at the time and which the Belgian designer Raf Simons became the new promoter of. "The new perversion of young style attacks the codes of education and of the son from a good family, transforming him into a little devil, a junky in short culottes," continued the French daily. This regression made its mark in women's fashion with the return of *corsaire* pants with little laced-up tops in cotton that were inspired by 1960s Saint Laurent Rive Gauche and were dedicated to the lolitas of the fine neighbourhoods. On the Milan and London catwalks (Clements Ribeiro, Amanda Wakeley, CopperWheat Blundel) the pantacourt suit gently took sway. In Paris, the American Jeremy Scott, originally from Kansas City, Missouri, went against the general fashion consensus and cut short only one of the legs. Hoisted up on spiked heels held to the foot by simple adhesive strips, his divine beauties, springing from some other world, celebrated the energy of a new millennium. In Los Angeles, rappers made pants with huge legs their uniform — a market that would see a 30% annual increase according to *The Wall Street Journal of Europe*.

Exercises
in Style

Pants from Every Angle

Drawings and photo-montages with exclusive rights by:

Giorgio Armani

Éric Bergère

Dolce e Gabbana

Jean Paul Gaultier

Marithé et François Girbaud

Rei Kawakubo (Comme des Garçons)

Christian Lacroix

Alexander McQueen

Issey Miyake

Thierry Mugler

Dries Van Noten

Sonia Rykiel

Martine Sitbon

Paul Smith

Yohji Yamamoto

Giorgio
Armani

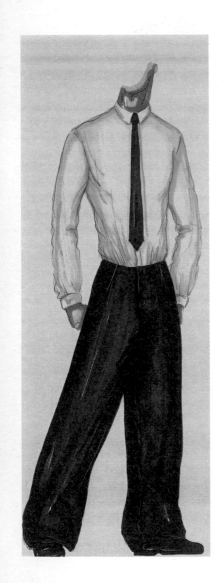

« If I tried to think of the history of clothing without pants, I would see nothing more incomplete! Even in its most primitive forms, above all ethnic forms, pants are truly the element that has given men's fashion a dignity, a look, an equilibrium. And it was in the 14ᵗʰ century, many centuries later, when the Venetian comedy 'Pantaloon' was performed. Today, in men's fashion, pants are much more important than the jacket — a distinct sign of the advent of a 'metropolitan tribe.'

Young people have all become identified by their jeans, businessmen by their four-pleated pants with cuffs, intellectuals by their workman or gentleman farmer pants, men in the creative fields by their pants à la mode — either slim, cigarette pants that come just to the ankle, or wide, oversize pants held up with a belt. But pants have also become inescapable in women's fashion. It is true that they appeared in the 1930s, but through the post-war period, they were relegated to the ranks of clothing for playing sports or reserved for the elite. The great 'boom' in women's pants came about with the social and intellectual rapprochement of the sexes, and with women's new equal role, to the point where, during the 1980s, pants became the status symbol of the professional woman. In the year 2000, this rapport, strengthened through the mutual help of men's and women's fashion, will be like pants which, in the way of so many other articles of clothing will entirely lose all association with one sex more than the other. »

GIORGIO ARMANI

Éric
Bergère

« I grew up in the world of pants. It was the great era of the unisex, the androgynous style. It is easy. My girlfriends and I had the same ones. Extreme dictated style. You could no longer wear a pair of pants that didn't hide your shoes, the Buggy style compensated with rounded cuffs. Tight-fitting at the hips, they delineated the narrow leg and began to flare at the knees. We played, combining two fabric and two colours. I loved the idea of walking without seeing my feet — it was ecstasy. Men and women had the same obsessions. Icons from film and all wore pants. Joe Dassin, Michel Polnareff. And then, there was Catherine Deneuve wearing Saint Laurent who was my master *vis-à-vis* fabrics and pants. I also admire Azzedine Alaia for his super-structured styles that he makes in flowing fabrics.

I like pants that are a bit tight, but that don't cut. Ones that 'pour' over the body, as Chanel said. Pants that are too tight, are unforgiving. They don't escape deadly fashions: ski pants with an underfoot strap and a boot, leggings with a suit jacket.

I hold a passion for this piece of clothing that refines, elongates, even if it is particularly demanding Women who prefer to conceal themselves would do better to choose a long skirt. My great aunt, who made pants, instilled in me this precision: a concern to the millimetre in the placement of the fly, the rise of centre seam, the inseams. You can play around with a house dress, but not a pair of pants. With them, you must be a master of material. And as such, jeans are what require the most. »

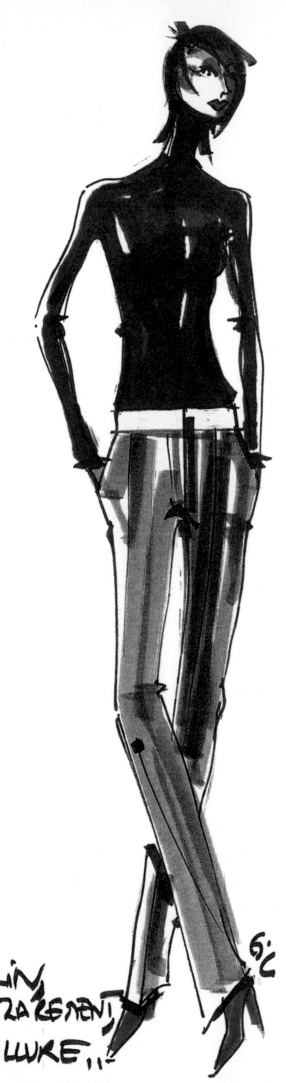

Le pantalon
vêtement masculin,
il exacerbe bizarrement
la féminité, l'allure...

Dolce e Gabbana

« For us, the mythology of pants is linked to two key images: photographs of Italian women after the war, like my grandmother, and the Helmut Newman photograph of Madonna in an Yves Saint Laurent suit. Pants allow women to express their masculine side, to play at role reversals, something always fascinating and seductive. It's a key part of the wardrobe, linked to movement, to the absolute freedom of the legs and their allure. We love all pants — ski pants, gauchos, with tennis stripes, in reflective fabric with shiny silver sequins. The most important thing is that they're sexy. It's not a matter of shape, but of attitude, of how it's worn, how it's lived. Everything comes from the head. Our pants were inspired by those of Sicilian men, pants that we find very erotic. We have always held this predilection for men's fabrics, as well as those stolen from lingerie. Today, we're experiencing the advent of a new unisex: fifteen- to twenty-year-olds, whether boys or girls, are wearing the same pants. This inspires us, but we definitely prefer glamour. In our eyes, the absolute master remains Yves Saint Laurent. »

Dolce & Gabbana

Jean Paul
Gaultier

« I only make men's pants with an invisible zipper hidden in the side seam, transforming them into a skirt from behind. Pants are clothing that makes one feel less vulnerable. With a skirt, air passes from below. It can rise up. Pants are more modest, more closed, concealing, they protect more. In a kilt, one is not supported, it floats, it moves. Pants follow the legs. A skirt lives its life, pants live yours. For a long time, skirts have imposed certain obligatory movements upon women, like crossing their legs. Pants have freed them of that imposed propriety. »

Jean Paul
GAULTIER

30 R. FG ST-ANTOINE
75012   PARIS

Marithé et François Girbaud

« It has been thirty years of my life that I have spent before this crotch. Imagine such a thing. There is the neck, and there is the crotch. Once one understands that, one can begin to attempt to dress the body. Nike brought the sweatsuit out of the stadium and into the street. We have taken jeans out of the ranch and brought them into the city. We are children of the war who grew up in the shadow of the great American dream, the publicity caravans that followed the troops after Liberation, nylon stockings, chewing gum, B movies, jeans, John Wayne killing Indians. At Golf Drouot, we dreamed of refinding that dream. It was the days of button-down shirts, UCLA sweaters and cowboy pants. A story that continued until 1968. Couturiers invented the ready-to-wear and we, the young look. Courrège was another planet, not fashion of the street. With an eye toward Goa, we made a collection of peasant work clothes, but in denim with, for example, 'grandpa' pants, the 'Toulouse-Lautrec.' Styles evolved, hips were swung, indigo was discovered. Our tubes were called the 'Goulue' and the 'Boutonneux' with its fifty buttons. People set about inventing fantastical stories inspired by comic strips like Pilote, Gotlib and Brétécher. From Neuilly ladies to ministers, with pants, people changed their skin. Washed, faded, baggy, never before had jeans been so shaken up. Since 1968, we created more than three thousand kinds. The, 'Compagnon,' the 'Pedal Pusher' — the first construction in X — the 'Metamorphojean,' the 'Sirène' for the changed body of a pregnant woman, etc. They all had names, I have always refused to give them numbers.

"Since the beginning of the 1990s, we moved away from

Pourquoi dessiner assis ?
le regard sur la ligne d'horizon

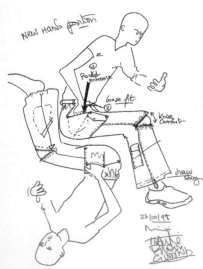

jeans to work with other materials. I continue to have a passionate rapport with denim. But I know that we have only scratched the surface. From where the concept, for example, of the stealth airplane, the result of research that transcends fashion and biannual collections, and calls upon the laboratory more than the studio to bring it to fruition. Earth, wind and fire are the natural elements that engender innovation from which arises ceramic textiles, laser cuts and thermal fusion. We have called upon chemists to isolate the indigo molecule and create a permanent blue. Jeans in the third millennium? I see them without seams, cut with a laser. Flexible, they will be twenty-four-hour-a-day jeans, but adapted to a new way of life, identifiable with the internwear. The future imparts less to those who walk than those who fly. These are who interest today. »

Rei Kawakubo
Comme des Garçons

《 For me, the wearing of pants by women at the beginning of the century represented the start of their liberation. They could take on an equal role in society with men. "Today, at the end of this century, paradoxically, pants are nothing other than a part of men's and women's wardrobes. They have lost all significance attached to a given sex. These pants, somewhat special, at once both a skirt and pants, can be worn by men and women. It is typically 'Comme des Garçons' in the respect that the border between skirt and pants is ruptured. 》

Christian
Lacroix

« From which side ought we consider pants? Technically, they are certainly one of the most preoccupying exercises in style. Be precise, even when all is vague. For, they capture the epicentre of the body, and conceal as much as they offer, the point where the perfectly straight line must negotiate curves, roundness, as well as angles. The bone structure, the hip, the crotch — girl-boy-man, masculine/feminine woman. The question is far behind. An individual affair, without ambiguity. What is the perfect pair of pants? The 'andalou' which passes over the 'S' of the arched thigh, high-waisted with a dry and impeccable fall upon a booted leg? Pants with open pleats, very straight, that makes one feel he is moving not without giving a nod to the zazous of the 1940s with their 'skirted' look, as well as to the same era that rendered Marlene impeccable? An affair of architecture. Of look, of stride, of gawkiness. Tighter against the body, or absently floating around it, it will certainly remain one of the symbolic images of the century which has perhaps not exhausted all of its permutations: the casual low waist, the thumb stuck in the belt loop, austere and ceremonious, almost Byzantine on Savile Row where the science is quasi-cabalistic. The most exaggerated of civilizations is nested there in the slope and the nature of each line. Work in geometric, there is nothing without the mechanics and the modelling of this half of the body to serve. Nothing than a scarecrow or a work of art like the giant photographs of Patrick Tosani, images of jeans rolled up in a ball,

the negative of a body becoming 'disembodied.'
"Pants with under-the-foot straps for children and for skiing in my generation. The first pair of pants for school after years of wearing short knickers. Checks. Herringbone. The entire washed-out range of mini-cords. Rough fabrics, essential creased skintight pants, timeless flares, thirty-year-old baggies. Buttoned down a flat front, stitched down the back. Belts somewhat also making the pants. Chocolate-coloured peasant pants with buckles and straps on the back. All the clever corporate techniques for pants, with those magnificent brain-teasing details that not one amongst us wouldn't invent. Superb stylistic feats of military pants the world over. The mythology of pants with a fold-over flap. The hideousness of sweat pants. The liberation of the tipsy widows of my adolescence. There would be an entire cartography of pants. For each ethnicity, each different folklore has surpassed the imagination. It is all these pants that I prefer: utilitarian ones, ones of pure grace, from the dawn of time, the eccentric calculations. I love them with overstitching, torn, with hidden details. A case, a cover, a pedestal for my personal use, according to the mood of the season, for others, that is to say for collections, from the tip of my pencil, I want them only perfect, but almost absent, complements, accessories, leaving to other specialists this purple passage, as I prefer the pretences: the pants-skirt, pants-pareo, pants-portfolio when there are no basics. (Ah, the basics, that tapestry of Penelope that each day she undid so as to imperceptibly balance the formula and to bring together the codes subterraneanly exhaled by the era.) The domain reaches to infinity. Whether it be origami, a compass or a second skin, a manifesto, a provocation or politically correct, orthopaedics, carelessness or ease, pants is in saying long, since they clothe the roots of men and women — torsos that we are — adorning our body movements, speaking as much as hands and gesticulations, declaring as well, the colour of our states of soul, of our work and our days. »

Alexander
McQueen

« By creating the "bumster", my intention was to elongate the female torso, thus utilising the proportions of her natural form to create an exaggerated silhouette. »

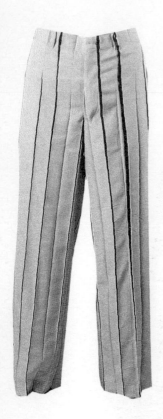

Issey
Miyake

« When a pair of shorts meets a skirt, it becomes a skort
When a long skirt meets a pair of trousers, it becomes a pantskirt
When a shirt is connected to pants, it becomes a jumpsuit
And when a pair of shoes meets a pair of pants limitless possibilites abound for the shapes of clothing. »

Thierry Mugler

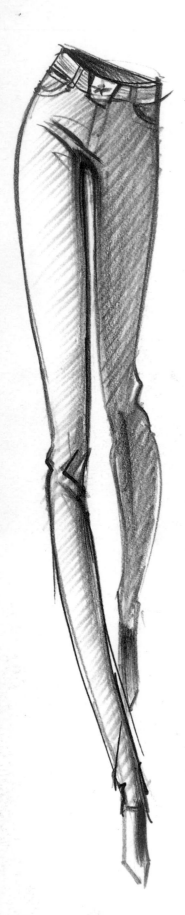

« I love pants for what they free, not for what they hide. For their spirited, nasty, provocative, glamour, rock side. Because they clothe the legs and everything that runs around, I have always used them to taper a presence, to ameliorate a figure. From there, my first jean-girdles, leather pants-boots, pants-garters, vinyl leggings, the haute couture leggings of the summer of '99 that revealed unexpected parts of the thighs, redesigning the leg in the shape of a tulip. In truth, I hate the bundles of fabric that hinder the step.

My first memories of pants? Rompers with a pocket in the shape of a heart. A little Scottish outfit with very pretty Austrian leather shorts, that had a bib, notches, buttons made from horns and goats cut out of felt.

It was with pants that I made my debut in the fashion world. 1972. King's Road. We wore bellbottoms that were super-tight at the knees with Tom Jones — Louis XIII shoes with buckles — size twelve Shetland sweaters stolen from the Scotch House, worn over satin shirts with the sleeves hanging out. My bellbottoms, I dyed them like a rainbow, the leg going from red to turquoise. No one dressed in colours. Especially guys. We made scandals on Cherry Lane, at Voom Voom in St-Tropez. That is to say, we looked like we should. To make the structure collapse. To liberate. To set free a generation from the post-war, and from its notions of chic and the obligatory new. We liked jeans because they aged with us.

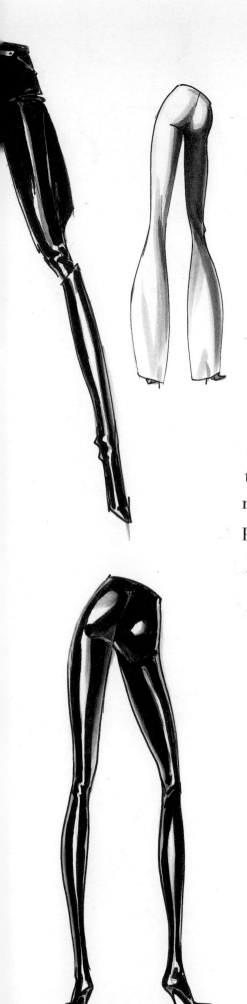

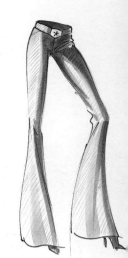

Pants, before all, I see them as clothing of seduction, an object of desire. It's Elvis, it's Louis XIV. The Duke d'Artois, Indians in chaps. Gene Kelly — more virile than Fred Astaire — in pants made from a heavy cloth with cuffs and a little short. Marlon Brando, James Dean. Dolorés del Rio. Katherine Hepburn, her hands in her pockets, comfortable shoes. Not to forget Marlene in the Red Empress, for the military side. Nancy Sinatra, then Bardot in her gingham corsaires. Janis Joplin, jeans, fringe, hanging earrings.

Pants, they are solution to life. I love the idea that they can be part of the strictest outfit, or to the contrary, utterly disobedient. That they define the step. That they live for a body, through it, to help it, to sublimate it. These is why women are often poorly panted. Those that shoot a figure? Men's pants worn with flats. Very thin heels with sports pants. That makes me think of bourgeois women with the short-sighted vision on evening gowns.

Every shape has its own lengths, its own proportions. I have very set principles about this. Bellbottoms must be very low-waisted, rock, hugging the knee, starting with a bell-shaped curve, being too long or too short. Having an nervousness in the line. Jeans, Popeye ones are pretty, crumpled up. I remain loyal to my leather pants. For their presence, physical and carnal. With them, one feels ready and prepared for and against everything. But I don't hate snakeskin or bull leather pants. »

Dries
Van Noten

« My first pants? They were dark blue, as I was a boarder with the Jesuits.

My ideal pants? A Moroccan sarouel with lots of folds and embroidery, for comfort, an Indian dhoti, used work pants, a pair of classic men's pants. The ideal pants doesn't exist. It would be a mixture. When I think about pants, I think of the Flemish saying 'I'm the one who wears the pants," indicating the husband's authority over the wife. For men, pants is the only choice. For women, it is one possibility among others. It is a cult image, like Lauren Bacall, for example. Pants are linked to power, but also to travel, to elsewhere, as one wears them loose, in the summer, for example. I like the idea of travelling through clothing. Jeans, which once symbolized the anti-establishment, have become a solution, almost 'safe.' Today, you can have them with a little pleat or even ironed. I prefer them with a mix of ethnic-urban, male-female that escapes uniformity. Women in pants — I like them in dresses with the pants worn like an undergarment. Absolutely not the Star Trek pants. But rather a blend of all styles from Dutch fishermen's pants, to the very long Rajasthan, as well as Yugoslavian pants that are similar to Turkish pants. Because these pants relate the riches and poverty, they are the jewels of the memory. I buy them, I collect them because they relate all of a life. Each time I learn something from looking at them, from studying them about the secrets of the cut. »

Sonia
Rykiel

« Pants. It's equality with those who have pretty legs. Seduction pants…

First off, the pockets. Hands in pockets like a man with the movements of a woman.

A way of walking, of standing. With pants, you advance, you envelope the world It's life!

The skirt stops you; with pants, you're on the go.

The first time, it was in Hong Kong in the 1970s.

Women with wide pants, cut short above the calf. It was beauty itself, with an eternal youth, a timelessness, a superb sensuality.

Magic! »

Martine
Sitbon

» Pants, that's all I wear. I've lost the habit of wearing skirts. In my profession, pants have become a uniform linked to the city. My first pair was cigarette overalls with a low flap. Wearing them, I felt 'to the max.' I had the air of a 'Zaz'. Pants always represented and ideal for me, no doubt because of my two older sisters who went to surprise parties, went out with their boyfriends in convertibles, listened to Elvis Presley in houses like in Tati's film Mon Oncle, with their kidney-shaped swimming pools and everything was modern. My mother always wore pants. During the 1960s, she wore jeans with penny loafers and a Burberry trench coat. I thought she looked very 'Ingrid Bergman.' Pants followed me to Paris. In the nightclubs like the Bus Palladium and Au Rock and Roll Circus it was the low-waisted style worn with sandals. Pants, like mini-skirts and make-up were not allowed at La Fontaine high school. I also liked corduroys. I had one in beige, in orange and another in eggplant which I wore until they wore out. It was the great New Man time, and we wore them with Shetland crewneck sweaters that we boiled in because they were four sizes too small, and Clarks. I loved jeans that fell down onto your Clarks. I have always liked that look that's a little lanky, low waist, flat hips. That's why my pants never have pleats. When you design pants, there are at least two pitfalls to be avoided: the buttocks either too round or too flat. But the real problem begins when you assemble them — they must not ride up in the crotch. The crotch either being too low, or too cutting. They also have to be able to adapt to different shapes. Ultimately, pants are the most deceptive article of clothing. »

Paul
Smith

« When I opened my first shop, in 1970 […], I started by selling Levi's 501s jeans — you couldn't find them in London. I went to New York on a charter flight with an empty bag. I found painter and carpenter pants there which I matched with the first Paul Smith shirts, in flowered silk, hippie style. My jeans, I wear them with a V-neck cashmere sweater, "very country," and Anello and David boots, the famous "Beatles boots" in black leather. At the time, going to work in jeans was out of the question. They were something of rebel pants. Today, I sell them by the millions.

Everything has changed. And there's more of a choice. The same person can be very different, according to whether she wears combat pants or a pair of high-waisted pants, rather smart. In France, students wear jeans with a leather vest, in Italy, they love "panini" pants with Dockside moccasins and a scooter. In Japan, the teenagers are all in ultra-wide camouflage pants, the "skateboard look."

Things have evolved. Wearing jeans everyday sets a casual attitude that sometimes gets on my nerves — and I hate the idea of "Friday wear," an American invention for selling more. My chinos, I only wear them on holiday and Sundays to go to the flea market.

Pants remain something of a mythical element in contemporary fashion. For me they evoke Katharine Hepburn, Ginger Rogers. The real revolutionary in pant was Yves Saint Laurent. The mini-skirt and see-through defined the fashion of the 1960s, but it was pants that changed the way of getting out of a car, of life. Today, what is important is to know to choose them according to their morphology. The shape of a pair of pants can change your mood, your attitude, and must adapt itself to your personality as much as to your figure. Nothing is more vulgar than wearing them too tight. They have to show without showing. But at the opera, I prefer all the same that women wear dresses. »

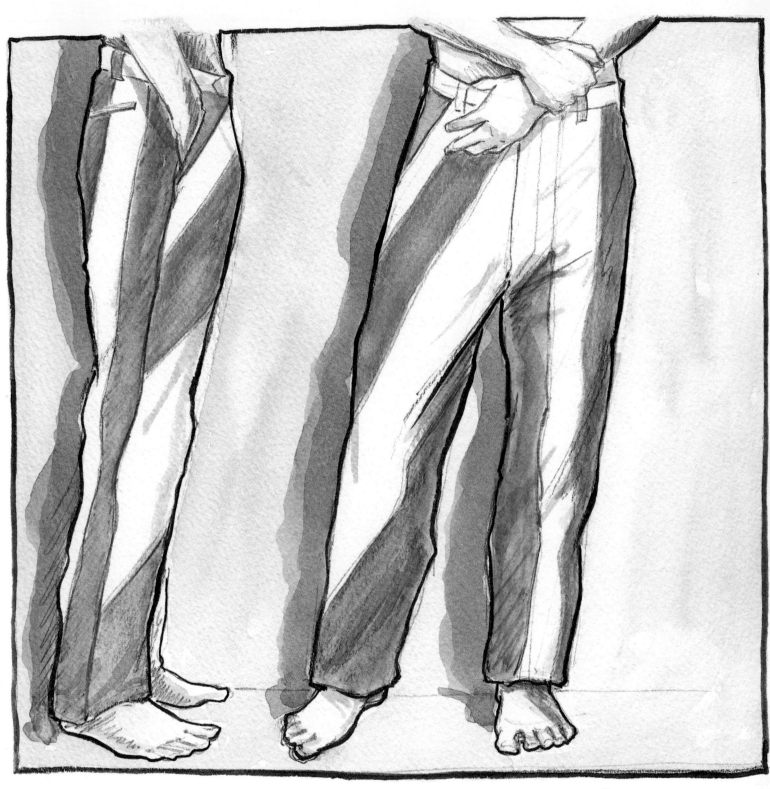

Paul Smith

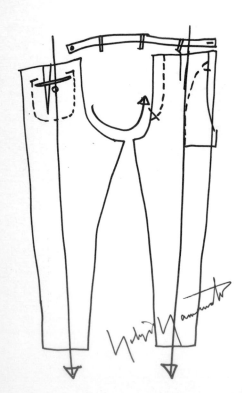

Yohji
Yamamoto

« My mother made me a pair of knee pants when I was four years old. I was ashamed because all my friends wore simple long pants. Now I know it was 'chic, à la mode,' but it's too much for me. I haven't really created pants. I've just proposed men's pants for women, black preferably. It wasn't a creation, but a choice. Pants have always had a utilitarian, functional character. I'm thinking, for example, about military pants in general. The birth of pants comes to mind, a pair of stockings that men of the upper ranks wore during the Middle Ages. Perhaps they wanted to cover themselves and to show the beauty of the shape of their legs. Or for war. I've been told that when the stockings became joined, pants were born.

"I don't know why, but for me, pants are 'battle.' Really, you simply had to be able to separate your legs! For women, it was an enormous revolution which was linked to liberation. For women, my preferences run toward men's pants, a little baggy, with four pockets. For me, since I'm small and thin, I prefer ones wide and loose, in a jersey. I hate jeans that are very tight, skintight, sometimes with embroidery and that are worn with high heels. A cult image of pants? It would be one of August Sander's farmer pants. He wears them three hundred and sixty-four days a year, and one day, for a wedding he wears a suit he inherited from his grandfather. His hair is well-groomed, he's elegant. »

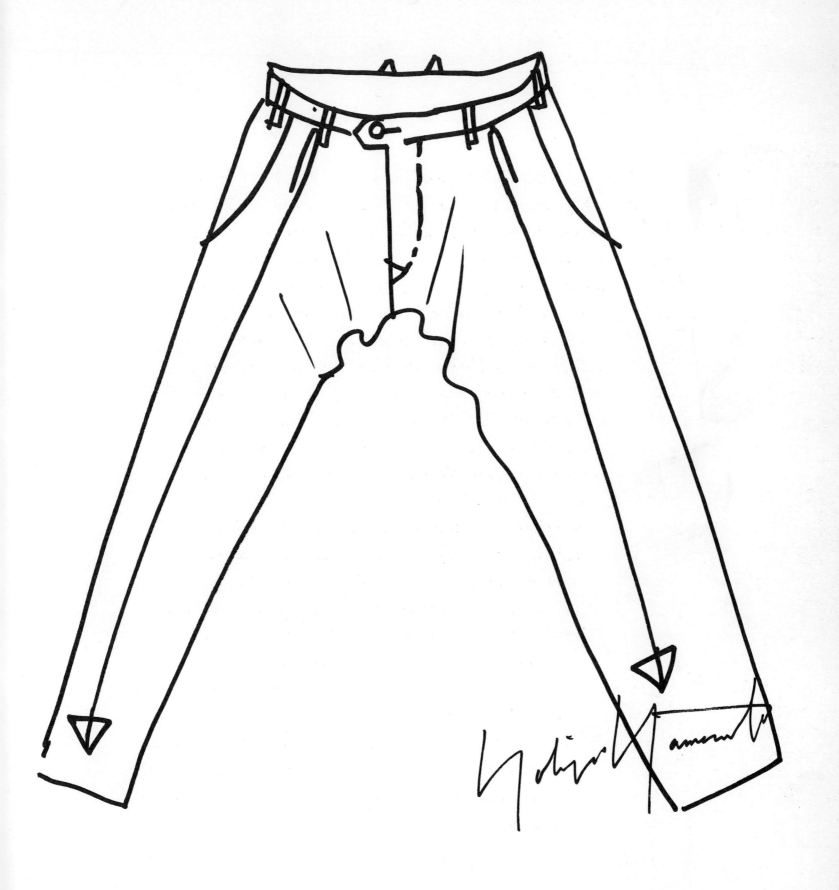

A Thematic Journey

Overalls, Short Culottes and Pajamas

"Little men, like embryos of café waiters, their heads plastered with pomade, walked with their legs spread apart so as not to stain their black culottes." **(Guy de Maupassant, *La Maison Tellier*, 1881.)**

"My childhood, during the 1930s, was defined by short culottes, golf pants and the few long pants that were saved for the rare, grand occasion. There's nothing less becoming, especially when we consider how elegant and fun children are today with their overalls, their Bermudas and the jeans that they start wearing at such an early age." **(Giorgio Armani, 1998.)**

Slit up the middle of the buttocks in China, and bouffant in the West, the pants of the nodding baby, in turn both functional and ornamental, bedecked the bulgy legs of the infant-king with fluorescent polyester and Swiss cotton.

For a long time, during the period when boys and girls were clothed in a long birthing shirt, the child's pants were a dress. Even a "progressive" thinker like Fourier waited to avoid "from early childhood the distinction of the two sexes by contrasting outfits like a petticoat and pants. It would be to risk preventing the birth of vocations and distorting the proportion of the sexes in each function." This was a long-held tradition in the upper reaches of society before dresses for boys were replaced by sailor suits with short pants, dating up until 1935, a point when little girls were no longer obligated to wear gloves when they went out. Girls would soon be able to wear shorts on the beach, while boys, freed of their ceremonial suit, would dare to wear short pants, an open-collar shirt and a pullover.

1

2   3

Knickers and Rompers

Ever since, pants have not stopped running rampant with the image of a child leaving his pastel cocoon and being exposed ever and ever earlier to the life of an adult. Although babies were wrapped up in rompers inspired by women's shirt-culottes, by the end of the 1930s, young boys began wearing knickers like their fathers. Bloomers, associated with the "anti-crino-linist" Amelia Bloomer (United States, 1851), found a new legitimacy as they were worn under English smock dresses. Children's pants reflected an evolution of morals which generated their acceleration. Created in 1895 as work clothes,

OshKosh overalls became a symbol of leisure wear in the United States during the 1950s, and was linked to a new way of life and consumerism (the mail-order catalogue was introduced in 1962). The appearance in force of synthetic fabrics affected these changes. "I was a child when acrylic and polyester reached my village to be transformed into school uniforms. Everyone believed that they were more expensive than silk or ordinary cloth. Our uniforms didn't crease, they dried quickly and they didn't need ironing." Memories of the Japanese designer Hideaki Matsuura.

Short Pants and a Rash of Buttons

During the same period, the introduction of stretch fabrics and *Babygro* "the clothing that grows with

the baby," defined a new stage: the recognition by parents of a child as a person completely unto himself. OshKosh overalls, sold at large department stores such as Bloomingdale's, Saks Fifth Avenue and Macy's starting in the 1970s, marked the advent of the "daredevil" — the same child who, at the beginning of the century, had been kept away from everything and protected to the extreme, finally entered a limitless realm of fun and games with sand boxes, sharp pebbles and muddy knees.

Success came. In 1997, OshKosh, a brand distributed in eighty countries, saw 95% of its sales derived from children's clothing. They had employed an advertising campaign based upon the complicity of the company, of the parents and their children. "James Dean Clothes. Give him no cause to rebel," read the caption of a photo titled *James Dean Oswald, 12 months, Portland, Oregon.*

For a long time, playgrounds were synonymous with knee pads, those pieces of leather, a bit rough with wear, sewn on to corduroy pants and the short pants with a rash of buttons being in the collected memory associated with scraped knees, red with mercurochrome. In 1940, *Marie Claire* suggested to its readers to make " a pair of pants for the young boy" from "leftover ticking." Flannel pants could also be included in a chapter of bad memories along

with Sunday sermons, boring marriages, lanky and sad kids, blushing little boys.

Too small, too big, pants ended up by adapting to the desires of a generation for whom the name "junior" avoided the torments of adolescence, of a changing body that overly identifiable clothes cubby-holed to the point of suffocation and the despised pimples of self and others. The XXL would certainly be the saving grace of those too fat or too thin, sparing one of all unpleasant confrontations with the mirror. The playground, a social microcosm, had come to life at a time when pants were more and more resistant and, in a bulimia of necessary consumption, were changed more and more often. Washed velvet pants under an Avirex aviator jacket, and as the prevailing mood dictated, fabrics were mixed: sweat jerseys with velvet, nylon and cotton patches.

Fashion-Crazy Kids

Going from babydolls to daredevils, from classic households to "non-conventional" families, the child of the 1990s has grown up in co-ed classrooms where girls in "trumpet-bottomed" pants and boys in low-waisted khakis — Classic or Slim fit (GapKid) — wear them like T-shirts on the bottom, while sneakers have served as the new indicator, replacing the uniform of yesterday. Also, defining colours have been dispensed with: pink for girls, sky blue for boys. Pants with a fold-over flap clothe little sailors kids, and raw jeans have become the indispensable accompaniment for hooded sweatshirts inspired by rappers. The *vintage* phenomenon has not escaped the world of the young. In 1992, during the first international auction of jeans, organized by Levi's, a pair of children's overalls dating from the 1920s sold for 18,000 francs.

Never before has the child been emancipated to such a degree. However, a new obsession did come on to the scene with the "baby object" (725,460 births in 1997 compared with 800,000 in 1980). Between electric baby bottle heaters, "securing" bed valences designed to create a "cocoon of tenderness" and other "sweet dream" swings, the "booties-pants" knitted by grandmothers since the 1940s had to confront the advent of "Babygro" in a polar knit that could be transformed into a bodysuit with separate legs. A system present-

8

Pantsmousse
Overalls, Short Culottes and Pajamas

ed at the *Salon de la Puériculture* 1998 and which, according to its manufacturer Jean Poyet, located at Pont Trambouze, "enables the changing of the baby without undressing him, but also to put him in a high chair or car seat. A revolution!"

1- Young boy in a summer outfit. France (circa 1920). Collection of A. Vassiliev, Paris.

2- Children fishing. Neapolitan post card (1918). Private collection.

3- Young boy (circa 1917). Collection of A. Vassiliev, Paris.

4- OshKosh overalls.

5- *Le Fifre*. Édouard Manet, Orsay Museum, Paris.

6- The Chinese split pajamas. Beijing. Photograph by Ling Fei (1999).

7- Korean children wearing silk hanboks. Lee Young Hee.

8- Design for the Brazil (1920). Created by Jeanne Lanvin, gouache. Lanvin Estate (rights reserved).

9- Beach outfit. France (1933). Collection of A. Vassiliev, Paris.

10- Little girl in zipped pants by Sonia Rykiel, the first to dress children in black. Photograph by Nathaniel Goldberg (1998).

11- Issey Miyake. Hiroshima, Japan.

12- Martine Sitbon. Casablanca, Morocco.

13- Yohji Yamamoto. Tokyo, Japan.

14- Jean-Charles de Castelbajac. Casablanca, Morocco.

15- Christian Lacroix. Arles, France.

16- Yves Mathieu-Saint Laurent. Oran, Algeria.

17- Stefano Gabbana. Milan, Italy.

18- Domenico Dolce. Palermo, Italy.

Custom-made — The Tailor's tradition

*"I, who am a man who does not take care of my own dressing,
who finds such beneath myself and look upon it with scorn, I did buy
a pair of pants [...] for a change, for the humour of it, as one buys
a trinket or an orchid."* (Goncourt, *Journal*, 1888.)

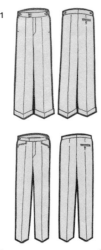

In a demand for quality encouraged by the post-recession, the 1990s rediscovered the "tailor". Italian industries, such as Pal Zileri, joined forces with French tailors (Beylerian) and introduced new "custom-made" signature labels. The French industrial Bernard Zins chose to present its line in the large department stores (Les Galeries Lafayette and Le Printemps). From London to Paris, shops set aside space for "custom-made," from Milan to New York the *sartorial* spirit gained ground, adapting a tradition know-how to a new morphology, looking less to distinguish it than to discreetly place it in the fore. Matched with a three-buttoned suit and a featherweight cashmere overcoat, the flat stomach pants revealed a sobriety with the fall of the fabrics that never bagged, perfect for the new international *business class* warriors in polished shoes. Cashmere-wool blends, super 100, fake plain fabrics and tiny herringbones were all quite in evidence, while the use of a light stretchable flannel softened the look of the *super spenders*, as the *Financial Times* called them.

At the beginning of the 1990s, the "Savile Row" style was recycled under the influence of several designers and clothed the young lions of the City (London's financial center) and the young Japanese dandies of the fashion world. Among the designers were the Ghanaian Oswald Boateng, whose clientele was almost 10% women, Richard James and Timothy Everest. Everest's *Ethan Suit* was inspired by the heroes of the 1960s American television series *Mission Impossible*, and were worn by Tom Cruise in the 1996 film remake. In the basement of his home-studio on Elder Street, the cardboard templates were arranged in tight rows. "The Italian style was too soft, the English too rigid. We softened everything while keeping the structure. We took the best of each and reinvented a style." In 1997, Timothy Everest announced sales figures of two thousand custom-made suits for the year. Beau Brummel had returned. "What's most sexy about pants is the cut. You can lengthen or shorten the legs," said Oswald Boateng. The *Jeans Look*, in the eyes of Timothy Everest, is much more comfortable than a jogging suit which makes the figure shapeless. In 1997, Hugh Grant called Mulberry's for three custom-made suits — each entailed an eight-week wait.

The Bespoke According to Paul Smith or "Mr. Bean on Savile Row"

Beginning in June 1998, Paul Smith, who sold millions of jeans per year, welcomed his posh clients in his new house-shop in Notting Hill Gate. There, in the Classic Room, one could order custom-made suits from the two in-house Savile Row tailors, the master and his heir apparent, who trained from age sixteen at Anderson and Shephard. Pin-stripes for the bankers, velvet for pop stars, the suits were delivered in a Rover mini-van (violet exterior, apple green interior) designed by Paul Smith, for whom the art of pants was defined by "showing without showing". "The height of vulgarity? Choosing them too tight." Marks and Spencer began offering a specialized service in its London store. Terrance Conran opened a restaurant he named Sartorial using tailor's mannequins as decoration. Paul Smith, great uncle of *Cool Britannia* and a member of Tony Blair's governmental committee on cultural politics, created a symbol in his Westbourne House located in London's *hype* Notting Hill Gate sector — the top floor was devoted to orders for custom-made suits. "I make money from selling jeans and under-garments. This is my whim, my folly," explained the designer for whom, "eccentricity is to be oneself". Christopher Tarling (who was addressed "maitre d'"), an old friend of Paul Smith, welcomed his guests as if in a luxury villa, a dacha of *nouvelle* shopping during the Blair years, where the waiting list for custom-made suits had already reached some twenty names before the opening. It was behind a door on which in pink calligraphy was written "fitting in progress" that two Savile Row tailors officiated. "There, tradition is rigid. One must wear a shirt and tie. Here, as well," explained Nick, a cutter for twenty years who had done his training at Anderson and Shephard, where Alexander McQueen had also studied. "The difference, is that I can choose my colours." The craft and metre templates found themselves in the unusual setting of a salon-club: mirrors and screens, Warhol's Marilyn on the walls and leather Conolly chairs that were routinely reserved, as Paul Smith asserted, for the heads of Bentley and Rolls-Royce. Euro-gentlemen and working ladies could, for a price ranging from 960 to 2,000 pounds, treat themselves to a custom-made suit. For those unable to come during opening hours, a technicolor Rover mini (signed by Paul Smith) would deliver the latest-style clothes. "We are the only ones who can work for ministers and rock stars," explained Paul Smith who took on the spirit of the place. "Mr. Bean on Savile Row."

Slit Pockets and Fobs

Piped pockets, extended waistbands, double linings, cloth stirrups at the bottom of the pants — the art of the custom-made fed upon the never-ending demands of the large Paris houses like Lanvin. Thus, the client could choose from sixteen thousand fabrics (from linen to whipcord), with the pants being delivered three weeks after the cutter had noted the desires and measurements of the client. Pockets on the slit, patch or

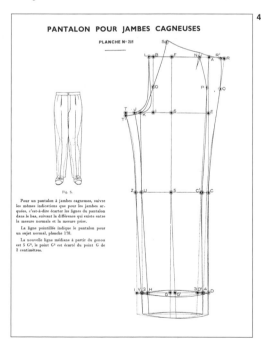

PANTALON POUR JAMBES CAGNEUSES

PLANCHE N° 201

Fig. 5.

Pour un pantalon à jambes cagneuses, suivre les mêmes indications que pour les jambes arquées, c'est-à-dire écarter les lignes du pantalon dans le bas, suivant la différence qui existe entre la mesure normale et la mesure prise.

La ligne pointillée indique le pantalon pour un sujet normal, planche 178.

La nouvelle ligne médiane à partir du genou est 5 G³, le point G³ est écarté du point G de 2 centimètres.

cowboy pockets, hip pockets; buttoned or zippered flies, turned-up cuffs, pleats, piping, moveable waistline, fobs. The manufacturing was done by a *culottiere* working between twelve and twenty hours on a single pair of pants. More, if there were a lot of detail work, or if the detail were particularly arduous as was the case with hip pockets, that could require an additional two hours.

Haute couture found in the tailor a kind of permanence. At Yves Saint Laurent, who was the first after Chanel to hijack men's fabrics, as well as professional clothes, luxury obeyed a simple, unpretentious ritual. According to Monsieur Jean-Pierre, technical director of the house, a pair of haute couture pants required forty hours of work. "It is very controlled, very arduous, very focused. We take dry fabrics, fine grained gabardines and flannels, and work a lot with ironing. All the lines lie straight. One feels that the pants live, that they follow the movement." Pleats sharply ironed, organza cut on the bias on the inside of the pocket to prevent stretching out, the waistband reinforced with grosgrain, the crotch ironed smooth, everything being a question of millimetres. "What is important is the balance and the fall as the model moves. If the crotch is too short, the pants pull, if it is too long, they fall."

6

8

9

"Pants with a Clean Look, No Hitches"

"Our pants are never crushed or folded, but always hung. One doesn't sleep in clothing, one respects it," stated Bernard Zins, the pioneer of the stretch waistband. He applied for the patent on May 20, 1959, and was awarded it on May 13, 1960. "One of the problems that pants tailors encounter frequently," he explained in the descriptive memoir about his patent, "is the automatic adjustment of the waistband whether for the same user as his body in the hip area varies during the course of a given day or during the usage of a given article of clothing, or [...] to prevent a store from having to stock large quantities of different sizes." At Zins, the industrialized manufacturing system borrowed the know-how from the tailor's technique. "Your pants walk all by themselves," as one could often hear this entrepreneur say regarding the signature labels who had entrusted him with their sales: Pierre Cardin, Yves Saint Laurent, Lanvin, Yohji Yamamoto, Givenchy, Sonia Rykiel, Hermès and Chanel.

10

11

12

It was in 1967 that this engineer, who was a student along side Courrèges at the École Supérieure du Vêtement de Paris in 1948, founded his business and was on the way to establishing himself as the French leader of pants. Situated in Lens, in Pas-de-Calais, the Bernard Zins factory knew to seek in tradition and the love of "beautiful work" its industrial and commercial spirit. A fashion house that defined itself by "the cut, the choice of materials (five thousand fabrics), the balance of the pants, the finishing touches and all the essential details — the back and front always being placed in a straight line, preventing the pants from twisting." Everything is sewn with an overcast stitch to prevent fraying. Every part of the pants that is susceptible to loosing its shape, is double-sewn, and to soften and perfect the essential components of the pants — the waistband, the under-foot strap, the opening of the side pocket, the opening of the hip pocket, the piping. Nothing is left to chance — the lines, like the checks and the wale of corduroy, everything is aligned with the side pockets and the waistband. Sewing machines must make flat stitches that do not "bunch up". The corners of pockets are closed with a security point to prevent layering. Visible on the right side and invisible on the inside, the "half moon" edge of hip pockets are measured and worked to the millimetre. All is controlled layer by layer, piece by piece. Symmetry is premium. Every year, some four hundred thousand pieces are produced in the Lens factory, with the manufacturing of women's pants beginning in 1981. Thirty per cent of its production is exported to the United States, Japan, Hong Kong and Latin America.

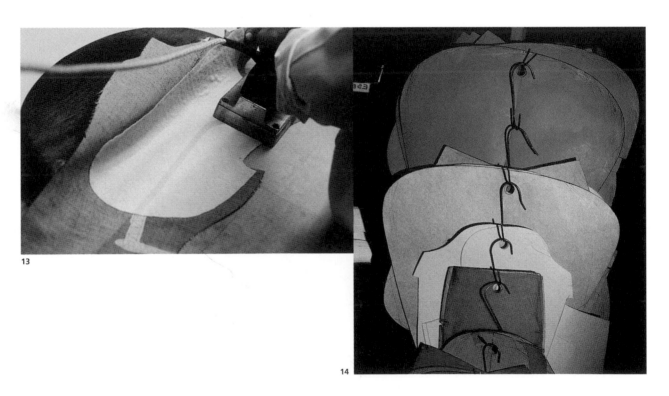

13

14

Pants in the Time of the Industrial Cut

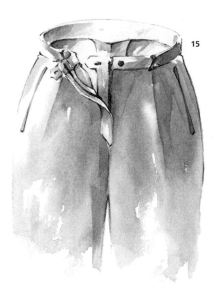

15

"I only wear pants, and so I am as comfortable as a truck driver. I have only one dress for evenings, and it's long." This quote from Lauren Bacall can be found in the *Livret du Pantalon*, edited by Bernard Zins, where watercolour figures were presented with fabric samples and explanations of techniques, and linked to "finishing touches" from buttonholes to "doubling knees" that prevent some fabrics from puckering to the "pre-breaking of the crease" which is dependent upon a strict balance. The mythology of Hollywood refound the soul of its tailors in the pleated pants in the style of Marlene Dietrich and Ava Gardner, along with riding pants, overstitched down the length of the leg, golf pants with their "rounded legs," and the classic "cigarette" — Italian crease, two slit pockets, one back pocket, slim legs and turned-up cuffs. If the automatic machine controlled by computer enables perfection, it does not constitute, according to Bernard Zins, "the criterion of the cut" *par excellence*. Between robots and the forest of cardboard templates, the "tailor" spirit has been reformulated, still fed by the hand and the eye of man, by a certain love for the craft. A well-conceived design is constructed based upon a balance of line. It is the lines that allow the pants to lie flat, and perfection is dependent upon calculations to the millimetre. Curves of the profile, marks for assembling and widening — it is the template that, with great precision, identifies the design. Made of hard cardboard, it serves to calibrate the assemblage.

The technical contributions, such as pressing or computer-assisted conceptions, according to Bernard Zins, have allowed the production of "an ameliorated final product, to perfect it and ultimately, to obtain a pair of pants with a clean look and no hitches." Thus, in 1997, with an initial selection of fabrics (about one thousand choices), the Fitfor concept created with the Lectra System enabled the fabrication of a pair of pants in a delay of only fifteen days and bearing a label with the client's name, as well as a certificate of authenticity. Tradition then entered into the third millennium with orders made on the Internet. Style remains. According to Bernard Zins, "a successful pair of pants is the one that allows you to forget that which you have come to leave behind. A good pair of pants must give the impression of having already been worn. It must not make the leg heavy, but rather must make the step light. It is an article of clothing that follows us from morning to night. The whole secret is in the crotch — one must never feel anything. The most reliable test happens in the store. A good pair of pants does not need to be tried on more than twice." The requirements are there, in the words of a slogan: "I hate pants that smile".

1- The Sartorial spirit. Sketches by Timothy Everest, London (1999).

2- Dandy Rock: silk pants by Alexander McQueen. Summer 1999. Photograph by Ling Fei.

3- The flat stomach for the new male chic. Paul Smith (1999).

4- Study for pants with knocked-knees. Private collection.

5- The tailored look. Sketch by Yves Saint Laurent for an haute couture style (1978).

6- With a sepia ribbed sweater, the timeless look of men's pants in dark brown linen and crêpe. Hermès by Martin Margiela (summer 1999). Photograph by Ling Fei.

7- Trying on in the studio of Monsieur Jean-Pierre (technical director at Yves Saint Laurent) on Avenue Marceau in Paris (1999). Photograph by Ling Fei.

8- In Bernard Zins' factory in Lens. Curves and profiles, marks for assembling. It's the template that identifies the design.

9- Table for adjusting and cutting plaids. Bernard Zins factory.

10- Pieces of fabric ready to be assembled step by step. Bernard Zins factory.

11- Plaid and striped fabrics being cut by scissors for a perfect match. Bernard Zins factory.

12- As in a tailor's shop, the ironing of pants at the Bernard Zins factory is an art. Photographs 8-12 by Gabriele Basilico, 1998.

13 & 14 – Templates at the Zins factory. Each template carries a name whether or not it is part of a collection. Photographs by Ling Fei (1998).

15- "Anatomical cut" illustrating the Femme Bernard Zins catalogue with finishing touches.

Fatigues, carpenter's and chinos

"On the sill of a ravishing square window, a pair of red pants completely spread open, let its two legs fall down the length of the wall and unfurled with a mad impudence its large flap with its grey lining." (**Gustave Flaubert,** *Champs et Grèves,* **1848.**)

*"**Zucco: I'm looking for my fatigues.***
Mother: Your what?
Zucco: My fatigues. My khaki shirt and my combat pants.
Mother: That trashy military clothing. Why do you need that trashy military clothing? You're crazy, Roberto. We should have understood that when you were in the crib and should have thrown you into the garbage." (**Bernard-Marie Koltès,** *Roberto Zucco,* **1988.**)

Some pants seem to escape fashion and pass through time unhindered, as to better dress the new end-of-the-century advertising heroes — adventurers on skis, women firebrands in low-waisted khakis, pacifists in the open air, the asphalt Icarus fearing neither inclement weather nor heights.

Reduced to pieces by the Dogons of Mali who make them into ritual masks (the madder-red of Zouave's pants), and the twirling around by the hands of the caricaturists of *L'Assiette au Beurre* who sketched Jeanne Dieulafoy in fatigues, military pants have lasted through the centuries with the assurance of the incorruptible. It was in the *grand siècle* that armor was abandoned and replaced with the first regular uniforms. The bouffant styles and the padding disappeared, and the culotte, worn with jerkin, a tie, boots and a three-cornered hat became widespread under Louis XIV upon the urging of Louvois. Soon the colours would set the tone.

Brown cap, white tie, blue tunic, white pink-striped belt, matching culottes, blue stockings. In the eighteenth century, the seaman in the Royal Navy looked as if he had emerged from a fashion engraving. The first notion of a "uniform" dates from the sixteenth century with the Swiss mercenaries and their "kits" replete with ribbons and German lansquenets, however the formalizing of the outfit occurred with the French Revolution, which saw the end of embroidery and overly bright colours. This phenomenon became more pronounced in the nineteenth century with, for example, the creation in 1811 of crews for both huge ships and small vessels. The blue cloth pants that the men wore only on inspection days and when they received permission to go on shore became more widespread. The white pants hugged the body above the waist and suspenders were no longer used. Seaman, who had sported long hair and spit curls, had to submit to short "bowl" cuts. Officers' wore blue pants on board and white pants while on shore. The function defined the outfit, codifying through ordinances and decrees the jacket with epaulettes, the drummer's cardigan, the white pants with "bone buttons" and the pants with a "big flap" that "fall to 100 millimetres from the ground and are, by half, 270 millimetres in width at the bottom of the leg". (Ordinance of October 2, 1825.)

Horizon Blue and Madder Red

Pants established a new relationship between space and body. "Let us keep pants narrow at the knee and tight cuffs," a certain P. Jullien, chief naval administrator, had already stated at the beginning of the nineteenth century. "It must be, when necessary, that a seaman can quickly be barefoot and with his pants rolled up to the knees and his sleeves also rolled up." Pants also established a rapport with the order, well expressed by this popular saying "the little finger on the seam of the pants" which clearly relates the image of the rigid position adopted by the soldier at attention giving his respects to a superior. "La Guillaumette is a step ahead, having taken his place near the non-commissioned officer who is with heels aligned, feet spread and squared, he lets his arms fall without pretense or rigidity, his little finger on the seam of his pants." (Courteline, *Le Train de 8:47*, 1891.)

This formalizing of dress for the ground-based army subsisted of an abandoning of vibrant colours. In France in particular, to indicate the placement of troops and their progression, beforehand, it had been necessary for the uniforms to be loudly coloured, dust from the cannon powder demanded such. Thus, the horizon blue and the madder red of the French soldiers stood out against the fields of maneuver, their outfit calling to mind the "rabbit fur coat" of Marshall Foch, and as well, the grey attire of the Russians and the "Japanese in khaki" *(Principes en Guerre*, 1911). But the prestige of the uniform was there. "The garrison on leave, at this point, and red pants, braggarts, are not bothersome," wrote Colette in *La Fin de Chéri* in 1900. "Already, when coming to diner, our little band was escorted by smiles, the clicking of tongues and the smacks of kisses."

On August 2, 1914, the day of general mobilization, the French army was still dressed in colours, while the German army had already adopted the "reseda" which enabled them to blend into the landscape. The madder red still inspired popular sayings like "giving to the red pants," meaning to give preferential treatment to the military. Red pants would be found

APRÈS LA BATAILLE
Deux amis deux frères

2

on naughty illustrated cards, one of which showed a woman in culottes with the caption: "Wearing red pants./She has the red; lives the line/It'll be good, my old man/Fish with her on the line".

It was at the end of 1914 that "horizon blue" first appeared in the trenches filled with *Poilus*, while the Americans adopted the earth brown "cachou" that would herald in the long march of the khaki. The etymology of khaki derives from Urdu and Hindi where it indicates a yellowish-brown, a "dust colour". From 1916, the English chose to use this colour for the uniforms of their troops in India. The army resembled thus "a farondole with soldiers in grey, soldiers in green and soldiers in khaki," wrote Roland Dorgelès in *Les Croix de Bois*, in 1919. The debate took root in the French army. In 1931, the blue-white-red was restored, leaving some, like Blaise Cendrars to comment ironically about the young conscripts coming from a box of crayons. "The big clods came along to the front in khaki mauve and pastel blue, their tall starched kepi soaked in watercolour dyes." *(Bourlinguer*, 1948.)

Fatigues and Camouflage

It would have to wait until 1947 for fatigues to be officially regulated by the French army. The French word *treillis* from the Latin *trilix* ("with three threads"), indicates a fabric originally from Saint-Gall in Switzerland where they make *trellis* called German, in a cloth rubbed, satiny or shiny, initially used for making caps, hats, jackets, linings, the outer side of mourning doublets, jerkins used on the hunt and, in the United States, in the manufacturing of gaiters and culottes for valets, country folk and labourers. It was in the middle of the twentieth century that the word *trellis*, associated up until then with a heavy

hemp cloth used for sacks and peasants' clothes, signified pants. Using this word, one speaks of total endurance and resistance. "He dodges in and out of his best and his departed, no point so fast, nevertheless, the officer's sole did not come to graze lightly upon the greasy bottom of his *trellis* pants." (Courteline, *Le Train de 8:47.)*

If Dior's New Look marked the return in force to haute couture in Paris, as the advent of a decade dominated by seasonal change in lines, fatigues, on the contrary, extolled the idea of permanence with only five minor modifications between 1947 and 1997. The notion of camouflage corresponds to a change in tactics. The camouflage fatigues of the next millennium will be designed not to reflect the rays of detection devices and to offer protection from radioactive rays. Protecting from "views" and blows, fatigues became splashed with colours during the war in Indochina, the Americans not hesitating to adopt the "jungle" motif during the Vietnam war and the "sand" motif during the Gulf War. But the splash of colours did sometime receive bad press, particularly in France where it was associated with the paratroopers in Algeria. They will be dethroned by khakis, the infra-red green of NATO, the earth-of-France.

It was at the point when technology invaded the army that military pants, fatigues and chinos, found once again in the civilian world a multi-faceted public and extended its combat zone into daily life. Adopted, for very different reasons, by anarchists and hunters (one million seven hundred thousand in France in 1997) who matched them with their inevitable Barbour jacket, and by hairstylists in fashion photography studios, who wore them with a black T-shirt and Caterpillar work shoes, fatigues lived out the last thirty years of the century along a thread of gradual demilitarization. This is not contradictory with the development of paramilitary organizations. In the United States, for example, the combat wardrobe presents pages of glazed paper with articles distributed by mail-order or through the Internet. In the *Rothco* catalogue, there are thermal "camouflage" leggings side by side with a machete, a pair of suspenders and grey sweat pants stamped "Army" or "Navy".

"Cargo" Pants, Outdoor Version

If army green is always a bestseller with the French manufacturer Paul Boyé, fatigues (six hundred thousand pieces produced in 1997) have become a basic and less militant in attitude. They're worn on weekends, at picnics and on vacation, based upon Paul Boyé's "bivouacer" style with its loop for attaching a Swiss Army knife. The vogue for outdoor clothes, sales figures for which in the United States went from one to five billion dollars between the 1960s and the 1990s, is the basis of new "hijackings". Inspired by a "knowledge of nature, the rustling of the leaves, the lapping of a stream, the feel of the damp earth under one's feet," Wrangler's *Trail Summit*, outdoor pants in a herringbone weave, with reinforced patched knees, brought into existence a whole line of styles, like the *Coll* hiking pants with

patch pockets, that also came in a children's size, the *Hill-Y* and a slimmer cut for women called *Valley*.

At the end of the 1990s, the emergence of *street work* took hold over such brand names as Levi's and brought on to the scene "functional and authentic products" like the *work pants* that champion skiers and surfers adopted, along with the oversized, "surplus-coloured" jeans. "The military look invades junior fashion" (Levi's winter 1998 catalogue). Even Levi's 520 jeans in twill metamorphosed and appeared in "army green" and "dark grey" versions. Nineteenth-century American trainman's overalls came back in an XXL style that made the rounds at "camouflage" nights at the Blue Note in London and the Respect in Paris. *Cargo* pant, with no pleats, reinforced belt loops and side pockets in "antelope-coloured" gabardine or in narrow-waled corduroy (oak, dark brown, moss), became the new god-send for jeans-makers. A group of young people gathered in the mountains, the forests or along rivers replaced, in the advertising world's Eden, the image of the lone cowboy smoking in the desert. "May the force be

with you" — an advertisement on the lifestyle page the British *Elle* in 1998 that appeared under the title *Combat Zone* at the same time as fatigue pants by Next were advertised side by side with a watch from Timberland and a GI-style T-shirt from Pied-à-Terre.

Work Pants

But these are the professionals who set the tone, like Alpha Technical Clothing, purveyor for the US army of camouflage fatigue pants made from Gore-Tex, that is waterproof and breathable, and protects from cold and wind. At Duthilleul and Minart, specialists in professional clothes from 1850, work pants were coordinated with their purpose: those of the Maitre d'hotel were made of a fine wool weave; for the bartender, a quick-drying, easy-to-iron polyester (when the employer or the workers' collective were responsible for up-keep); for movers, a tear-resistant leatherette; for carpenters, a black velvet called *largeau*; for policemen, a serge of no less than 600 grams per square metre; and for the baker, a neutral polyester (because of the flour). Ever

since the herringbone appeared in 1914 along with the new dyes and was used for the "food trades," it has remained a classic.

The "chef" vogue, along with all the cooking shows, drew in a new public and broadened the available range (some fifty in 1998), including innovative fabrics like polyester and stain-resistant Tefal-treated cotton. At Duthilleul and Minart, people came from Japan to buy the "bartender" pants, the chef's/baker's pleated pants, the fishmonger's smock, the blue overalls, the "Vilette" shirts, valet's apron. The 1439 style, made with a double-needled machine and of two-ply fabric was particularly durable. But declarations came: "Dry cleaners do not accept more than four-ply fabrics because of time constraints."

Surplus Chic

Like the "policeman's sweater" and the New York firefighter's red "multiscratch" jacket, "trade" pants became a part of the new urban wardrobe, along with the T-shirt, the down jacket and the Cordura Plus waterproof backpack from East Pack. Whereas the students of May 1968 carried their photocopied tracts in bags bought at flea markets, Webbies slid their cell phones into combat pants signed by the likes of Replay, Kulte and Paul Smith. Jean Touitou (APC) contacted the creator of Xuly Bët fashions for advice on stocking his surplus store which he opened in 1994 in the Saint-Germain-des-Prés quarter of Paris. There, one could find Dutch army shirts and alpine hunting pants in snow and pine camouflage motifs. "I would never have dared. One would have said, a Hartungs" stated Jean Touitou, so crazy about camouflage that he went as far as presenting it in adhesive tape in his VPC winter 1998 catalogue.

At a time when Russian officers were seething with anger about not being paid, and the Chinese were selling their uniforms around Tienanmen Square in Beijing, Europe was rediscovering, via wise importers, classics guaranteed for life that for a second time young women would wear, slung low off the waist. Defying the economic crisis, surplus flourished along Tokyo's Omotessando, attracting a mob of young Japanese preoccupied with distinguishing themselves… with pieces originally made to escape the view of the enemy. Fashion has passed, already captured by science fiction with, for the third millennium, an infantryman in an NBC (Nuclear, Bacterial, Chemical) protective camouflage jumpsuit presented in November 1997 in Paris by the DGA (Direction Générale de l'Armement). Mission operational around 2005.

The Post-Chino: context relaxed surfer, the itinerary of a pair of pants without a fake crease

In the history of clothes "hijackings," chinos, or khakis as they are sometimes called in the States, trails a mythology more lively than its colour. Introduced onto the European market in 1995, the Dockers brand sold more than two million pairs in 1997, and would double that in 1998. For the first time since the creation of The Gap in 1969, the company reserved their expansive advertising campaign for chinos utilizing both film and television. From Paris to New York, and as far as Tokyo, the brands war intensified. In Europe, Avirex, which sold more than twenty thousand pairs in 1996, cleared over a million in 1998, winning over a most exacting clientele with

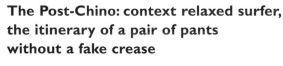

the quality of its long-fibered gabardine imported from Peru and Colombia. At Avirex, manufacturing a pair of chinos took three times as long (some sixty minutes) as a pair of jeans. "We have a military tradition, and we cannot avoid it." In the United States, today some hundred manufacturers share the chinos market. If jeans dressed the rebellion of the 1950s, then chinos symbolized the relaxation of the 1990s. IBM, the first company to permit "dress-down Fridays," unquestionably contributed to this new found interest in twill pants that GIs stationed in the Philippines bought from the Chinese during the second World War. In the 1920s, chinos were manufactured in Manchester and exported through colonial China to expatriates. If James Dean and Marlon Brando immortalized Levi's 501s, it was John F. Kennedy, who wore chinos at the beach as well as in the White House, who made these twill pants the uniform of leisure, and which became the key product of The Gap, sold under the name "khakis."

Different from the United States, where the best-selling style remained the two-pocket, pleated classic, in Europe, was gluttonous for new styles. Having seduced executives, Dockers set it sights on a new set of consumers: the young. The Gap, which five years earlier had extolled it khakis with images of Hollywood superstars from Gene Kelly to Marilyn Monroe, made an appeal to skateboarders and rollerbladers as they swerved and flew. The traditional line ranged from flat fronts, to low-risers, along with "cargos" that had side pockets and were inspired by combat pants. Beyond the sixteen hundred sales outlets throughout the world, customers could buy their khakis over the Internet.

Following the period of the politically correct, came the era of technologically cool. And thus, Dockers, the first brand to introduce *easy-care cotton* that needed no ironing, began offering in 1999 styles whose functionality would become

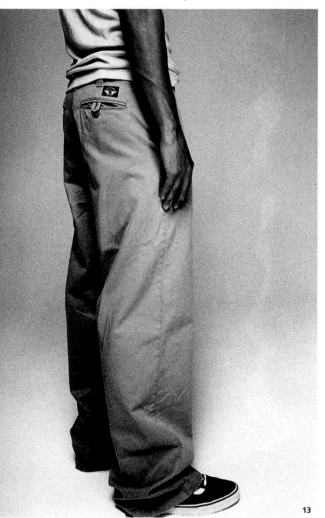

an "alibi-fashion." For example, the *duck pants* made of a waterproof material, the *element pants*, a veritable firefighters outfit that was fire-, water- and air-resistant. And one must not forget the ones that were reflective to two hundred meters. Twill-cotton/nylon, brushed cotton with the feel of suede, the line became widespread, recycling the image of the adventurer.

1- Soviet soldiers (circa 1944). Collection of A. Vassiliev, Paris.

2- "After the battle, two friends, two brothers". Post card (circa 1918). Private collection.

3- Soviet army uniforms. Private collection.

4- Chinos and khaki cotton shirts. Headquarters Hawaiian Department (1942). Avirex archives.

5- Avirex chinos manufactured according to the 1942 US army style.

6- The Travel cover-pants invented by M. Strom in 1932 for automobile drivers.

7- English women steelmill workers in overalls (circa 1942).

8- Denim overalls style 110Z, manufactured by Lee since 1911.

9- The blue hydrone, *on the banks of the Seine. Paris. Photograph by Ling Fei* (1998).

10- Herringbone chef's pants. Duthilleul and Minart.

11- Rollerblades and baggy fatigues. Photograph by Ling Fei (1998).

12- Camouflage *petit marquis.* Jean Paul Gaultier haute couture, summer 1998.

13- Dockers' chinos introduced in France in 1995.

13

From work clothes to *vintage*

*"Dean was wearing washed-out tight Levi's and a T-shirt
and looked suddenly like a real Denver character again."*
(Jack Kerouac, *On The Road*, 1957)

*"Bluejeans wind up being the cleanest thing you can wear, because it's
just their nature to be washed a lot. And they're so American in essence.*
**(Andy Warhol, *The Philosophy of Andy Warhol (From A to B
and Back Again)*, 1975.)**

When heroes become tired, denim makes a return. Its history is one of an outlaw turned loss leader. Hard to fade, in turns frayed, washed-out, bleached, it never ceased to dye the city with its colours. Bought like blue gold from surplus stores, it was from then on sold at supermarkets from Nashville to Belleville. The uniform of the adventurer, throughout the entire second half of the twentieth century, denim became the universal colouring of legends from cowboys to rockers, the student pacifist to the bourgeois lady in a Chanel jacket, from the yuppie to the kid, from America to Asia, where the *vintage* market broke all records.

This plebian cloth manufactured in Nîmes clothed the peasants in Cévennes and Liguria, before a certain Levi Strauss, a Jewish peddler of Bavarian origin from New York, bought supplies in 1853 and brought tent cloth and canvas sheets to San Francisco. Jeans would be born when a gold seeker found the fabric on Montgomery Street. "Don't need tents, but pants. There aren't any here that hold the cut. Impossible to find solids." In 1860, the peddler, along with his brothers, founded the Levi Strauss Company. In 1873, a miner named Alkali Ike complained about the weakness of the pockets under the weight of gold nuggets. Jacob Davis, a tailor from Reno, Nevada suggested to Levi Strauss that he reinforced his jeans with the copper rivets that had previously been used only for horse harnesses, placing them in all the strategic points: front pockets, back pockets, the small pocket and the base of the fly. The *number one*, with it tightening cuffs, was created and saw such a success that Levi Strauss could

not meet all the demands. In 1875, an orange overstitching was added to the two pockets, symbolizing the flight of the Rocky Mountain eagle. "All over the West they wear Levi Strauss and Co," as a poster with cowboys and lassos promised. The first counterfeit jeans appeared in 1886. In response, Levi Strauss marked his product with a leather patch depicting two horses, and a legend was born.

Gold Seekers and Western Wear

One century and a lot of dust later, puritan America embarked upon a more intimate cavalcade. Levi's *shrink to fit* were shrunken as soon as they were first washed to hug the figure. Bought unwashed and not pre-shrunken, the interactive jeans were the ones that aged on their own. These were added to an already complex family of jeans peopled with the traditional

stone-washed, streaky denims and dirty used, that existed in the shadow of such whims as the rolled-up cuffs, the open button and the ones with an end surgically removed on the spot of Jeremy Scott's left tibia, he being the new mascot of the Parisian avant-garde.

What remains of this band of gold seekers nicknamed the Forty-niners that made the little town of San Francisco into the Golden Gate? Nothing, other than the elegance of a memory that manufacturers, overrun by a street without etiquette, do their best to cut to the shape of our times. Thus, in 1998, in the small Louisiana town of Opelousas, population twenty thousand, the police booked people wearing baggy pants on grounds of indecency, an infraction that could carry a six-month jail sentence. The Cajun sense of morality took offense at seeing these boys decked out in pants at least one size too large, and that sometimes revealed a good portion of their underwear. The only good thing in this story, according to the police, was the tactical advantage they were afforded. "The young suspects had trouble fleeing when their pants fell down to their knees."

Fit better. Look better. Wear better. So promised the 1930s advertising campaigns of selling Western Wear. In 1997, the multinational textile group Tavex, cited a figure of forty-five million metres in terms of its denim production, which represented a 50% increase over a three-year period.

"I have only one regret — not to have invented jeans," declared Yves Saint Laurent, who was the first couturier, back in the 1970s, to have offered in his ready-to-wear collection dresses and long coats made from denim. "Fashion is what everyone wants to wear, just to what everyone is wearing." So stated Bob Haas, executive of the Levi Strauss Company, whose personal wealth was an estimated nine hundred million dollars in 1997. Jeans have already been worn by many generations and individuals ranging from carpenters to miners, kings to rodeo performers, aviators to rockers and the angry college student. Sold on the black market in Moscow during the 1980s, adopted by the masses in China who had abandoned the blue Mao suit for them, jeans had, for a long time, been the symbolic outfit of the "free world". Reviled in the interior of the United States itself, would they be able to surmount the menace of the new religious, moral conservatism?

With time, the agitator, having been the object of so many exercises in style and fabrications by Marithé and François Girbaud, those adventurers in denim, that it lost its aura. At the beginning of the 1990s, jeans competed with politically correct chinos, the weekend beige cloth of dynamic executives, as well as with the fatigues of the urban

"fighter" and even with leggings, against which a five-pocket stretch version battled. (One million pieces were sold by Cimarron in 1996.) By the end of the century, 50% of jeans were bought by women. Would the cowboy be able to counter the fashion assault? In the United States, the "big three" — Levi's, VF (Lee, Wrangler, etc.) and Guess were subjected to an attack by brands like Calvin Klein whose standing soared among teenagers, but also by Ralph Lauren, Donna Karan and Tommy Hilfiger (adored by rappers). There was also a myriad of signature brands based in Los Angeles, such as Arizona (whose sales figures soared from fifty million dollars in 1991 to one billion in 1996), Penny's, River Blues and Pacific Sunwear of California, that were closer to their clients than the "established giants".

Signed, Coded, Chameleon

7

Funky look against *old folks?* The new signature labels like Kik Wear Industries (ten million dollars in sales in 1997, double that a year later) and above all, Revatex, Inc. which brought out the JNCO brand, the first to market the super-large jeans they named JNCOs (pronounced "jinkos") became dominant. *The New York Times* documented the battle under the headline "A big pie". Jeans sales in the United States would see an increase of 8% in 1996, reaching ten billion, six hundred million according to analysts of the NDP group (March 17, 1997). The latest teen craze announced by the *Wall Street Journal* (November 12, 1995) were jeans with a bottom circumference of as much as 107 centimetres, more than double classic jeans at 41 centimeters. "I love them because it feel like your wearing shorts. You can't feel the behind," as a Brooklyn eleven-year-old was quoted as saying in the daily columns. The *loose style* naturally became popular in the streets.

"Soon's I get to Denver I'm selling this suit in a pawnshop and getting me jeans," declared the hero of Jack Kerouac's *On the Road*, a cult book of the Beat Generation. Although having become commonplace, jeans would continue to place claim on an ever-more subtle identity, in a game of brands and codes from Ralph Lauren's red fly to the seagull cut "brush stroke" by Evisu. Chameleon, narcissistic, jeans of the 1990s became an essential, discretely signed, coded, whose soul was not merely a product of the cut, but also of the materials, like hemp which needed neither pesticides nor insecticides (from Giorgio Armani) and "cotonina," a cloth used in the eighteenth century for the sails of boats in the Adriatic. At Replay (forty-eight hundred sales outlets throughout the world in 1998), the three hours of stonewashing was replaced by two hours of a cellular enzyme treatment, a more ecological process.

Blue jeans became all colours. In the "clean" category, the *"bain de tonello"* for Calvin Klein's fine luster black jeans; in the "vintage" category, Replay's soft wash stimulated the oxidation of blue creating a yellowed appearance so sought after in vintage jeans. "Each generation, hereafter, has its own style of jeans," stated the *Financial Times (How to Spend It*, no. 25, May 1998).

In France, where the sale of jeans reached forty-five million pairs (compared with forty-six million nine hundred thousand in 1997; source: Secodip), brands like G. Star created in the Netherlands in 1991 posted impressive returns through the marketing of a variety of jeans in twenty different styles, thirteen sizes, six lengths, twenty-two shades ranging from used, to stiff unwashed denim, to grey-coloured. Novelty once again arose from the attention paid to image, as was evidenced by the advertising campaigns by Deisel and G. Star's summer 1999 catalogue, showed the body in three-dimensional movement, contrasting greatly with the "blonde Coca-Cola girl in cowboy boots" communications standard of certain brands that had not anticipated the sea change. "How to make jeans with the air of having been worn while being new?" Pierre Morrisset, a designer at G. Star and creator of several pants-cults like the Liberto's *Cody* of the 1980s asked in 1994. He was also responsible for the famous *Elwood*, a G. Star best-seller, recognizable from others by its distinct fold at knee level — the "body-cut effect". "It was in February 1994. I was on the terrace at Félix in Carcassonne, explained Pierre Morrisset in his sing-song accent. I saw a biker get off his motorcycle. Dazed. His knees bent. I had a flash." In France, in 1998 there were eighty sales outlets and three hundred orders were placed in 1999.

Haute Couture Denims and Limited Editions

11

Upon the eve of the third millennium, jeans once again became a cult object and an object of controversy. In turn victimized, in turn suspected of betraying its origins in a thousand and one twists (for some, work clothes, for others, anti-establishment garb), in 1999, jeans recaptured with panache their difference. Codified to the extreme (in its 1999 collection, The Gap went so far as to offer a line with the serial number imprinted on the label), jeans reappropriated an authenticity that young Japanese were crazy about, as the exclusive process perfected by Girbaud (pioneers of fading jeans back in 1965) attests. What was setting the runways ablur: Helmut Lang's signature jeans in black and white and Miu-Miu's khaki version. Between the Fendi bag sold at Colette's and the Chanel bag (6,100 francs for a square metre of jeans), the last spring of the century placed denim in the realm of luxury. As provocation, it was just to the point of perfection. For the summer of 1999, Jean Paul Gaultier unflinchingly presented as haute couture a sheath dress in faded denim layered with ostrich feathers, individually appliqued at the Lemarié studios (two hundred twenty hours of work), and baptized "L'Écume des jours". Two months after the showing, four customers, one of whom was Aretha Franklin, fell prey.

12

13

14

The blue jean planet

From work clothes to vintage

Pants, A History Afoot

In ready-to wear, Tom Ford at Gucci's buried minimalism and the "androjeanly" correct by way of recycling, with jeans hand-embroidered by Indians brought to Italy for the purpose. His line was among those most photographed during the summer of 1999. Multicoloured plastic pearls, Latin cock feathers, the hippie-chic style strutted down Sloane Street in London and the Via Montenapoleone in Milan.

"Two thousand pounds for a pair of jeans?" Hilary Alexander openly wondered on the pages of the *Daily Telegraph* (February 12, 1999), and offered to personally embroider on sequins and holograms purchased at Fantasy Fayre in London. The phenomenon was there. By February 1999, the waiting list for Gucci jeans from the summer collection had already reached one hundred names. And a columnist acknowledged that the Guccis had already set a style trend partly because in 1999 "denim, once again, is back in style." But the English market, very affected, saw its sales go from forty-four million pairs in 1997 to thirty-eight million in 1998 (source: Secodip). Will it continue? The truth is that from now on, for jeans to be dominant, they must join the club.

The height of chic: limited edition jeans, jeans woven on special narrow-width looms, custom-made jeans (computer-assisted designs) for order at the Levi's store on Regent Street in London. Manufactured in Belgium, they were delivered three weeks later. A few steps away on Sloane Street, Gucci, for the summer of 1988 disseminated its faded jeans that were individually ripped by a sworn seller. The Italians and the Japanese fought with the Americans over their monopoly, the end-all hereafter would be the Denime woven in Kobe and sold in London for 2,500 francs, sealed in a vacuum-cleaner bag.

Japanese Ring Ring Madness

The *Ring Ring* is to ordinary jeans what cold first-pressed olive oil is to engine oil. Who had thought of it? Often manufactured on looms dating to the 1950s, these Japanese jeans with their irregular woof called "ring ring," copper rivets and the famous red border (indicating a narrow-width weave), first landed on European soil at the end of the 1980s and were held in a rare prestige by purists enamoured with the originals. Connoisseurs loved these jeans raw or yellowed with special tannins capable of creating this effect.

From Domingo (1946) who manufactures and dies raw cotton thread the old-fashioned way and relaxes out the fabric by hand using small stones and brushes, to Edwin (1961) created by the Tsunami family, importers of American jeans since 1947, success ruled. Ten sales outlets in 1996, by 1998, Edwin had three hundred outlets and manufactured and dis-

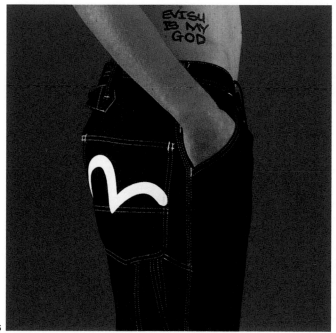

tributed Lee jeans under license throughout Japan, as well as resuming the manufacture of its original jeans from the 1960s. Even more coded certain brands which were sold at Killiwatch, Kulte, MKDM and raw Essentials enjoyed a veritable cult appreciation. Two were the beloved Denime, whose cloth was woven by hand in Kobe and the post-modern Evisu ("God of Money" in Japanese) recognizable by the white seagull on the back pocket and whose manufacturer was bought in 1999 by the leading Italian jeans maker, the Allen Group SRL of Turin. For Yves Dumora, who distributes Domingo jeans, as well as those of Haimai Koji made from Japanese paper which have already been on exhibit at MoMA and sold at Harrod's, "people want the authentic".

The Blue Generation

In the United States, jeans became the all-terrain dress of the militants who demonstrated against the Vietnam War and refused to pay taxes that funded arms. "Yes, we shall overcome one day, we shall live in peace, we shall all be brothers" sang Joan Baez before thousands of people gathered around the White House on August 28, 1963. Music and politics celebrated the advent of the blue generation at the end of the 1960s, breaking into gospel and libertarian refrains on the grass at Woodstock. Embroidered with pearls, abloom with messages, jeans became the uniform of those denouncing the army.

Levi's 501s, a Hundred-Year Myth

"Nothing in fashion, except for 501 jeans, is good for everyone" confirmed the American designer Marc Jacobs, named artistic director of Louis Vuitton in 1997 *(Vogue GB*, April 1998). Levi's, which had made the 501 its battle horse, posted earnings in 1996 of seven billion dollars. This did not keep the world leader from dismissing more than seven thousand workers and closing eleven of its twenty-seven American factories in 1997.

The 501 remains a legend. It appeared in 1890. It was the first time that a reference was used to designate a pair of jeans, the name coming from the lot number of the fabric used at the time of manufacturing. In over a century, it has only undergone some half-dozen changes: the belt loops and the reduction of the width of the bottoms (1922), the Tab (the little red label sewn to the left of the right back pocket), the small "e" on the Tab (1971), the end of the red edge (1981). Avoided by the fashion world (enthusiasts of skin-tight jeans did not much appreciate its cut that lowered the behind), 501s saw a new-found glory in the vintage market, with prices reaching as high as 10,000 francs in 1992 at Tokyo's Haradjuku flea market, thanks to such details as the "Big E" (authenticating models made before 1971) dear to devotees. Distinctive features, taken up in part by the top-of-the-line brands, were placed upon a pedestal: separate pockets for cigarette lighters, pockets reinforced with six rivets, top-stiching on the sides, hemmed cuffs and finally, a leather label indicating the legendary number of the fabric, the size and the length of the inseam. But above all, devotees of 501s preferred to buy them raw, not pre-shrunken. The first washing was seen as a veritable rite — some preferred running water, others still water and even others, let the

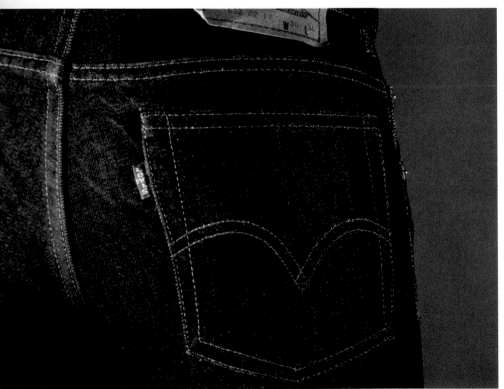

new jeans float through the water behind a boat. With its first washing, a pair of 501s would shrink approximately five percent in length. The particular softness of its feel can be explained by the tiny cotton hairs that emerge from the denim remain unburnt. Exhibited at the Levi's centre in San Francisco, the oldest pair of 501s, dating back to the 1890s, is estimated to be worth 25,000 dollars.

Raw or otherwise, the 501 hangs on this account from the 1930s. "He didn't have a rope or a chain, but he did have an old pair of Levi's in the trunk of the car, and he attached one leg on our car and the other, to the front of his. We really had to pull, but the pants held and his car started."

16

Thirty-three Processes for a Pair of Jeans

Different from most fabrics, denim is dyed before being woven. It takes five to seven indigo baths for the surface of the thread to permanently take the dye, then four baths of washing to eliminate the excess indigo before being dried. Cone Mills, the sole mill for Levi's since the end of the nineteenth century, performs a dozen tests according to an assault course conceived by the US army, enabling them to verify the resistance to rips, tears and strength of the edges. Three successive washings guarantee the degree of shrinkage, the change in weight and the hold. In several hours, the fabric undergoes the wear of several years. This is to say nothing of the fifteen washings of the buttons and the six tests inflicted upon the zippers. Thirty-three processes are required for a single pair of jeans.

Jeans According to Calvin Klein

If Yves Saint Laurent was the first couturier to have hijacked jeans to make dresses and coats, Calvin Klein opened the way to "designer jeans" when he introduced his first signature styles. In 1986, Brooke Shield created a scandal when she claimed on advertising posters that "there's nothing between my Calvins and me". An image that stated its distance from the country chic of Ralph Lauren and the cowboys of New York's Upper East Side.

In 1999, Calvin Klein, nevertheless, readapted the raw look of the jeans worn by Brooke Shield. "For pants, I have always been influenced by jeans, which have their own identity that inspires me. There's a purpose, a point of view with jeans which translates anywhere, at anytime. They exhibit a sexy spirit. A look associated with a relaxed elegance and a personal style. Because the cut is not constricting but precise, the leg can move freely and the figure is free," declared the American designer.

1- The oldest pair of Levi's jeans documented (1880). Levi's Museum, San Francisco.

2- Patterns for the first pair of Levi's jeans with button for suspenders and narrow legs. Levi's archives.

3- American workers wearing Levi's. Levi's archives.

4- Women wearing Levi's on a ranch (1930). Levi's archives.

5- Patchwork jeans by Andrew Yiannakou (1971). Victoria and Albert Museum, London.

6- *Vintage* jeans from the 1970s, bought in the United States. Diesel Collection.

7- Jeans with cock feathers. Gucci summer 1999 collection. Photograph by Mario Tetino.

8- Marithé and François Girbaud 1986 jeans advertising campaign. Photograph by Gilles Tapie.

9- Baggy jeans in the streets of Seoul. Photograph by Ling Fei (1995).

10- Jeans by G. Star, summer 1999.

11- Jeans outfit by Gaspard Yurkievich. Levi's fashion show, September 1998.

12- Repainted jeans with pockets torn off. House of Martin Margiela (1999).

13- Wide wool flannel paints with vintage jeans appliqued on front and back. Jean Paul Gaultier winter collection 1999-2000. Photograph by Gislain Yahri for the exhibition catalogue Pantalons, *Affaire de Liberté*, Printemps de la Mode, 1999.

14- Jeans outfit by Jeremy Scott. Levi's fashion show, September 1998.

15- Japanese jeans maker Evisu's white seagull signature label.

16- Levi's 501s.

17- Washing jeans at Levi's.

Slits, Flies and "Stroke it": Pants Hell

"He took me in his arms, lifted up my pajama with a cautious movement, threw it in a ball on the floor. I made him notice that it would get all crumpled up. He started to laugh softly. Every move he made arose from an incredible softness. He gently kissed me, my shoulders, my mouth. He continued to speak. Do you smell the hot grass? Do you like this room? If not, we can go elsewhere. It's really nice, Cannes..." **(Françoise Sagan, *Un Certain Sourire*, 1956.)**

Slit, prominent, unbuttoned, skin-tight, of all the unisex clothing, pants are the least morally correct. A close-up, and there for all to see, the curve of a buttock, the bulge of a fly, the phallic relief of that the fabric claimed in an attack judged at times to be morally scandalous. As proof, the photo-cult of Robert Mapplethorpe showing the penis of a man dressed in a suit and tie, a beautiful black stalk shooting out from a snowy grey suit.

The satin of the toreador and the crocodile of the rocker, pants have implanted power. It was in the sixteenth century throughout all of Europe that the *braye*, a moveable triangular piece, became a horn-shaped padded pocket that symbolically proclaimed the sex and the virility of those who wore it. The word *braguette* (today, meaning "fly," originally, "codpiece") appeared for the first time in Rabelais' *Pantagruel* (1532). "Would you, said Pantagruel, maintain that the *braguette* is the first piece of military equipment? This doctrine is very new and paradoxical, for we say that we do not wish to start being armed."

"Tumblers," "Secretives," "Sassies": Underpants

One legend attributes the birth of women's leggings to "a woman, falling from a horse." In 1532, Rabelais in *Gargantua* described the sumptuous undergarments of the lady residents of Thélème. "The ladies, at the foundation of the order, dressed according to their pleasure and desires. Then, by their own determination, they changed in the following manner: they wore scarlet or pink breeches, and these aforementioned breeches were pulled up to just above the knee." Elsewhere, the excitement birthed a glance. "In picking up her glove, she lifted the edge of her dress making visible enough of her legs for the unhooded boy to see her blue stockings

1

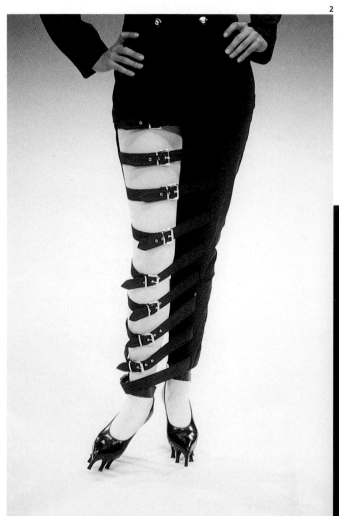

"live-wires" and "stroke it." While the "gust of wind" became one of the favourite subjects of snuffbox manufacturers, some women unhesitatingly sent the count of Caylus a Request to Obtain Stockings, asking him to "procure for them a pair before they would consent to the shortest of walks." His response was final. "What bad intention to augment precautions. It was a nun, sister Véronique, who submitted the most convincing plea in favour of the controversial undergar-

and her black velvet mules, elegances that made him pant with lust." (Pietro Baci, *Dialogues Putanesques*, 1535.) For others, stockings were the best guardian of morality. Thus, in *Le Moyen de Parvenir* signed by Henri Estienne (posthumously, 1610), the character Philausone explains, "They use these stockings because they have all great honesty. Furthermore, these stockings keep them very clean, they retain the dust, as well as they protect from the cold, they prevent [sight] when she falls from a horse, and otherwise do not show..." And to continue, "These stocking insure her from some dissolute ones, for when placing the hand under the petticoat, they are unable to touch any flesh."

There did exist stockings that were "open" for fast women, and others "closed" for virtuous wives. The eighteenth century would be the most generous in terms of named invitations: "sassies," "secretives," "cheekies," "tumblers,"

ment. Look, it is done such that from behind and from in front, unbuttoning its two flies, that I believe are artistically made, letting one use his "windmill" or his "watermill" without any problem." *(Le Caleçon des Coquettes*, anonymous, The Hague, 1763.)

Three centuries later, intimate photographs and news clips gave free rein to scandal. "This thirty-eight-year-old man from Brest obviously did not handle the separation that kept him from his ex-girlfriend. He was found with a machete hidden in his pants, and a rope with a slip knot." *(Télégramme de Brest et de l'Ouest*, August 22, 1998.) In a clinch with the fabric, the skin-tight pants of Rome's *ragazzi* became a language for Pasolini, a silent invitation that spoke to him. "The curly-headed guy in his tight trousers with slanted pockets, sculpting his youthful, stallion haunches." "This tight clinging, it was to each position as much as the radiating tubes around the fly, one tube on the right, one tube on the left, one tube high, one tube low, and when he leaned against the wall or against the pool table with his legs crossed, it dif nothing more than one extended, calm, menacing swelling." *(Les Ragazzi*, 1955.)

Spikes, Lumps and Phallicisms

Throughout western history beginning with the Renaissance, this "inflation" was often one of the attributes depicting power. In 1565, under the brush of Giovanni Battista, Antonio Navagero, the podesta of Bergame, is depicted sporting under his ermine-trimmed velvet coat, a red dou-

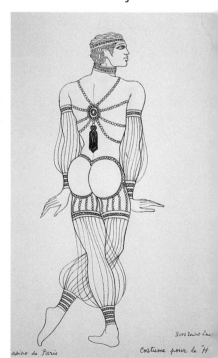

blet and stockings replete with a spiked pocket, accenting the phallic attributes. In France, the minions of the court of Henry III would bring into vogue the *panse* and the *panseron*, a padded doublet that created a voluminous lump that reached down the length of the leg in the shape of a horn. They were to be found at Polichinelle's and at the Commedia dell'Arte, where Pantaloon, the old merchant with the long red legs and the enormous phallus personified the role of the dirty old man.

The religion of artifice held sway just to lower Brittany where wide bouffant culottes called *bragou braz* that either had very fine or broad pleats were worn "under the buttocks." Intended to facilitate walking through thorny bushes, they accentuated the rear, a symbol of power and virility. An utter expression of liberty this protruding member bestows: from the *Sticky Fingers* album cover by the Rolling Stones (1971) to that of Bruce Springsteen's *Born in the USA* (1984), virility has put the polishing touches on its media-subversive finery: here the most lightest fly in the world, designed by Craig Braun after a Polaroid by Andy Warhol, was banned in Franco's Spain where it was replaced by another; there, a pair of buttocks in jeans with cap in the back pocket photographed by Annie Leibovitz would become the icon of the gay revolution during the 1980s.

The Helmut Berger androgynous style of the satin Yves Saint Laurent pants would step aside allowing the "homme-fatal" to emerge. It would be Jean Paul Gaultier's rendition that would be triumphant, dresser of a body rippling with muscles that determined new attitudes. "The fly could be worn opened or closed. These gestures are a bit provocative, I don't do it to that end. For me, they are glimpses of certain rites of propriety and taste," he would say regarding his winter 1983 collection. Worn nonchalantly with a Marcel, Brad Davis' white pants, alias Querelle, the eponymous hero of the 1982 Fassbinder, eclipsed those of John Travolta in *Saturday Night Fever* (1977).

6

7

Crotch and Inseam: Pants of the Skin

A question of mood, a question of style: made commonplace by the stretch revolution, at the end of the century "panta-sex," with the advent of new treatments and materials and neo-erotic styles, has come back to haunt the imagination. Thierry Mugler's swan feather version, Versace's fringed leather, the cowboy chaps that appeared in the backrooms of gay clubs during the 1980s and those that appeared in a variety of women's styles for parading down the catwalks since the beginning of the 1990s. Low waist, long legs, these were the choice pants of Tom Ford, creative director at Gucci. "A sexy pair of pants, are those that reveal your strength, whether you are a man or a woman. Tight pants are for men what a mini-skirt worn with high heels is to a woman with shapely legs. Everything is in the look, the way of carrying it, to be sure of one's body. This is why I like more narrow hips, which to my mind, are the most erotic part of the body. When I

Slits, Flies and "Stroke it": Pants Hell

think of pants, I think of a toreador, of Marlene Dietrich, of the *hipsters* of the 1970s, of the Rolling Stones' *Sticky Fingers* album cover. My first pair of pants had to have been a pair of jeans, Levi's 501s. Today, I tend much more to wear black pants. I must have a good fifty pairs. I feel comfortable in them. What gives you power, is confidence in yourself. Some clothes will give this to you, because they're functional. And that, that's the height of luxury.

Pants flaunted themselves like a tribal symbol of belonging. The success of Jean Claude Jitrois' *skin jeans*, stretch leather temperature-sensitive jeans stands as evidence. "When they crease, they change colour and react to muscle contractions." In September 1998, the date they went on sale, five thousand pairs were sold. As Jean Claude Jitrois confirmed, among those who bought a pair was the Canadian singer Céline Dion. "Women had bought pants to distinguish themselves from men, now it's to distinguish their age and themselves. Pants, it's the ass. Everything is in the cut. It's the way of placing the waistband to get the right height of the triangle that more or less carves the curve. What makes the buttocks gay or sad, happy or sagging."

9

1- High-waisted leggings in red and black latex
with a zipper along the buttocks seam. Phyléa, 1999.
Photograph by Gislain Yahri for the exhibition catalogue Pantalons,
Affaire de Liberté, Printemps de la Mode, 1999.

2- Multi-belted leather pants. Jean Paul Gaultier, summer 1993.

3- Jean Colonna's skaï pants. Photograph by Thierry le Goues,
Glamour, 1992.

4- Leather pants with metal codpiece. Jean Paul Gaultier,
rock stars collection, winter 1987-1989.

5- Drawing by Yves Saint Laurent for the magazine *Le H,*
Casino de Paris, 1970.

6- Zipped leggings. Jean Paul Gaultier, winter 1987-1988.

7- Swan feather chaps by Thierry Mugler. Summer 1982.

8- Three-meter leg sculpture, adorned with leather
by Jean Claude Jitrois. Photograph by Helmut Newton, 1998.

9- Stretch leather pants. Jean Claude Jitrois 1997-1998
winter collection. Model, Sarah Marshall. Photograph b y Tyen.

Pantaloon, Harlequins and Drag

"I am accused of being too active, too virile. It seems that,
in England, Hamlet has to be played like a gloomy German professor...
My acting is regarded as untraditional. But what is tradition?
Each actor brings his own traditions to the play".
(Sarah Bernhardt, *L'Art du théâtre*, 1900)

On the sets of Hollywood studios, a mysterious fate seems to have swooped down upon the actors and actresses whose pants, before having become a classic of the contemporary wardrobe, had always clothed that otherness, whether at balls, scenes or cross-dressings. From Sarah Bernhardt appearing as Hamlet in 1886 at the Porte Saint-Martin theatre in Paris, to Marlene Dietrich in a white tuxedo in Josef von Sternberg's 1932 film *Blonde Venus*, pants played the role of "the other," personifying all sorts of dreams and demons. "The customs official at Charing Cross ought to have confiscated her doublet and black breeches," decried a critic regarding Sarah Bernhardt who, wearing them, had seduces other judges more sensitive to her metamorphoses. A thoroughly paradoxical article of clothing, pants are chameleon. Prohibited in cities, stage pants "protected" privacy, and thus the dancer Mademoiselle Camargo (1710-1770), a pioneer of the short skirt to shield herself with the protection of leggings. "Her companions accepted the skirt but rejected the leggings, with many jokes about the prudery of the famous dancer. [...] Mademoiselle Mariette, one of the mockers, one day was suspended upon a swing, which put her in a state similar to Eve's before the fall. The crowd below applauded, but the police got angry and an ordinance required from thereon that pants were obligatory for all the dancers." *(Grand Dictionnaire Universel du XIX Siècle*, Pierre Larousse, 1873.) It was at the beginning of the nineteenth century that a certain Monsieur Maillot, supplier of hosiery for the Opera, made the first knit stockings that hugged the legs for the dancers. Heralding in the athletic body of the twentieth century, leggings clothed a movement devoid of all artifice. It was in *Le Spectre de la Rose* (1911) that Nijinski, wearing a costume by Bakst, soared to the skies as if to harvest the glint of the stars.

Chosen for dressing fauns and cherubs, pants always transgressed the rules of morality and convention. They inspired all sorts of metamorphoses that only the stage could make possible, upon the grounds of an ambiguity that would naturally appropriate the city. This was the case with Monsieur Maillot's leggings, but was as well with the male-female style, overalls. Its power of expression enabled it to have rooted legendary roles. Certainly Marlene Dietrich's tuxedo would come to mind, but just as well, would be Charlie Chaplin's falling-down pants, eternally associated with his cane, his bowler hat and worn-out jacket.

The Story of Pantaloon

He carries along with him, centuries of prohibitions and myths. "Pantaloon: a man who took on all forms and who played all sorts of roles to come to his end," as the *Dictionnaire de l'Academie* stated in its first edition which appeared in 1694. It was the name of a Venetian merchant, Pantaloon, that before indicating a single stocking had, in the sixteenth century, set a type of role in the theatre of farce. Between comical fights and amorous dances, the tirades Sire Pantalone provoked laughter.

Gesticulating, he was often shown with his hand in a fist, even though he never killed anyone and was always the recipient of the blows. Married, he was ever the cuckold. He coughed, spit, stammered. All calamities befell him. If he had girls, whether Isabella and Rosaura, or Camille and Smeraldine, and the maids Fiametta and Zerbinette, all made fun of him. Gold, gold. They always asked him for gold. Libidinous, scabby, gouty, wheezy, this "child of a hundred years" is the dupe *par excellence*.

The people called him tooth-gnasher, stitch-pincher, bread-beggar *Pantalone dei bisognosi*, *cagh'in acqua*… Pantalone hid a treasure under his straw mattress: *bolognini* in old silver and ducats. His ancestor was none other than Euclion, seen by Plautus. "He is so miserly, that when he lies down, that he takes pains to tie up his mouth to keep from losing his breath during the night. There have been times when the barber cut his nails and he carefully gathered up the cuttings and so as not to lose anything, carried them off." In his will, Pantalone wrote "I leave to my valet twenty-five good blows of the whip, bloody ones, for having made a hole in the bottom of my urine bottle, making me completely wet my bed."

Nasty tongues confirmed that in his worst debaucheries, he only ate soup made from greyhounds or alley cats, that his wine was drawn from the corner fountain and that his meals most often consisted of a duck egg. Red legs, floating black coat, the *zimarra*, his beard tapered in the wind, Turkish slippers and red woollen bonnet, he was dressed in the colours of Venice, queen of the vessels and the colonies, this city where "its old cocks, according to Joachim du Bellay, will marry the sea, as they are the husbands and the Turk commits adultery." Iconography from the sixteenth century presents the oldest representation of Pantalone — a painting held in Bayeux in France, it depicts him amid a troupe of improvisers in the court of Charles IX, while the painted murals at the castle in Trausnitz, Bavaria and the prints from the Fossard collection (circa 1580) depict a Pantalone dressed in a tight-fitting red-orange court jacket and long leggings of the same colour that had stirrups. Amorous, his physical reactions are caricaturised and he finds himself endowed with an enormous phallus.

From the Gros Guillaume to the Harlequin

Many actors succeeded one another in the role of Pantalone, who was also called Magnifico: from Giulo Pascati in Padua (circa 1587), to Colato, the author of

Three Venetian Twin Brothers, and not to forget the actors in the Mazarin troupe at the Petit Bourbon and those of the Duke of Modena's troupe at La Foire. The family of Pantalones spread and through its ridiculous avatars, enacted the French farce (Gaultier Garguille), the theatre of Gherardi (Brocantin and Gaufichon), as well as that of Molière (Orgon, Gorgibus, Arpagon).

Too thin, too fat, bizarre. Everything took places as if a curse had struck a certain type of character, marginalized from the start by his costume. And thus came Gros Guillaume, a character in the troupe at the Hôtel de Bourgogne, famous for driving away melancholy with his false stomach that was underscored by two belts and his face dredged in flour being associated with a miller. One can also mention Gros René, who wore a bodysuit with a padded belly, yellow crêpe and cloth culottes that were piped and trimmed with red braiding. Mascarille was rigged out in a Swiss-style get-up of culottes and a doublet in a heavy green cloth, placed over a fine green cloth that was visible between the bands of the culotte and the bottom of the slashes.

Harlequin wore wide pants, a loose blouse and a peasant's *blanche* that was tied at the waist with a cord. This last article of clothing was made of irregular pieces of cloth sewn onto fabric, which by the seventeenth century would become standardized with red, green and white triangles placed in a diamond-shaped pattern. Treated as an unrefined valet by Marivaux and a sombre character by Watteau, it was to him that, on an engraving one of his feats were addressed in the following terms: "I place my life and my honour in your hands, Harlequin, my friend, take as much pleasure as you desire, but do as never any man, as he would without having had known…"

With his hooked nose masked, by the eighteenth century, Polchinello had supplanted Harlequin. For him, there was a fat leather belt, a pair of loose, pleated pants and around his neck, "a sort of half-tabaro, half-ruff rag" edged with a green braid. And there was Pierrot, sometimes also called

Gilles, who came from the Italian Piero or Pedrolino. With a "loony" character, he wore loose white pants and dispensed his fuzzy thoughts from a pasty face.

Sarah Bernhardt in Drag in *L'Aiglon*

"She wanted to gain the familiarity that would allow her to play her role of a man as a man, unconsciously, and without remembering that she had ever worn a corset or a skirt," wrote Gaston Jollivet about Sarah Bernhardt in the revue *Le Théâtre* (1900). "She had had the courage, that women playing in men's attire did not have enough of, to wear these

9

10

uniforms long before the such became the way of performance and, one could say, she did so like wearing a shoe [...] All the gestures that she made were those of a young man. The actress did not have the air of doubting herself as she wore the attire of a soldier."

On March 15, 1900 was the date of a triumphant premiere. At fifty-seven years old, Sarah Bernhardt, on the stage of her own theatre, enacted Napoleon's heir, the tragic Duke of Reichstadt, the hero incarcerated in the gilded prison of Schönbrunn. The performance was all. "Fine, yes. Ask the first actress who comes by to play a similar role, if she has not, as Madame Sarah Bernhardt, not only, good God, slogged away at her diction, but also thus controlled her every movement, her every step, and above all, if she is not accustomed to wearing men's clothing to the point where it seems to be her body, to be moulded on her like a uniform on an officer, the hair shirt on a saint!" once again wrote Gaston Jollivet.

For this play, written two years earlier by Edmond Rostand,

Paul Poiret, then the assistant to Jacques Doucet, "signed" the costume that would set as never the figure of the king of Rome entered in to the mythology in a grey frock coat, leather boots and white culottes. Famous for her extravagances, the actress reached the height of her glory. "In truth, I don't prefer men's roles, but men's minds. Hamlet, L'Aiglon, Lorenzaccio are minds haunted by doubt and despair, hearts always beating harder and ceaselessly tortured by their evocative dreams. The soul burns the body," she wrote. "The artist must be stripped of virility. He makes us see a phantom combined of the atoms of life and of the expirations that lead to death. It is a mind ever battling with things."

11

Many actresses such as Véra Sergine, Madame Simone, Fanny Heldy, Mary Marquet and the American Maud Adams would follow her model. "These roles will always stand to gain by being played by intellectual women who alone can preserve their nature of insane beings and their scent of mystery." (Sarah Bernhardt, *L'Art du Théâtre*, 1900).

12

Pantscene
Pantaloon, Harlequins and Drag

1- Pantalone. Commedia
   dell'Arte, circa 1577.
2- Lucie Lavigne as a toreador,
   1872. Collection of A. Vassiliev,
   Paris.
3- Harlequin at the beginning
   of the 20th century. Brussels.
   Private collection.
4- Masquerade. Romania, 1926.
   Collection of A. Vassiliev, Paris.
5- Jeanne Richard in a harlequin
   costume. Collection
   of A. Vassiliev, Paris.
6- Sarah Bernhardt in stage
   in *L'Aiglon.* Costume
   by Paul Poiret, 1900.
7- Charlie Chaplin in *City Lights,*
   1931.
8- Greta Garbo in an *amazone*
   outfit in *The Queen Christine,*
   1933.
9- Left: Marlene Dietrich
   in Josef von Sternberg's X27.
   Right: Marlene Dietrich
   at the St. Regis Hotel.
   United States, 1941.
10- Fred Astaire in *Top Hat,*
    1956.
11- The Nicholas Brothers,
    1940s.
12- Irène McBride (the mother
    of Jean-Paul Goude),
    Jackson Heights Queens.
    Taken from Jean-Paul Goude's
    Jungle Fever, 1927.
13- Carmen Amaya, the first
    woman flamenco dancer
    to wear pants, 1950s.
14- Roberto Ximenez in *Duende
    y Misterio del Flamenco,* 1951.
15- *West Side Story,* 1961.
16- Stage costume
    for Johnny Halliday
    by Yves Saint Laurent, 1970.

Pants, A History Afoot

Sarouels, Hakamas and Faraway Dreams

*"She learned the French language, said farewell forever
to her embroidered jackets and her pink silk pants."*
(Alphonse Daudet, *Nabab*, 1877)

*"Her black leggings were studded with mandrake, and in an indolent
manner, she clicked her little hummingbird-feathered slippers."*
(Gustave Flaubert, *Hérodias*, 1877)

Bouffant pants made from the skins of reindeer worn by the Kamchatkans and the Siberian Ghiliaks, culottes made of llama skins in the land of the Quechua Indians of Peru, the China blues worn with white Bensimon sneakers adopted in

Deauville (Normandy) by Parisians in the beginning of the 1980s and the Korean *paji* that Buddhist monks did not hesitate to wear with Nikes at the beginning of the 1990s: pants cross fashions and continents like the millennium traveller.

Pants can offer an indication of social status. In the court of Japan, the traditional attire had consisted of pants-apron with very long legs that trailed along the ground worn under the kimono. Like the Argentine gaucho's pants, the Japanese *hakama* magnified the space between the body and the fabric, defining a different manner of living and moving in a rapport with others and the environment based less on constraints and seduction, than the forgetting of oneself to the point where age and sexuality were erased. An older woman does not wear pants in the same fashion in the West as she does in Asia. Here, she would choose to wear them in order to prove something such as a splendid physique, a figure that the years had not mis-

shapen. There, pants naturally clothe the actions and gestures of daily life subjected to uninterrupted movement for over four thousand years. Although the "little feet" attracted great fascination and taboos, pants crossed the centuries in China with no difficulty, worn by concubines as well as their emperors.

In several civilizations, pants are an undergarment that constitutes a part of the traditional women's attire. The sarouel remains one of the better examples. As the chevalier of Arvieux remarked in the seventeenth century, Syrian women from Aleppi "wear long leggings like men, over which they put a long and ample blouse made of striped chiffon or another fine material, that is in no way different from the men's."

Regarding the women of Fez, Marmol Carvajal noted in 1751 that "When she goes out,

and in particular, the women of Andalusia, she wears rather longs leggings that are deeply pleated in order to make the leg beautiful, as the pants come only as far as mid-leg." Here again, the sarouel offers an indication of social status. The larger and the more fabric used, as Leyla Belkaïd reminds us, "the more horizontal pleats of the leggings are close together, the more the shape of the legs is demarcated, the more the city-dweller indicates a superior position." *(Histoire du Costumes Méditerranéen*, 1998.) The sarouel for outdoor wear must be white, an immaculate version reserved for married women, whereas for young ladies it is striped or coloured. In the eighteenth century, the English traveller Thomas Pellow commented that "only women of rank wear long culottes whose pleats circle the ankles." *(La Relation de Thomas Pellow, une lecture du Maroc au XVIII siècle,* M. Morsy, 1983.) In Algeria, only the most conservative women, the Tlemeciennes, adopt the *fouta*, a kind of loin cloth that they drape around their short sarouel, as they find it indecent "to show their culotte."

217   *Mauresque d'ALGER. — LL*

5

Juive Tunisienne

6

Exoticism and Revolt

It was during the nineteenth century that the great women travellers had added travel attire to their vocation of explorations: we cite the English women pirates Anne Bonney and Mary Read "buccaneers of the sea," Jeanne Dieulafoy,

archaeologist who, with her husband, unearthed the "frieze of the Archers" in Susa in 1885, Alexandra David-Neel who crossed India, Ceylon, Korea and China, and later, Isabelle Eberhardt, a young writer of Russian origins, who at twenty years of age discovered Algeria and Islam. Starting in 1899, disguised as an Arabian horseman, she travelled through the northern Sahara only to die five years later carried off by the floods of a wadi. "As for dressing like a man," wrote René Lois Doyon, one of her first biographers, "to wander on horseback, to run with the tribes, to sleep in shacks along side the peasants and horsemen, it was more than what was needed to present Isabelle as a dishevelled bacchante, or as a provocateur of the revolt."

It was with Paul Poiret that "harem pants," in a whiff of exoticism, coloured the stampede toward the Orient, that painting and literature were largely stylised in the nineteenth century. "The *toilette* of Soujia-Sari is completed. [...] Here is how it was done: pants with black bands, on a tawny golden background, that rise just to the hips and stop a little above the calves," wrote Théophile Gautier in *Fortunio* (1838).

Along with the gandoura, the Turkish sarouel became the indoor garb that eccentrics at the beginning of the 1920s affected. Women like Eveline Dufour and Jeanne Massoutier were the first in Paris to sell clothing made in Algeria and Morocco and that were embroidered according to their sketches drawn from ancient Arabic documents. If Pierre Louÿs' Salomé (*Aphrodite*, 1896) wore black leggings studded with mandrakes and her queen Bérénice "slit leggings," it was because

eroticism fed upon references to Oriental culture, exalting at once both the body's lascivious movements and its perfumed secrets. "I still see her, the dear little Aziyadé, sitting on the ground on a pink and blue Turkish carpet, erect and serious, her crossed legs in Asian silk pants." (Pierre Loti, *Aziyadé*, 1879.) And at the "Arabian Nights" ball held in London in 1913, Baroness Meyer made a remarkable appearance in the attire of "a strange Arabian princess" about which *Femina* complimented its "suppleness and grace."

From the Indian Dhoti to Toreador Pants

Under the influence of the hippie revolution and of Kenzo, the 1970s would pursue travel, while in the shadows of the cities, steps lightened in an Indian *dhoti* fashioned from a rectangular piece of cloth wrapped around the haunches like a Malay sarong, but with a tail drawn through the legs and passed through the waist or a Cambodian sampot. The infatuation with countries of the East, which dates from the beginning of the 1970s, brought back the tweed Muzhik pants, worn with riding boots, along with the China blues (more than twenty-five thousand outfits sold by the *Compagnie de l'Orient et de la Chine* in 1974) that continued their long march.

But soon, pants from "faraway" would become a sophisticated accessory worn with high heels in golden kidskin. From 1976, Yves Saint Laurent, with his *ballets russes* and then *opium* collections (1977) with their flamboyant evening pants, would celebrate the marriage of the bazaars and haute couture. It was the invitation to the seraglio. Muzhik pants, worn with jersey tunics the colours of precious stones and with cords tied as belts, created a certain air. "A completely new style and a new way of being, living in movement, with these bouffant pants, their ample seats that curve the thin and envelope the round with the same grace." *(Elle,* July 3, 1978.) "Ethnic" pants would soon lose their initial design, emphasizing the bias of the fabrics and the colours inspired by Venice and Istanbul. The end of the 1980s would put them on the scene. With the arrival of such designers as the Italian Roméo Gigli and the

Belgian Dries Van Noten, whose vibrant silk pants were worn with men's jackets came an expansive new taste for the far-off, offering crossbreedings to all.

Isabelle Eberhardt, A Russian in the Orient

"In an outfit appropriate for a young European woman, I would never have seen anything, the world would have been closed to me, for the outer world seems to have been made for men and not for women," wrote Isabelle Eberhardt. At twenty years old, this errant princess boarded a boat in Marseilles for Algeria, taking off on a voyage "toward the blue horizons" which would be the one of her lifetime, a life cut short at age twenty-seven. Dressed in "attire d'emprunts, chosen according to place and circumstance," she would come to call herself Mamooud Saadi, "the little Turk escaped from a French school." An early-day hippie, she explored the Algerian-Tunisian border, pursuing her "dream of a tribe within a tribe," wanting "to live far from the world so as then to try to say that which she had said." In 1904, she died, swallowed up by the floods of a wadi, leaving behind her the memories of golden plains, violet dunes and narrow black streets where this writer of Russian origins had lived and had metamorphosed into another, "the peace of heart." She was, for Lyautey, "the one who draws me most into the world, a resistor."

13

1- Chilean gaucho girl. Santiago, 1928.
   Collection of A. Vassiliev, Paris.

2- Buckskin Bill with mutton chaps. Private collection.

3- Traditional Chinese pants from the Zhejiang province.
   Photograph by Henri Cartier Bresson, 1949.

4- Mother and daughter, or the ideal Chinese revolutionary
   in wide cotton pants and flat canvas shoes.
   Private collection.

5- *Mauresque* of Algiers wearing a sarouel.
   Private collection.

6- A Jewish Tunisian woman in "grand attire." 1920s.
   Collection of Philippe Guez, Paris.

7- *Odalisque à la Culotte Rouge*. Henri Matisse, 1921.
   Musée National d'Art Moderne, Paris.

8- Iranian girls playing soccer. Photograph by Abbas.

9- Young shepherd from Rajastan, India.
   Photograph by Bruno Suet, 1990.

10- The Stowitts in a revue at the Folies Bergère, 1924.
    Private collection.

11- Toreador couture. Sketch by Yves Saint Laurent.

12- Bullfight. Photograph by Isabel Muñoz, 1994.

13- Isabelle Eberhardt in 1895 at age 18.

14- Korean peasant. Beginning of the 20th century.
    Collection of Lee Young Hee.

15- Korean fashion at a Buddhist temple;
    ceremonial hanboks by Lee Young Hee.

The Korean Hanbok: Pants in the Wind

As women are again dressing in the china *(a long skirt) and a bolero, men have adopted the* pagi *(bouffant pants), worn with a chogori. The history of the hanbok, which in Korean means "clothing," is tied to that of Korea and its three kingdoms: Koguryo (37 BC to 688 AD) from the north of the peninsula extending to Manchuria, Paekche (18 BC to 663 AD) from the start installed in the present-day capital of Seoul and Silla (57 BC to 688 AD).*

The first traces of the hanbok can be seen in the frescos on the tomb walls of the Koguryo kings and noblemen. This was the first kingdom to adopt Buddhism which had come from China. The influence that came with the adoption, by the court, of the dress of the Chinese Tang Dynasty can be noted. In silk, cotton or moshi *(natural fibres), the hanbok remains a traditional article of clothing which villagers living along rice paddies, during festivals, and city-dwellers celebrating certain ceremonies such as marriage and the full-moon festival adopt equally as well. The first to dye her fabrics with colours of the temples and the outfits of monks, Lee Young Hee, designer of hanboks, knew to find, through a thousand and one shades, the soul of the country of tranquil mornings.*

14

15

The Imagination of Pants

*"The little girls whom I have seen, with a mastery of gestures
that give a perfect suppleness to their bodies and a sincere
contempt to the rest of humanity, came straight before them,
with neither hesitation nor rigidity, executing exactly
the movements that they desired, each of their limbs
fully independent of the others."*
(Marcel Proust, *À la recherche du temps perdu)*

1

A "unileg" that is boxy, full of buttons, zipped
down the ankle, pants excite the imagination.
Featherweight and paranoid, reinforced at the knees
and the seat, fireproof, coldproof, stainproof, they
amble through the mind as much as they do along
city sidewalks, where from now on they would take
off, struck by the energy of skateboarders and
rollerbladers. Starting with tops, its skin-tight thighs
and the androgynies of the 1970s, pants are falling
down, literally, puking, blue-grey, baggy, along the
asphalt and the unknown territories of a unshaped
future. It is from below, bouffant above the ankles,
that they made their entrance upon the puritan ways
of the late nineteenth century when *La Mode Illustrée*
pronounced, "Up until the present, we have wanted
to ignore that honest women, in a word, women of the
home, in all respects being the concern and the
respect of conventions, can, without blushing, show
themselves in public in that accoutrement you know,
and abandoning themselves to sports which impas-

2

sion to the point of delirium the present generation."

It is also from below, brushing atop vintage sneakers, that they henceforth distinguish themselves, yielding to the implacability of the codpiece, to the virile glories of times past, from where the radiant future has drawn its line. Here they are, naked before themselves, this faceted destiny that painters, fashion designers, theatre and opera costume designers have many a time coloured with their dreams, from Bakst to Fernand Léger, from Picasso to Jean-Charles Blais, from Malevitch to Yves Saint Laurent and Jean Paul Gaultier. There, where an infinity of possibilities crosses the route of needs and functionality, and a body pure in movement. François Girbaud has gone so far as to make a membrane with two legs, a carapace that is almost invisible, adorned with messages and sketches. At the end of this century, all work on ever-changeable pants recalls the experiments performed by the futurists of the 1920s who dreamed of a universal piece of clothing like the Tuta. But pants always break out.

4

Glossary

AGLETS. Tagged laces for assembling or closing garments or armour parts.

BAGGIES. Very wide pants which became fashionable in 1974 and again in the 90s owing to the influence of rap and techno music.

BELT. Long strip of leather, fabric or metal fastened at the waist. (idioms: below the belt, to tighten one's belt).

BERMUDAS. Close-fitting shorts reaching to the knee, adopted by the British Army in India and then by the Bermuda police in the 30s. The emblem of holiday wear in the United States, they are made from cotton, denim or seersucker.

BLOOMERS. Pants for women invented in the United States by the reformer Amelia Bloomer and unsuccessfully presented in France and Great Britain in 1851 despite the support of her "Bloomerist" followers. An anti-crinoline symbol, it was designed to rationalise women's clothes by replacing the wide skirt by long puffed pants tied at the waist and of the same fabric as the bodice. The word came to mean the puffed pants of small children before being applied to an article of women's lingeries in the 1950s.

BLUE-STOCKING. Name given to literary/intellectual woman. After the Blue Stocking Club formed in London in 1750 in which Mr Stillingfleet always wore blue stockings.

BOOT CUT. Generally refers to low-waisted jeans with a slight flare for wearing over boots and which has become a fashion classic, linked to the fashions of the 1970s.

BOUFFANT KNICKERS. Puffed knickers (18th century).

BRAGUETTE. Fly.

BREECHES. Pants worn by different peoples in Antiquity. The Romans, who wore roomy and unsown garments used this men's garment, ancestor of stockings, tights and culottes, fastened at the waist with a belt, which they had borrowed from the Gauls.

CALECON. Tights.

CAMOUFLAGE (pants). Very sturdy hemp pants used for military exercise or combat.

CASUAL. Style of Californian and surfing origin from the 60s. Synonym of everyday and urban comfort in the 90s.

CHINOS. Canvass pants adopted in 1846 by an English lieutenant in the Pundjab to replace the traditional red flannel pants. Following a recommendation made by Indians, he dyed them with the leaves of a plant called "mazari" to give it a beige-green colour known as "khaki", or "dusty", a standard colour registered in Manchester in 1844. The American President Teddy Roosevelt was the first to popularise this material during his expeditions in Kenya. In the 1920s, these pants were manufactured in Manchester and exported to colonial China for expatriates. During WW2, the GIs stationed in the Philippines bought them from local Chinese traders.

CIGARETTE PANTS. Close-fitting pants.

CORSAIRE or CORSAIRE PANTS. Or "Capri pants". Young women like Audrey Hepburn wore them in the 1950s with black ballet shoes and, a few years later, Brigitte Bardot in Saint-Tropez.

CULOTTE. Men's forked undergarment covering the body from waist to knees (originally fastened at the knees), each part after the fork covering a thigh. French tight-fitting culottes were worn by courtiers in the 17th century. The Revolutionaries adopted loose pants and called themselves "sans culottes" (without culottes). At the end of the 18th century the Bavarian culotte appeared, closed in front by two buttoned plackets.

DENIM. Popular serge manufactured in the Nîmes region in the 18th century. An elliptical form of "serge de Nîmes". Another source given for it is the Hindi word "deenim", meaning course cotton.

ECLAIR. zip-fastener. Brandname registered in France in 1928 for a fastener using a sliding clip binding a double row of teeth. The inventor is said to have drawn his inspiration from the burdock's hooking device that enables it to stick to animals and garments.

FLAP (pants with a foldover flap).

FLY. Part of pants or shorts forming a vertical opening in the middle. At the end of the 15th century it referred to a piece of cloth hiding the opening of the knickers and attached by buckles or laces to the front of the knickers.

FOB. Small pocket slit on waistcoat or on the waist band of pants, for holding a watch.

GARANCE. Madder red pants of the French army from 1829 to 1914 when soldiers' visibility was regarded as crucial.

HABIT. Monk's habit in 12th century. Later came to mean pants in 18th century France.

HAKAMA. Traditional Japanese pants.

HIPSTER. Low-waisted and tight-fitting pants.

JEANS. Originally, fustian made in Genoa, popular cotton fabrics exported to England from the end of the Middle Ages and worn by Genoese sailors. Produced in the US from the end of the 18th century, the fabric was intended for workers. In the 30s and 40s, the name came to mean denim work pants. It was

adopted as a garment of cowboys whose mythology inspired the leisure society of the 50s and 60s. Jeans went through the full gamut of fashion in the 70s.

JERKIN. Ancient garment tight at the waist and with long sleeves and tails or skirts. Today it is a knitwear vest covering just the trunk, used for dancing and gymnastics.

JODHPURS. Riding pants wide across the thigh and tight-fitting from knee to ankle. From the Indian city of Jodhpur, the name was adopted in the 19th century by English colonialists who had adopted this style for riding. It was brought back into fashion in the 1980s.

JOGGING. Sweatsuit or running suit.

JUMPSUIT. Appeared in the 40s in the USA, made fashionable by Yves Saint Laurent from 1968 on.

KHAKIS. See Chinos.

KNICKERBOCKERS. Word derived from a hero of Washington Irving. Pants used for golfing, skiing or mountain-climbing.

KNICKERS. Ancestor of pants.

LEOTARD. Close-fitting one-piece garment launched in 1968 by André Courrèges, before appearing in stretch versions: "body stocking" for dancers and "leotard" for city wear.

LEVI STRAUSS (1829-1902). Bavarian peddler who arrived in

San Francisco in 1850 with tent canvass and fabric carriage covers. According to the legend, a gold digger asked him for a comfortable and solid pants made from denim.

LYCRA. Brand name registered by Du Pont de Nemurs for its elasthane. Well known in lingerie, tights and swimwear, Lycra fiber was mixed in the 80s with other fibers to produce garments of great comfort and flexibility. The first fashion designers to use it for city wear fabrics were Marc Audibet and Azzedine Alaia.

OVERALLS. Work garment worn over garments to keep them clean, and child's garment consisting of pants and front kept in place by braces.

OVERALLS. Worker's boiler suit, generally in blue canvass.

PAJAMAS. pajama pants. From Hindustani, meaning "leg garment". Loose-fitting garment worn by women in certain regions of India. Since 1908, a light and loose-fitting night or indoor garment made up of a pants and jacket.

PAJI. Traditional Korean pants.

PANTALON. Pantaloon.

PANTALOON. Figure of the commedia dell' arte who wore long pants, a lecherous and avaricious old man. Figuratively speaking, an untrustworthy person.

PATCH POCKETS, varying in size, made by attaching a piece of fabric

Chronology of a Scandalous Attire

550-329 BC

First known appearance of pants worn by the Medes during the Persian Empire.

1350

The wearing of a doublet necessitated tight leggings that went high up.

1430

Charges against Joan of Arc. "The aforementioned Jeanne cut her hair in the manner of a valet, and that she took to wearing shirts, breeches, gipon, long leggings of a single piece, attached to said gipon by twenty aglets."

1431

Date that sailors from Genoa would first wear pants woven from fabric coming from Nîmes; "denim serge".

1534

The word "braguette" (codpiece, later: fly) appears for the first time in *Gargantua* by Rabelais.

1538

Separation of "chausse" into "bas" and "haut" (long- and knee-breeches).

1555

In a sermon marking Assumption Day, Andreas Musculus, professor of theology at the university of Frankfort, warned his students about evil, and about sinners who, possessed by the devil, wore the breeches that had been adopted by Hosenteufel, the devil of culottes.

1567

The first mention of the word "jeans," a corruption of Genovese.

1599

The first mention of the word "trousers" according to the *Oxford English Dictionary*.

1779

A change in the uniformality of French attire that would last for sixty years; a jacket from woven cloth and pants of a knitted fabric.

1790

In his "call to the nation," Marat spoke of "long culotte without feet."

1792

The *sans-culottes* adopted pants, in reaction to the culotte worn by French aristocrats. The carmagnole, a short jacket originating in Italy, lent its name to a revolutionary chant.

1794

The decree of 16 Pluviôse, year II (February 4) indicates that the "sacks of old clothing" which were to provide for the sailors and the novices embarking upon the vessels of the Republic would contain, along with all else, "two large cloth culottes".

1800

In the ordinance of 16 Brumaire, year IX (November 7, 1800) of the Napoleon Code, the prefect of police stated that, "all women desiring to dress like men would have to present themselves before the prefecture of police to obtain authorization to do so." At the same time, Monsieur Maillot, hosier for the Opéra, made the first tight-fitting knit stockings for the dancers.

1820

Arrival of the "madder red" pants, one of the inventions, along with the shako (1804) and the tunic (1845) that most defined the military outfit.

1821

The arrival of the word "pantalette".

1830

Under the reign of Louis Philippe (1830-1848), pants came to the fore, opening with a vertical slit. The canteen women of the artillery in Algeria made them their military outfit and wore them in "royal blue with red bands" with boots and a tunic with three rows of buttons and a sailor-like waxed hat.

1848

The Saint Simoniens presented a look comprised of a tunic and a pair of pants. On April 6th *La Voix des Femmes* launched an appeal for George Sand to be elected a deputy.

1851

Amelia Jenks Bloomer became one of the heads of the *anti-crinolinist* movement in the United States and presented her invention of a pair of long, bouffant pants that were tight at the waist in London and in Dublin. They were to create a scandal. She advocated them on the pages of her feminist journal *The Lily*.

1853
Oscar Levi Strauss (1829-1902) sewed the first jeans from a cloth for tents, and sold them to the California gold-seekers.

Oscar Levi Strauss. Levi's archives.

1858
With Charles Frederick Worth, English couturier based in Paris, the crinoline petticoat and women's undergarments became widespread.

1860
Founding of the Levi Strauss Company. The first 501s with the logo of two horses tearing apart a pair of jeans.

1863
Mary Edward Walker, the first woman surgeon in the army, wore pants and would often be stopped for impersonating a man.

1870
Jacob Davis, a tailor from Nevada, reinforced the pockets of jeans with copper rivets.

1873
First changes to the 501s: the arrival of a double arc on the back pockets and a button-down fly.

1874
Jacob Davis and Levi Strauss register a trademark for the 501s.

1875
Calamity Jane, dressed like a man, took part in the "George Cook Sioux Expedition," but was thrown out the day it was discovered she was a woman.

1877
In Norway, the creation of Helly Hansen, the oldest manufacturer of "outdoor" clothes in the world.

1880
Appearance of the "modern pleat."

1885
In Great Britain, Charles Poynter, the director Redfern, created for the princess of Wales (future Queen Alexandra) an outfit inspired by a man's jacketed suit. The vogue of a "tailored suit" was launched.

1886
Construction of the building on 14-16 Battery Street in San Francisco that would house the home office of the Levi Strauss Company. Appearance of the leather label with the "two horses" on the 501s.

1889
The Globe Superior Company, specializing in denim work clothes, is founded in Abindgon, Illinois. After waiting in vain

for a deliver of work clothes, Henry David Lee, owner of a general store in Salinas, Kansas, decides to make his own under his own name. He created the HD Lee Mercantile Company in Kansas whose star product was the Bib Overalls, which had many pockets and was exclusively intended for manual labourers. American farmers adopted them *en masse*. Backed by its slogan "Lee, the jeans America builds with," Lee would become the brand second only to Levi's (which had added to its 501s a small pocket for a watch at the top of the front right pocket).

In Paris, was the opening of the Moulin-Rouge, dedicated to the triumph of the French Can-Can and to the "little women of Paris" in their swishing undergarment pants. The same year, Alpine hunters adopted knickers in a "bluish steel grey" that were worn with banded puttees made from a dark blue cloth. Infantrymen remained loyal to the "madder red" pants that gave them the nickname "red

"Fireman," from the "Women of the Future" post cards series. Beginning of the 20th century. Private collection.

asses." The skirt-culottes of "cyclewomen" make their first appearance.

1891

Invention of the zipper in the United States. A Swedish engineer, Gideon Sundback, would perfect it in 1913, and thereafter it would be marketed in France by the company Eclair.

1892

On October 27, a circular emanating from the minister of the Interior would remind all police prefectures that "the wearing of men's clothing by women is not tolerated, save for the case of cycling sports."

Woman in pants "à la Montparnasse." Beginning of the 20th century. Private collection.

1895

The English ironed the crease of the pants crease, the hem "reawakened" each morning. The French ironically remarked that "one "reawakens" his pants in Paris because it is raining in London."

1896

Creation of the brand OshKosh in the United States, makers of the famed striped overalls. One century later, OshKosh products would be sold in seventy countries around the world.

1898

The golfer Harry Vardon, soon to be followed by George Duncan, Charles Mayo, Tom Ball and P. J. Gaudin, is the first to launch the vogue of knickerbockers.

1900

In March, Sarah Bernhardt appears in men's dress in Edmond Rostand's play *L'Aiglon*. Paul Poiret, then employed by Doucet, designed the costume.

1902

Death of Levi Strauss. He left a fortune estimated to be worth six million dollars.

1904

C. C. Hudson and his brother create the Blue Bell Overalls brand in Greensboro, North Carolina. Their products are sold to workers at the local railroad company. A few hundred kilometres away in Tennessee, R. W. Baker founded the Big Ben Manufacturing Company.

1908

Founding of the Lee Cooper brand by Morris Cooper.

1909

In France, the year when a law providing eight uninterrupted weeks of maternity leave is enacted, women are officially authorized to go out in culottes, provided they are riding a bicycle or at the reins of a horse. Harem pants make their debut

in Paris in *Shéhérazade*, choreographed by M. Fokine, with sets and costumes by Bakst.

1910

Globe Superior Company, Blue Bell and Big Ben merge to form the biggest American manufacturer of work clothes. In France, one of the first "Amazones" to wear pants and cause a scandal is Colette.

1911

On February 18th, *L'Illustration* reproduced four drawings signed by Poiret under the title of "Four ways to dress women in pants." On June 24th, at the Persian ball given by her husband, Madame Poiret appeared in a skirt-pants. Two couturiers, Bechoff-David, introduced the idea of having the skirt-pants go down to the street. The Vatican set off a war against the "immorality" of harem pants. The state of Illinois declared itself against bloomers, but no ordinance was promulgated.

The first skirt-pants, 1911. Collection of A. Vassiliev, Paris.

1914

German police banned the wearing of ski pants off the slopes. During World War I, the blue horizon of the "poilus" replaced the madder red. In factories, women's pants became a necessity.

1917

The first advertisements in the United States for work clothes (Lee).

1918

Horseback riding women who began to ride astride adopted jodhpurs, the culottes worn by English officers in the Indies that were inspired by Hindu fashion.

1919

In the United States, jeans, work clothing, took on a relaxed look. Lee invented the "Sanforized" jeans that did not shrink in the wash.

1920

Gabrielle Chanel introduced her pants "à pont" that were inspired

Young French women in Moorish outfits. Collection of Françoise Kreif.

by sailor's pants. Jeanne Lanvin signed vacation and "interior" styles.

1922

Levi Strauss' old "Number One" became "7015SXX" referring to the number of lots of denim (7015) and their quality (double X).

1925

First pantsuit for women, signed by Paul Poiret.

1926

The first pair of zipped jeans: the "101Z" from Lee.

1927

The Parisian couturier Lucien Lelong presents tunics and ski pants. Women's craze for sports generates the evolution of its fashion.

1928

Creation of the airborne army that adopted the *"bleu Louise."*

1929

Overalls became the uniform of the Great Depression in the United States. In Great Britain, the Spanish tennis player Lilli de Alvarez is the first to wear pants at Wimbledon.

1930

In France, Armand Allard, master tailor at Mégève, designs the first ski-pants. They were straight pants, worn inside the shoes, that were very tight at the bottom with an elastic strap under the foot. The ski champion Hilaire Morand asked him to create a model for him that was more practical than the Norwegian pants. American tourists copied the police in

Bermuda who wore English shorts, thus giving birth to Bermudas.

According to Cecil Beaton, Greta Garbo bought her clothes at American Navy surplus stores where sailors and manual labourers got their overalls and sweatshirts.

1931

During the summer season, the beach pajama was triumphant on the Côte-d'Azur, and Juan-les-Pins became "Pyjamapolis."

Ski outfit. Jean Patou. Patou archives, Paris.

1932

Elsa Sciparelli presents overalls for women in her February collection. Marlene Dietrich, while walking along the Seine was beseeched by a policeman not to dress as a man when in Paris.

1933

The golf champion Gloria Minoprio made a scandal by playing in pants, worn with a matching navy blue sweater, white make-up and a single club. Her pants are on exhibit at the Women Golfer's Museum in Edinburgh.

1934

Shorts make their appearance on the shores of the Mediterranean. Claire McCardell, considered a pioneer of American sportswear, introduced "separates" — a coordinated sweater/pants outfit for women — in large American department stores. They would not be bought until 1941.

1935

A drawing of a pair of Levi's is published in *Vogue*, USA. It is the first appearance of women's jeans in a woman's fashion magazine.

1936

The appearance of the "tab device," the red label on the back right pocket, from Levi Strauss. For the second time in the world, after the Lacoste shirt in 1933 and to eschew counterfeits, a textile brand placed a label on the outside of the garment. The Blue Bell Overalls Company became the largest clothing producer in the world.

1938

Johnny Hess, who sang *Je Suis Swing*, introduced "zazou" fashion in Paris. In New York, the "zoot suit" with its huge pants made their appearance in Harlem jazz clubs.

1941

In the Philippines, the American GIs adopted "chinos," pants made in China from English cotton cloth. On November 10th, the War Department introduced chinos as the uniform for the US Army Air Force.

1942

Claire McCardell launched her first bodysuits called "leotards." During World War II, more and more women took to wearing pants.

1945

Reappearance of the word "bloomer" (women's pants invented by Amelia Bloomer in 1851) to indicate the little underpants worn by children under five years old and cut from the same fabric as their dresses.

Rodeo in jeans, 1940s. Levi's archives.

1946

On October 1st, *Elle*, a young French magazine, energetically defends pants under the title "Secrets of the New Fashion."

1947

On September 1st, the cover of *American Weekly* sported a drawing of worker in overalls sitting on top a globe. American railroad workers were the first consumers of denim. Their work clothes were guaranteed against any defects. Up until 1955, Lee's "Union Made" line would use the image of the American railroad in its advertising.

Blue Bell signs a contract with Rodeo Ben, a Hollywood tailor, to create a new collection of western-style jeans, with the famous 13MWZ (Men, Women,

Zipper; 13 a reference to the prototype). The birth of Wranglers, with its famous button embossed with a lasso, the leather patch, the pockets with a stitched "W" and a white ironed crease on the front. The dark blue colour is introduced. American jeans arrive in Japan with the US Army, and importation companies, like Tsunemi, appear. In France, the battle dress called *"treillis"* is officially regulated by the French Army. Dior's *New Look* — which marked the rupture between two generations, those of mothers and daughters who discovered American slacks —returns the dress to prominence.

1948

The first Wranglers for women. They closed with a zipper in the front, not on the side. The golf champion Jean Donald Anderson appeared during the finals of the British Open wearing custom-made pants. Teddy Tinling, couturier of the women champions, introduced his famous "panty" (lace pants)

Levi's advertisement in the United States, 1950s. Levi's archives.

worn by the tennis player Gussie Moran. Placed on the backlist by the England Club at Wimbledon, they established the glory of Tinling.

1950

The birth of rock and roll. Jeans become a part of the American counterculture. In Italy, Emilio Pucci opens the "Canzone del Mare" at the Marina Piccola on Capri.

1951

On October 22nd, 5.2 million readers of *Life* discover Casey Tibbs, the rodeo champion of the world, posing in jeans and a jacket by Lee. He follows Jilm Shoulders, chosen two years earlier by Wranglers. The "rodeo wars" begin between jeans manufacturers.

1952

The creation of "Confecciones Saez" by the brothers Manuel and Joaquin Saez Merino. The first articles of clothing produced are work clothes sold by travelling salesmen. A company that would give birth to a large Spanish textile group, notably the makers of the Lois and Cimaron, two French brands of jeans.

1953

July 4th, release of the film *The Wild One* which established Marlon Brando and Lee Marvin, as well as the "Biker Look." With the black leather jacket and Schott perfectos, Levi's 501s make up the clothing of rebellion. Simon Fisbein creates the brand "Sym." The new idols in pants and corsairs are called Bettina, Audrey Hepburn and Françoise Sagan.

1956

Joshua Logan's film *Bus Stop* with Marilyn Monroe is under-written by Lee. With *And God Created Women* by Roger Vadim, Brigitte Bardot, wearing skin-tight corsairs and Repetto ballerina slippers, becomes the idol of a generation.

1957

On September 7th, America discovers Elvis Presley in *Loving You*. A veritable advertisement for Levi's, he plays a former truck driver become rock and roll star loyal to the 507 jacket and the famous 501 jeans. A few years later, Johnny Halliday would take up the exact same outfit. Dressed by Hubert de Givenchy, Audrey Hepburn, appearing in Stanley Donen's *Funny Face*, sets the image of the young woman on the move, dressed in tight pants and balle-rina slippers.

1960

Wrangler is the first manu-facturer of clothing to become computerized. Lee dresses the entire cast of *The Misfits:* John Huston, Clark Gable, Eli Wallach, Montgomery Clift, Arthur Miller, Frank Taylor and of course, Marilyn (née Norma Jean). In Florence, Emilio Pucci introduces "Capsule," a "cat-suit" in Emilioform, a fabric composed of 45% silk and 55% Nylon, used as a ski suit. Pierre Cardin introduces a first men's collection presented by stu-dents. The French company Frafor introduces "Babygro, the clothing that grows with the child." On May 13th, in the north of France, Bernard Zins obtains the patent for "perfectly

providing articles of clothing with a waistband and pockets with a stretch waistband that automatically adjusts to the waist."

1961

The "Edwin" brand, makers of jeans from fabrics woven on old American looms, is introduced in Japan by Tsunemi.

1962

First grand-scale importation of American jeans into Europe. The most famous are: Wranglers' 11MWB and 11MWZ, Levi's 501 and Lee's 101. In his first haute couture collection, Yves Saint Laurent presents white pants with a navy blue reefer jacket.

1963

François and Marithé Girbaud fade their first pair of jeans in a laundrette in Saint-Germain-des-Prés and make their debut by buying raw Wrangler jeans that the resold at numerous stores.

1964

Levi's creates STAPREST. The same year, Courrèges introduces the mini-skirt and offers white pants to be worn day or night, in the city or the country, with futurist boots. The first bellbottom pants (Renoma and Marinette). Marithé and François Girbaud import cow-boy clothes into France for the first time. They are sold in Paris at Western House.

1965

The Girbauds develop the "stonewashed" process. Begin-ning of intensive research on denim in terms of its nature and washability, giving birth to Tubic, Crupro, Black Dye, Destroyed and Trichlojean, among others. In the United States, Dupont de Nemours comes out with stretch fabrics intended for work clothes.

1966

Yves Saint Laurent introduces his Rive Gauche ready-to-wear line. He puts women in pants and offers them their first tuxedos. In Paris, Betty Catroux will be booed upon arriving at the Opéra. In New York, Nancy Kempner will see herself denied entry at the *Côte Basque* restaurant.

1967

Bernard Zins creates his company, becoming the pioneer of industrial pants in France.

1968

Yves Saint Laurent introduces his "jumpsuit." With him pants, previously considered as recreation clothing, would make their entry into the city and the office where, save for at the bastions of great conservancy, but associated with the worlds of finance and politics, they would come to dominate. André Courrèges invents the word "pantacourt" but does not register it. The Renoma brothers introduce the "Lenin" suit with pants with very wide belt loops.

1969

André Courrèges introduces the "second skin" leggings. Jeans become the uniform of the Woodstock generation. Triumph of the low-waist.

1970

Jacques Esterel presents a collec-

tion of dresses for men. Yves Saint Laurent is the first to offer jeans in his ready-to-wear Rive Gauche collection. The twenty-eight-year-old Paul Smith opens his first store in Nottingham, and is among the first to sell Levi's 501s in Great Britain. The first Japanese designer to create a brand in Paris, Kenzo introduces pants inspired by folklore from around the world. Marithé and François Girbaud create their first collection under the label "Ça," using materials like moleskin, velvets, blue hydrone and denim which would bring to life such fashion lines as "Toulouse Lautrec" and "Boutonneux."

1971

The Rolling Stones album cover for *Sticky Fingers* after a Poloroid photograph by Andy Warhol showing the fly on Joe Alessandro's jeans caused a scandal. It was banned in Spain. Appearance of the little "e" on the Levi's Tab. Yves Saint Laurent created a scandal with his "retro" collection which brought back the pantsuit of the 1940s. Vivienne Westwood opens her store Let It Rock at 430 King's Road in London where she sold clothes from the 1950s.

Jean patchwork, 1970s. Levi's archive.

1972

Bellbottom pants reach their maximum width and become the uniform of both sexes. Jacques Esterel presents a unisex wedding outfit.

1973

Following a "Jeans Art" contest in which ten thousand people participated, Levi's presented in New York the first exhibition devoted to jeans, "Rebirth of the Blue Denim Art Show." The department store Les Galeries Lafayette authorizes its saleswomen to wear pants.

1974

The first baggy jeans came out under the name "Elephant jeans" by Marithé and Fran çois Girbaud. In July, Yves Saint Laurent opened his house of couture at 5, avenue Marceau in Paris, and introduced his "muzhik" pants. Vivienne Westwood's store is re-baptized "Sex" (the first "bondage" pants and fetish bodysuits). In France, the Karting stretch pants sees a success.

1975

The first pants for men and women signed by Giorgio Armani. The first leather pants for men signed by Marithé and François Girbaud under the brand name "Compagnie des Montagnes et des Fôrets."

1976

The first jeans by Calvin Klein. Malcolm MacLaren and Vivienne Westwood introduce punk fashion; the first pants with fettered legs. Jean Paul Gaultier presents his first collection under his own name in Paris.

Bibliography

Gisèle d'Assailly, *Les Quinze révolutions de la mode*, Hachette, Paris, 1968

Azzedine Alaia, ed. Steidl, 1999.

Eric Baschet, *Les Grands Dossiers de l'Illustration/ La mode*, Le Livre de Paris, Sefag & l'Illustration, 1987.

Nathalie Bailleux & Bruno Remaury, *Modes et Vêtement*, Découvertes, Gallimard.

Samuel Beckett, *Le Monde et le Pantalon*, Les éditions de Minuit, 1989.

Laure Beaumont-Maillet, "La Guerre des Sexes", *Les Albums du cabinet des Estampges de la Bibliothèque Nationale*, Albin Michel, 1985.

Leyla Belkaïd, *Algéroises, Histoire d'un costume méditerranéen.*, Edisud, 1998.

Patrice Bollon, *Morale du masque*, Le Seuil, 1990.

Anne Bony, *Les Années cinquante*, éditions du Regard, 1983.

François Boucher, *Histoire de la mode en Occident*, Flammarion, 1996.

Pierre Briant, *Histoire de l'Empire Perse de Cyrus à Alexandre*, Fayard, 1994.

Penelope Byrde, *The Male Image: Men's fashion in Britain 1300-1970* .

Calamity Jane, *Letters to her daughter*, Rivages Poche/Bibliothèque Etrangère, 1998.

Xavier Chaumette, *Le Costume tailleur*, MGPL, 1992

John Grand Carteret, *La Femme en culotte*, Flammarion, 1899, Paris.

Maruccia Casadio, Emilio Pucci, *Mémoire de la mode*, Assouline, 1998.

Farid Chenoune, *Des modes et des hommes*, Flammarion, 1993.

Colette, *Colette et la Mode*, Plume, Paris, 1991.

Yvonne Deslandres & Florence Muller, *L'Histoire de la mode au vingtième siècle*, Somogy, Paris, 1986.

« Les modes vestimentaires dans la société occiden-tale », in *Encyclopédie de la Pléiade*, Histoire des Mœurs, Jean Poirier, Gallimard, Paris 1990.

Yvonne Deslandres, "Le pantalon féminin: la guerre des sexes", in *Peplos*, numéro 15, juillet 1984.

Meredith Etherington-Smith, *Jean Patou*, Denoel, 1984.

Colette Guillemard, *Dictionnaire du Costume*, Belin, 1991.

Benoite Groult, *Le Féminisme au masculin*, Denoel-Gonthier, Paris, 1977.

Elisabeth Hardouin-Fugier, *Les Etoffes, Dictionnaire Historique*, 1994.

Bernard-Koltès, *Roberto Zucco*, Les éditions de Minuit, 1996.

Vydal Jan Vanek, *Civilosovana Zena*, Prague, 1929.

J. Join, *Documents sur le costume des musulmans d'Espagne*, Dozy.

Lydia Kamitsis, *Paco Rabanne*, Michel Lafon, 1996.

Jacques Henri Lartigue, *L'Œil de la mémoire*, Michel Lafon/Carrère, 1986.

Maurice Leloir, *Dictionnaire du costume*, Grund, 1992

Claude Lepape, Thierry Defert, *Georges Lepape ou l'élégance illustrée*, Herscher, 1983.

Gilles Lhôte, Christian Audigier, *Le Jean des héros*, Lincoln, 1992.

Richard Martin, Harold Koda, Jocks and Nerds, *Men's style in the Twentieth Century*, Rizzoli, New York, 1989.

André Maurois, *Lelia ou la vie de G. Sand*, Marabout, Hachette, 1952.

Morsy M, *La Relation de Thomas Pellow, une lectu-re du Maroc au dix huitième siècle*, Paris, 1983.

Ted Polhemus, *Looks d'enfer*, Alternatives, 1994.

Paul Poiret, *En habillant l'époque*, Grasset, 1986.

Colombe Pringle, *Telles qu'Elle*, Grasset, 1995.

Nicole Pellegrin, *Les Vêtements de la liberté*, Alinéa, Aix en Provence, 1989.

Nicole Priollaud, *La Femme au dix neuvième siècle*, Liana Levi, Sylvie Messinger, 1983.

Bruno Remaury, *Dictionnaire de la mode au vingtième siècle*, éditions du Regard, 1996.

Annette Rosa, *Citoyennes, les femmes et la Révolution Française*, Messidor, Paris 1988.

Bruno du Roselle, *La Mode*, Paris, Imprimerie Nationale, 1940.

Gérard Julien Salvy, *Mode des années trente*, éditions du Seuil/Regard, 1991.

George Sand, *Œuvres autobiographiques, Histoire de ma vie*, Pléiade, Gallimard.

Christian Schlatter, *Les Années 80*, Flammarion, 1980.

pants" in class, and not only during recreational activities. The mail-order catalogue *La Redoute* offers an Yves Saint Laurent tuxedo in the winter.

1997

In London on September 16th, during the "Rock 'n Roll Memorabilia" auction organized by Sotheby's, an outfit worn by Prince during his *Sign of the Times* tour, was bought by the Hard Rock Café for 6,470 dollars. At the same time, a turquoise satin Lycra caleçon worn by Emma, "Baby Spice" of the Spice Girls, was valued at 4,900 dollars. In Paris in October, Jeremy Scott, the 24 years old American designer originally from Kansas City,

Baggy pants in the streets of Seoul. Photograph by Ling Fei, 1997.

Missouri, presents for his second collection called "Rampage" women's pants that have one leg shorter than the other. The invasion of new jeans brands (Evisu, G. Star, Kik Wear Industry, Pacific Sunwear of California) and the readoption by teenagers of work and outdoor pants.

Levi Strauss announces eleven of its thirty-seven factories in the United States and Canada, reducing its North American workforce by 34%.

1998

In January, Thierry Mugler presents haute couture jeans for his spring-summer collection. Calvin Klein reintroduces his black jeans in a limited series. In association with Lectra System and Les Galeries Lafayette, Bernard Zins offers pants "custom-made" in the factory. The website Designers Direct (www.designersdirect.com) enables the buying of Calvin Klein, Ralph Lauren and Levi's jeans through the Internet. Dockers presents its "Equipment for Legs" line with its very technical pants, and announces a collaboration with the Italian designer Massimo Osti, creator of the new Vespa, designer of the sports clothing line Superga, "to create pants for the twenty-first century." The brand sells 400,000 chinos in France yearly (2.2 million in Europe in 1997).

Summer 1999 collection, jeans adorned with feathers by Tom Ford for Gucci.

"Dockers" chinos by Levi Strauss.

1990

Wrangler introduces the first jeans certified "Oko Tex Standard 100" in Germany according to environmentally sound standards. The one-legged "Splash" jeans adorned with sequins make their appearance in the "Hawaii" summer 1990 collection of Thierry Mugler.

1992

On September 7th, the first worldwide jeans auctions is held in Paris, organized by Levi Strauss; thirty-four lots are acquired for a total of 500,000 francs. An advertisement made on a wooden composite and dating from 1936, showing a cowboy in a hat, western boots and wearing jeans in real indigo cloth with the border (Big "E" label) is sold for 139,000 francs. Development of the "vintage" phenomenon, with the recognition of the "Big E" that indicates jeans manufactured before 1971. The craze for collection pieces takes shape. In November, in Paris a beach outfit by Jean Patou having belonged to Princess Nilfur is estimated at 170,000 francs at the time of the "La Mode dans l'Art" sale organized by Françoise Auguet. At the same time, research into new fabrics intensify in Japan. Issey Miyake creates the costumes for William Forsythe's ballet *The Loss of Small Detail*, presented in Frankfurt which are the prototype for her "Pleats Please" line. Jean Paul Gaultier introduces his first collection "Gaultier Jeans."

1993

Alexander McQueen introduces his "bumsters" that were so low-cut, they reveal a good portion of the woman's derriere.

1994

Issey Miyake introduces the "Pleats Please" line, with its featherweight pants that were easy to care for and that adapted to all the movements of the body, constituting a revolution in the history of fashion.

Elton John's 1973 "Yellow Brick Road" suit, estimated to be worth 11,000 pounds during the "Sotheby's at the Hard Rock Café" auction held on September 16, 1977 at Sotheby's.

1995

Levi Strauss launches its Internet site. IBM is the first American company to authorize "dress down Friday." In France, within a rather depressed women's ready-to-wear market (-4% in volume between 1994 and 1995), the "Pants for city and leisure" sector registers an increase of 22% (source: Secodip).

1996

The Avirex brand establishes itself in Europe. Sales will rise in two years from 20,000 pairs of chinos to 1,000,000 pairs per year. More and more, luxury brands introduce men's suits in a stretch fabric. Christian Lacroix is the first couturier to design a season collection of "Jeans." In Indonesia, the minister of Education authorizes female teachers to wear "city

Yohji Yamamoto's baggy jeans.
Winter 1996-1997.
Yohji Yamamoto archives.

1977

The Girbauds' "mountie" becomes popular; it is better known by Americans as the jodhpur. After the "Pépère" closed by a cord, the "Baggy" and the "Cowboy" would see a worldwide success. First pants for children with "scotchguard" under the brand Mille Sabords.

1978

First Levi's factory in France. Brooke Shields poses for Calvin Klein: "There's nothing between me and my Calvin's" declares an enormous poster in New York's Times Square. Thierry Mugler introduces his winter jeans-girdle with topstitching.

1979

American success of the film *Flashdance* and the aerobics craze.

1980

The number of Levi's 501 jeans goes from 7 million in 1980 to 34 million in 1984. The Girbauds introduce the "destroyed jeans" in Europe and establish their signature first with the X pocket, and then with the fly label, the belt loop and the tear-off label. Repetto offers fourteen shades ranging from hot pink to ocean blue.

In France, prisoners abandon the regulation outfit, the "drogué" jacket and shirt, of a heavy mouse-grey cloth. The tennis player Anne White creates a sensation at Wimbledon when she appears on court in a "catsuit."

1981

Agnès B opens her first store "Homme" on rue du Jour in the middle of Les Halles quarter in Paris. Vivienne Westwood pre-sents her "Pirate" collection at her first runway show in London. The creation of the Guess brand by the Marciano brothers and the triumphant debut for "sexy" jeans of which the "3-Zip Marilyn" will become the product leader; and beginning in 1994, advertising campaigns noted for posing all the top models from Mark Vanderlo to Claudia Schiffer, as well as Naomi Campbell, Eva Herzigova and Laetitia Casta.

Agnès B.
Photograph by François Halard.

1982

In France, Marc Audibet begins his research to introduce the idea of elasticity into city clothes. He will present his first collection in for the winter of 1983-1984.

1983

The first jeans with Lycra. Triumph of the extra-wide Naf Naf overalls in a cotton fabric "ready-to-dye"; three million pairs were sold. The first pants for women by "Joseph," a brand that in the 1990s would distribute 100,000 pairs a year.

1984

The Girbauds see great success with the "Cargo Pocket."

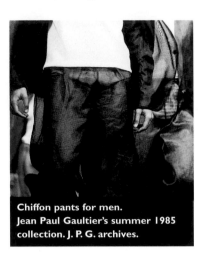

Chiffon pants for men.
Jean Paul Gaultier's summer 1985 collection. J. P. G. archives.

1985

Two Europeans, Milo and Jacques Revah, introduce their ultra-wide jeans in Los Angeles under the brandname "JNCO"; teenagers would baptize them "jinkos." These jeans would have a circumference as large as 107 centimetres, compared with 41 centimetres for classic jeans. For spring, Jean Paul Gaultier presents his "skirt for men." Marc Audibet works with bi-stretchable fabrics.

1986

The creation of the Dockers brand by Levi Strauss and the reintro-duction of chinos whose mythology is reinvented through a major marketing campaign. Azzedine Alaia incorporates Lycra thread into his knits and leggings.

1988

Marithé and François Girbaud introduce their "métamorpho-jean." The first leggings by Chanel inspired by the fitness craze. Issey Miyake begins to work on pleats. Thierry Mugler's vinyl pants create a scandal.

Valentino, *Trente ans de magie*,
Abbeville/Flammarion, 1991.
Pierre de Trévières, *Comment s'habiller*,
Librairie Garnier Frères, Paris, 1929.
Dominique Veillon, *La Mode sous l'Occupation*,
Histoire Payot, 1990.
Marc de Villien, *Histoire des Clubs de Femmes et
des légions d'Amazone, 1793-1848*, Plon, 1910.
Françoise Vincent-Ricard, *Objets de la mode*,
Du May, 1989.
Palmer White, *Paul Poiret*, Studio Vista, Londres,
1973.

Audrey Hepburn, Muséo Salvatore Ferragamo,
Leonardo Arte, Florence, 1999.
Histoires du jean de 1750 à 1994, Musée
de la Mode et du Costume, Palais Galliéra,
Paris-Musées, 1994.
Modes et Révolutions, 1780-1804, Musée
de la Mode et du Costume, Palais Galliéra,
1989.
Paris-Couture années Trente, Guillaume Garnier,
Musée de la mode et du costume, Palais Galliéra,
1987.
Paul Poiret & Nicole Groult, Maîtres de la mode
Art Déco, Musée de la Mode et du Costume,
Palais Galliéra, 1986

EXHIBITION CATALOGS

Pierre Cardin, Past Present Future, Victoria
and Albert Museum, 1990, Londres.
Costume, coutume, Galeries Nationales du Grand
Palais, 1987, Cinquantenaire du Musée national
des arts et traditions populaires, Paris, Réunion
des Musées Nationaux.
Femmes fin de siècle, 1885-1895, Musée de
la Mode et du Costume, Palais Galliéra,
Paris Musées, 1990, Paris.

THESES

Karine Azoulay, *Women's Dressing in America,
a historical perspective (1850-1920)*, Université
Paul-Valery, Montpellier III, 1993-1994.
Lydia Kamitsis, *Recherches sur l'archéologie
du vêtement. L'échange vestimentaire entre
les deux sexes*, Université de Paris Sorbonne
Paris IV. UER d'art et archéologie.

Photography credits

p. 92: Rue des Archives, Paris, rights reserved
p. 94 (1): Sipa/UPI/Corbis-Bettmann, Paris – (2): Roger-Viollet, Paris
p. 95 (3, 4): Sipa Press/Corbis-Bettmann, Paris
p. 96 (5): Roger-Viollet, Paris – (6): Harper's Bazaar/Photo Munkacsi, rights reserved
p. 97 (7): Harper's Bazaar, rights reserved
p. 98 (8): Rue des Archives, Paris – (9): Fotogram-Stone Images/Hulton Getty, Paris – (10): Keystone, Paris
p. 99 (11): Time Life, rights reserved – (12): Rue des Archives, Paris
p. 99 (13): Keystone, Paris
p. 100 (14): Keystone, Paris – (15): Fotogram-Stone Images/Hulton Getty, Paris
p. 101 (16): Sipa/UPI/Corbis-Bettmann, Paris
p. 102: Archives Emilio Pucci, Florence, rights reserved
p. 104 (1): Fotogram-Stone Images/Hulton Getty, Paris – (2): Archives Emilio Pucci, Florence, rights reserved
p. 105 (3): Magnum/Photo David Seymour, Paris – (4): L. Stanley & Marjorie Richardson, rights reserved
p. 106 (5, 6): Keystone, Paris
p. 107 (7): Magnum/Photo Philippe Halsman, Paris – (8): Rue des Archives, Paris
p. 108 (9): Rue des Archives, Paris – (10): Magnum/Photo Philippe Halsman, Paris
p. 109 (11): Archives Allard, Mégève, rights reserved – (12): Rue des Archives, Paris
p. 110 (13): Keystone, Paris
p. 111: Rue des Archives, Paris
p. 112 (15): Magnum/Photo F. Driggs, Paris – (16): Archives Yves Saint Laurent, Paris, rights reserved
p. 113 (17): Archive Photo, Paris
p. 114: Archives Yves Saint Laurent, Paris, rights reserved
p. 116 (1): Photo William Klein – (2): Marie Claire/Photo Willy Rizzo – (3): Magnum/Photo Burt Glinn, Paris
p. 117 (4): Sotheby's New York
p. 117 (5): Top/Photo G. Ehrmann, Paris
p. 118: Agence Scoop
p. 119: Archives Pierre Cardin, Paris
p. 120-124: Archives Yves Saint Laurent, Paris, rights reserved
p. 122: Photo Helmut Newton
p. 123 (18): Archives Sonia Rykiel, Paris, rights reserved – (19): Archives Hermès, Paris
p. 124 (20): Magnum/Photo Henri Cartier-Bresson, Paris
p. 125 (21): Archives Valentino, Rome, rights reserved – (22): Keystone, Paris
p. 127: Agence Scoop
p. 128 (24): Rue des Archives, Paris
p. 129: Musée Ferragamo, Florence, rights reserved

p. 130 (26): Rue des Archives, Paris
p. 131 (27): Rue des Archives, Paris
p. 132: Imapress/Camera Press, Paris
p. 134 (1): Imapress/Camera Press, Paris – (2): Magnum/Photo René Burri, Paris
p. 135: Uomo Vogue/Photo Oliviero Toscani
p. 136 (4): Archives Marithé + François Girbaud, Paris, rights reserved – (5): Archives Levi's, rights reserved
p. 137 (6): Collection U.F.A.C, Musée de la Mode, Paris, rights reserved – (7): Archives Marithé + François Girbaud, Paris, rights reserved
p. 138 (8): Archives Yves Saint Laurent, Paris/Archives Hermès, Paris, rights reserved – (9): Archives Sonia Rykiel, Paris, rights reserved
p. 139 (10): Archives Hermès, Paris, rights reserved – (11): Imapress/Camera Press, Paris – (12): Archives Emilio Pucci, Florence, rights reserved
p. 140 (13): ADAGP, Paris, 1999 – (14): Archives Yves Saint Laurent, rights reserved
p. 141 (15): Archives Pierre Cardin, Paris, rights reserved – (16): Archives Karting, Grenoble, rights reserved – (17): Musée de la Mode de Marseille, rights reserved – (18): Archives Marithé + François Girbaud, Gotlib, Paris
p. 142 (19): Imapress/Camera Press, Paris – (20): Stills, Vanves
p. 143 (21): Stills, Vanves
p. 144: Rue des Archives, Paris
p. 145: Croquis Agnès B, Archives Agnès B, Paris
p. 146: rights reserved
p. 148 (1): Stills, Vanves – (2): Imapress/Camera Press, Paris
p. 149 (3): The Face, Londres – (4): Archives Vivienne Westwood
p. 150 (5): Archives Yves Saint Laurent, Paris, rights reserved – (6): Archives Marithé + François Girbaud, Paris, rights reserved – (7): Imapress/Camera Press, Paris
p. 151 (8): Archives Azzedine Alaia
p. 152 (9): Archives Versace, Milan, rights reserved – (10): Archives Sonia Rykiel, Paris
p. 153 (11): Archives Yohji Yamamoto/Photo Max Vadukul
p. 154 (12): Archives Jean Paul Gaultier, Paris, rights reserved – (13): Cinémagence
p. 155: Archives Comme des Garçons/Photo Peter Lindbergh
p. 156: Archives Martine Sitbon, Paris/Photo Javier Vallhonrat
p. 157: Archives Azzedine Alaia, Paris/Photo Bruce Weber – (16): Archives Marithé + François Girbaud
p. 159: Archives Azzedine Alaia, Paris/Photo Jean-Baptiste Mondino
p. 160: Archives Giorgio Armani, Milan, rights reserved
p. 162 (1): Versace, Milan, rights

reserved – (2): Victoria and Albert Museum, Londres, rights reserved
p. 163 (3): Photo Ling Fei – (4): Archives Jean Paul Gaultier
p. 164 (5): Archives Yohji Yamamoto, Paris, rights reserved – (6): Archives Givenchy – (7): Archives Jil Sander – (8, 10): Archives Gucci – (9): Archives Ann Demeulemester
p. 165 (11): Magnum/Photo Ferdinando Scianna, Paris
p. 167 (12): Archives Louis Vuitton – (13): Archives Helmut Lang, New York, rights reserved
p. 168 (14): Archives Gucci
p. 169 (15): Archives Zana, Paris – (16): Gap – (17): Christian Lacroix, Paris
p. 170 (18): Archives Dolce & Gabbana, Milan – (19): Gucci
p. 171: Archives Hermès
p. 172 (21, 22): United Colours of Benetton
p. 173: Gap
p. 174: Archives Prada, Milan, rights reserved
p. 175: Photo Yasuaki Yoshinaga pour Issey Miyake. Archives I. Miyake, Tokyo
p. 210 (1, 2, 3): rights reserved
p. 211 (4): Osh Kosh – (5): Magnum/Photo Erich Lessing
p. 212 (6): Photo Ling Fei – (7): Photo Koo Bohn Chang – (8): Archives Lanvin – (9): rights reserved – (10): Sonia Rykiel
p. 213: Archives Issey Miyake, Tokyo – Archives Martine Sitbon, Paris – Archives Yohji Yamamoto, Tokyo – Archives Jean Charles de Castelbajac, Paris – Archives Dolce e Gabbana, Milan – Archives Yves Saint Laurent, Paris – Archives Christian Lacroix, Paris
p. 214 (2): Archives Timothy Everest, Londres/Photo Ling Fei
p. 215 (3, 4): Archives Paul Smith, Londres, rights reserved
p. 216 (5, 7): Archives Yves Saint Laurent – (6) Archives Hermès
p. 217-218: Archives Bernard Zins, Paris
p. 221-222: rights reserved `
p. 223 (5): Archives Ateca/Avirex, rights reserved – (6): Sygma/L'Illustration, Paris – (7): Fotogram-Stone Images/Hulton Getty, Paris
p. 224 (8): Archives Lee, rights reserved – (9): Archives Duthilleul & Minart/Photo Ling Fei, rights reserved – (11): Archives Jean Paul Gaultier, rights reserved
p. 225: Archives Dockers, Paris, rights reserved
p. 226: Archives Levi's, rights reserved
p. 227 (3, 4): Archives Levi's – (5): Victoria And Albert Museum
p. 228 (6): Archives Diesel, rights reserved – (7): Mario Testino/Art Partners
p. 229 (8): Archives Marithé + François Girbaud, rights reserved – (9): Photo Ling Fei – (10): Archives G. STAR
p. 230 (11): Archives Levi's, Paris,

rights reserved – (12): Archives Maison Margiela, Paris, rights reserved – (13): Archives Jean Paul Gaultier/Photo Gislain Yahni – (14): Archives Levi's
p. 231 (15): Archives Evisu
p. 232: Archives Levi's
p. 233 (17): Archives Levi's – (18): Archives Calvin Klein
p. 234: Archives Phyléas/Photo Gislain Yahni
p. 235 (2): Archives Jean-Paul Gaultier, Paris – (3): Archives Jean Colonna
p. 236 (4): Archives Jean-Paul Gaultier – (5) Archives Yves Saint Laurent, Paris
p. 237 (6): Archives Jean-Paul Gaultier, Paris – (7): Archives Mugler
p. 238 (8): Archives Jean Claude Jitrois, Paris/Photo Helmut Newton
p. 239: Archives Jean-Claude Jitrois, Paris
p. 241: rights reserved
p. 242 (6): Rue des Archives, Paris – (7, 8): AKG, Paris
p. 243 (9): AKG, Paris & UPI/Corbis Bettmann – (10): Cinémathèque française
p. 244 (11): Dance Collection, New York – (12): Collection Jean Paul Goude, Paris
p. 245 (13): Cinémathèque de la Danse, Paris – (15): PPCM/Kobal, Paris – (16): Archives Yves Saint Laurent
p. 246 (3): Magnum/Photo Henri Cartier-Bresson, Paris
p. 247: rights reserved
p. 248 (7): Succession H. Matisse, Paris, 1999/Photothèque des collections du Mnam, Centre Georges Pompidou, Paris
p. 248 (8): Magnum/Photo Abbas, Paris
p. 249 (11): Archives Yves Saint Laurent, Paris – (12) Isabel Munoz, Agence VU, rights reserved
p. 250 (13): Roger-Viollet, Paris
p. 251 (14): rights reserved – (15): Archives Lee Young Hee, Séoul, rights reserved
p. 252 (1, 2): Archives Marithé + François Girbaud, Paris
p. 253 (3): Photothèque René Magritte, Giraudon, Paris/ADAGP – (4): Bridgeman Art Library, Londres/ADAGP – (5): De Selva, Paris/Succession Picasso, Paris 1999
p. 254 (6): Archives Issey Miyake, Tokyo
p. 255: Galerie Yvon Lambert, Paris, rights reserved

CHRONOLOGY
ADAGP – Miloslav Sebek, Prague, rights reserved – Jean Patou, Paris, rights reserved – Levi's, rights reserved – Givenchy – Yves Saint Laurent – Marithé + François Girbaud – Jean Paul Gaultier, Yohji Yamamoto – Gucci.

PRINTED BY
INDUSTRIE GRAFICHE EDITORIALI MUSUMECI,
QUART (VALLE D'AOSTA), ITALIE.